AF615447

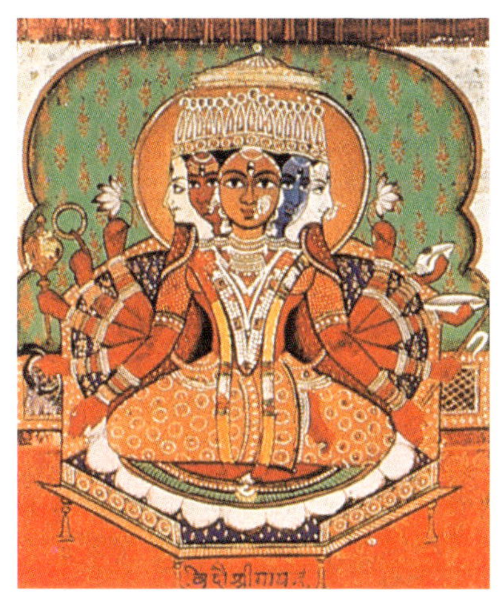

DIVINE ART

Dedicated to my loving sons Vikrant and Siddhartha

Previous page 1: The Tantras emphasise external ritual activity or internal Yogic practice.
Right: A performer doing the Zshana Cham dance, also called the black hat dance, during the Paro Tsechu (Buddhist festival) at Paro Dzong, Paro, Bhutan.
Following pages 4-5: The Basilica of San Francisco in Assisi, inlaid with precious stones and mosaics in gold, is considered an architectural wonder.

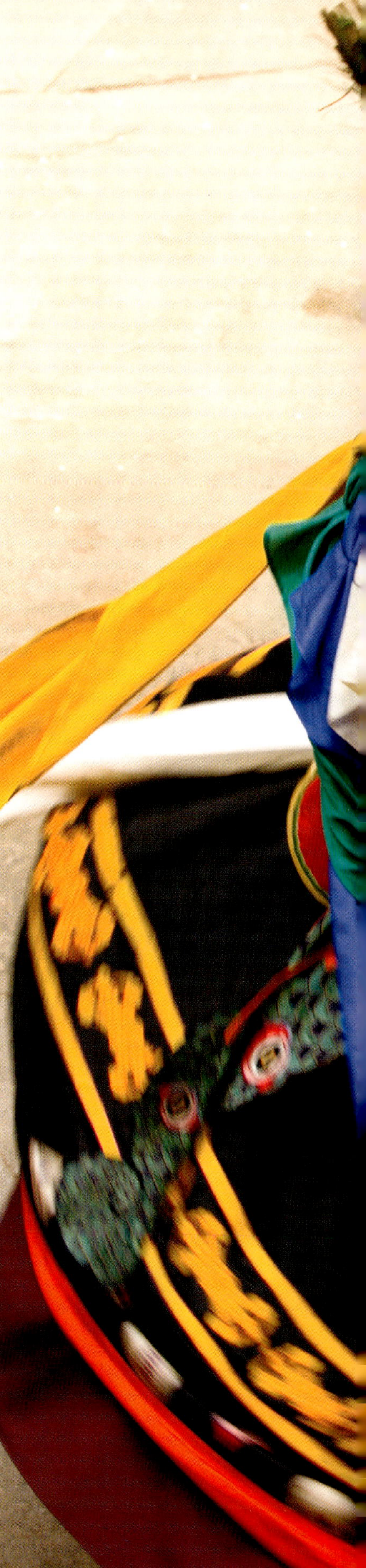

All rights reserved. No part of this publication may be transmitted or reproduced in any form or by any means without prior permission from the publisher.

ISBN: 978-81-7436-321-3

© Roli & Janssen BV 2007
Published in India by
Roli Books in arrangement with
Roli & Janssen B.V.
M-75 Greater Kailash II Market
New Delhi-110 048, India
Ph: ++91-11-29212271, 29212782, 29210886
Fax: ++91-11-29217185
E-mail: roli@vsnl.com
Website: rolibooks.com

Printed and bound in Singapore

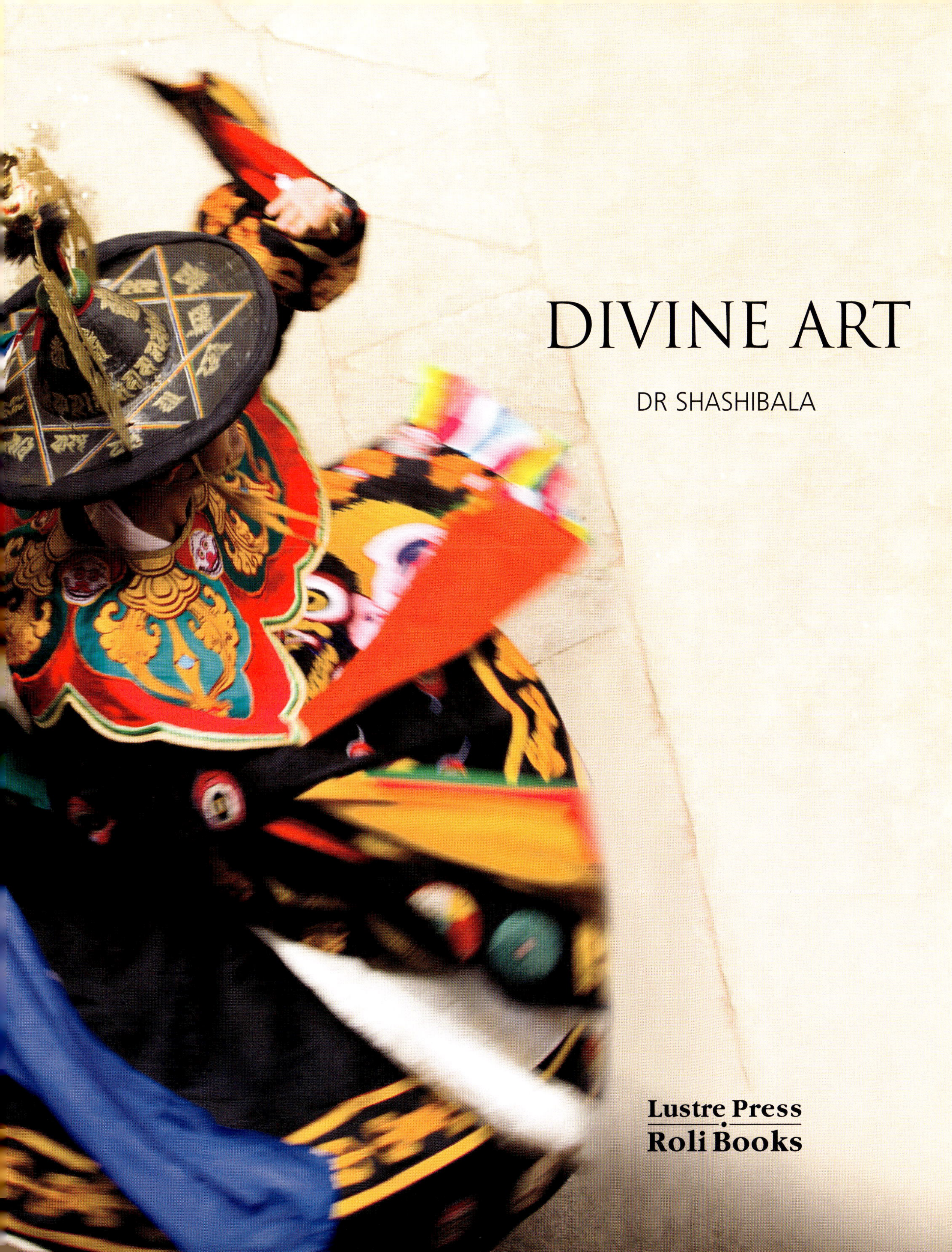

DIVINE ART

DR SHASHIBALA

Lustre Press
Roli Books

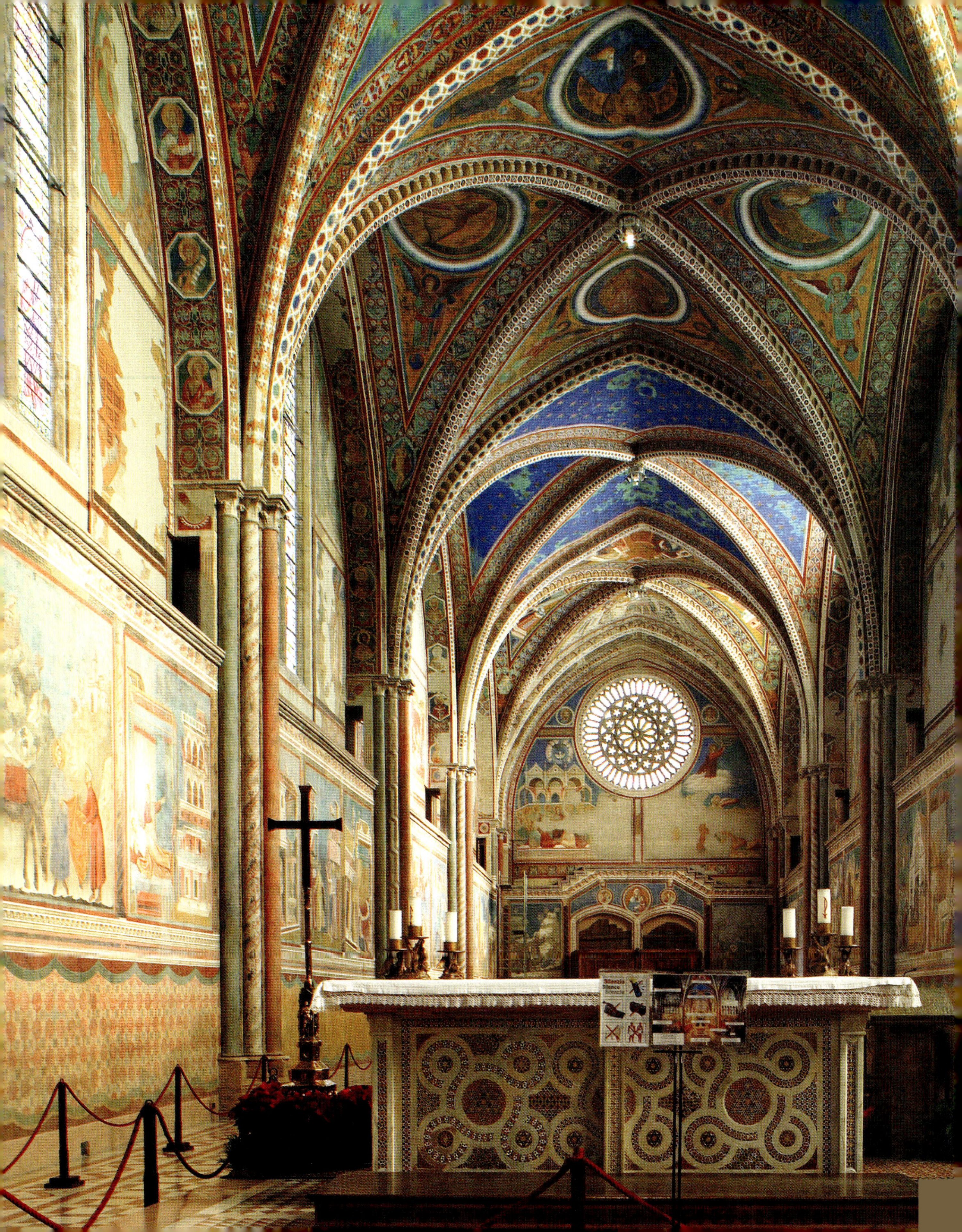

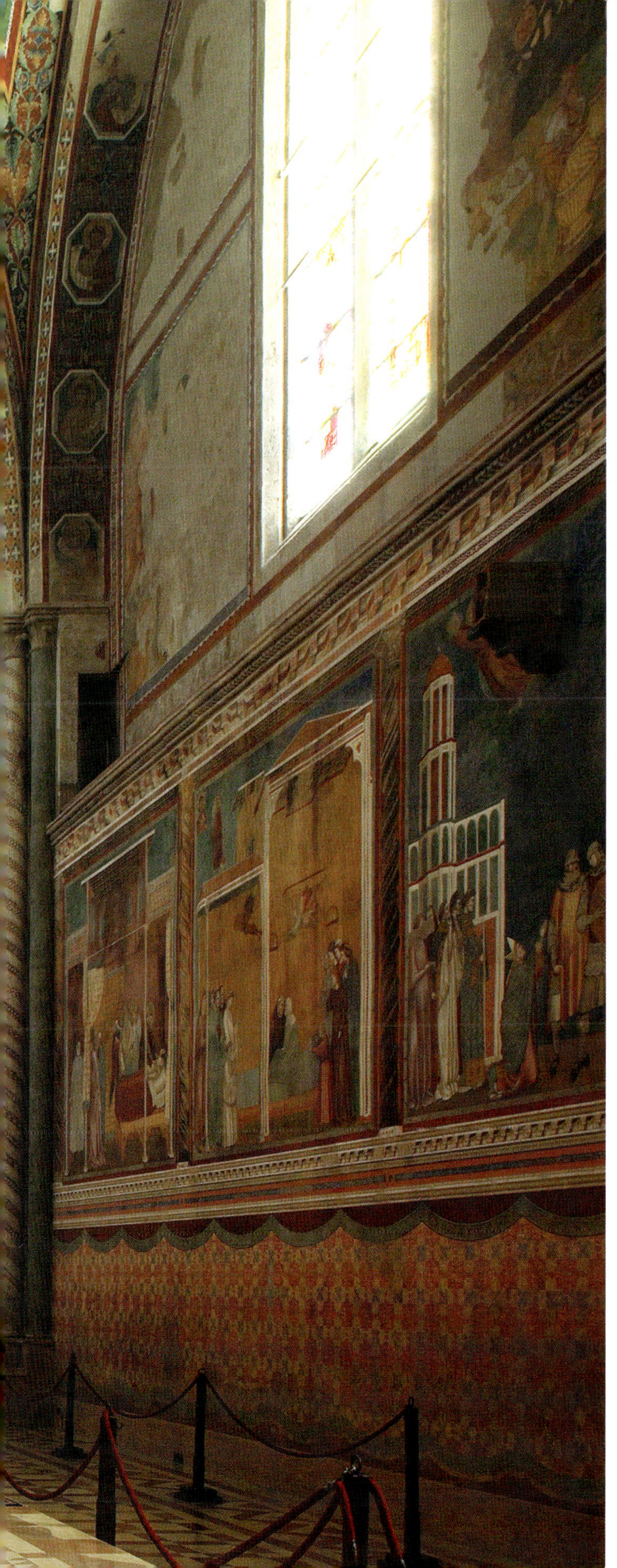

CONTENTS

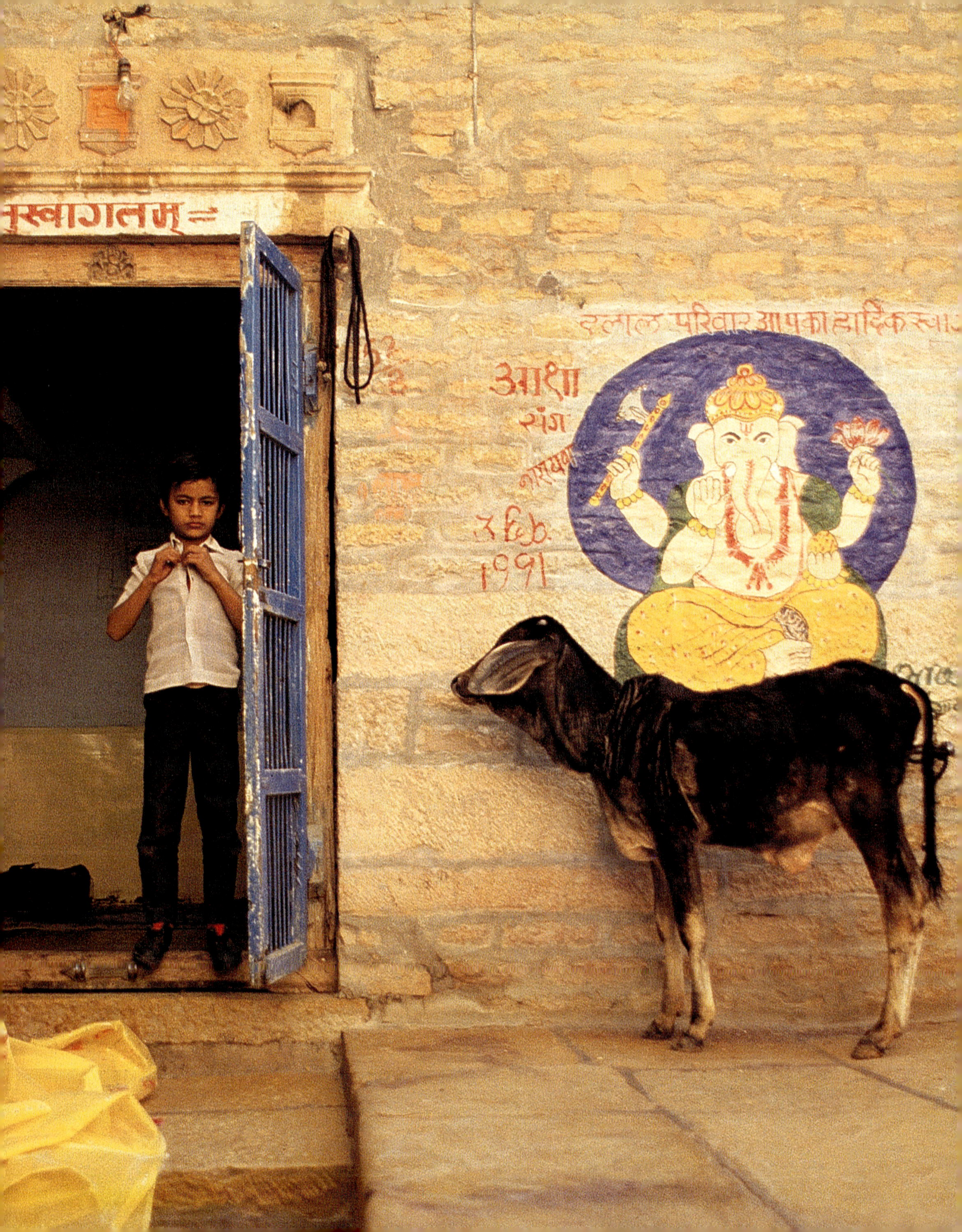
स्वागतम्
दलाल परिवार आपका हार्दिक
आशा
संग
1991

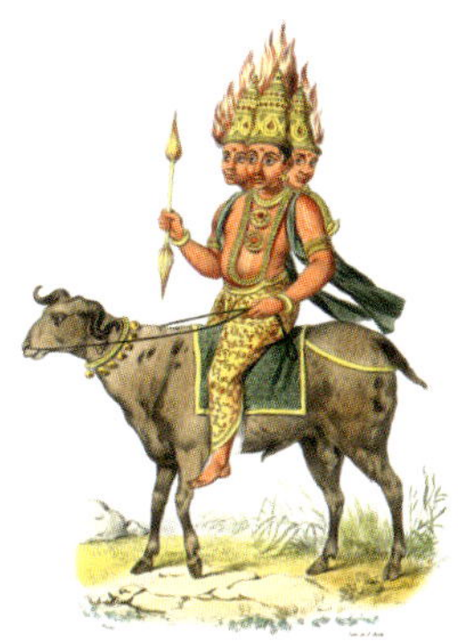

INTRODUCTION

Religions of the world have inspired divine art forms embracing the philosophical and metaphysical perceptions of people, their deepest insights and highest aspirations. Visionary in nature and produced by an artist's higher level of consciousness, divine art gives form to the intangible.

In this age of consumerism and materialism, divine art instils feelings of love and compassion, alleviating mental suffering. It cleanses the darkness of ignorance and arrogance. Unlike commercial art, it connects the modern world with the peaceful sphere of wisdom, spiritualism and ethical values. The term 'divine art' appeals to emotions; it is a pleasure in itself, a source of happiness and perennial inspiration. The ultimate goal of its creation is transcendence of humanity.

However, the artist is never completely able to represent philosophical truths through his art forms, because nature in its immensity is often overwhelming. Divine art represents universal truths, convictions and beliefs, rooted in the minds of the people and accepted as truth itself.

Nature itself is a creative artist whose beauty changes every moment and whose moods can be appreciated in different seasons and in varying forms at different places. Nature fills colour and gives life to this world, manifesting itself as an architect of

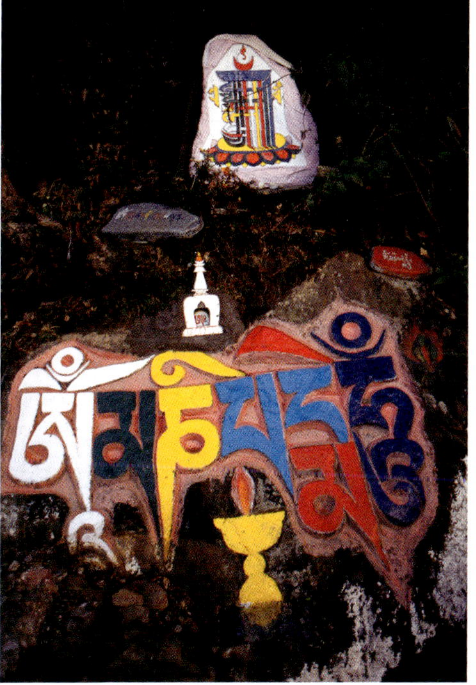

Facing page: A wall mural of Lord Ganesh in Jaisalmer, Rajasthan. Such paintings play a fundamental role in deity worship and are very commonly found in India.
Above: Agni, the god of fire in Hindu mythology, symbolises the capacity to both destroy evil and spread divine illumination upon the world.
Left: Painted Mani stones from Tibet, inscribed with '*om mane padme hun*', literally, hail the jewel in the lotus, the jewel being a symbol of the Buddha.

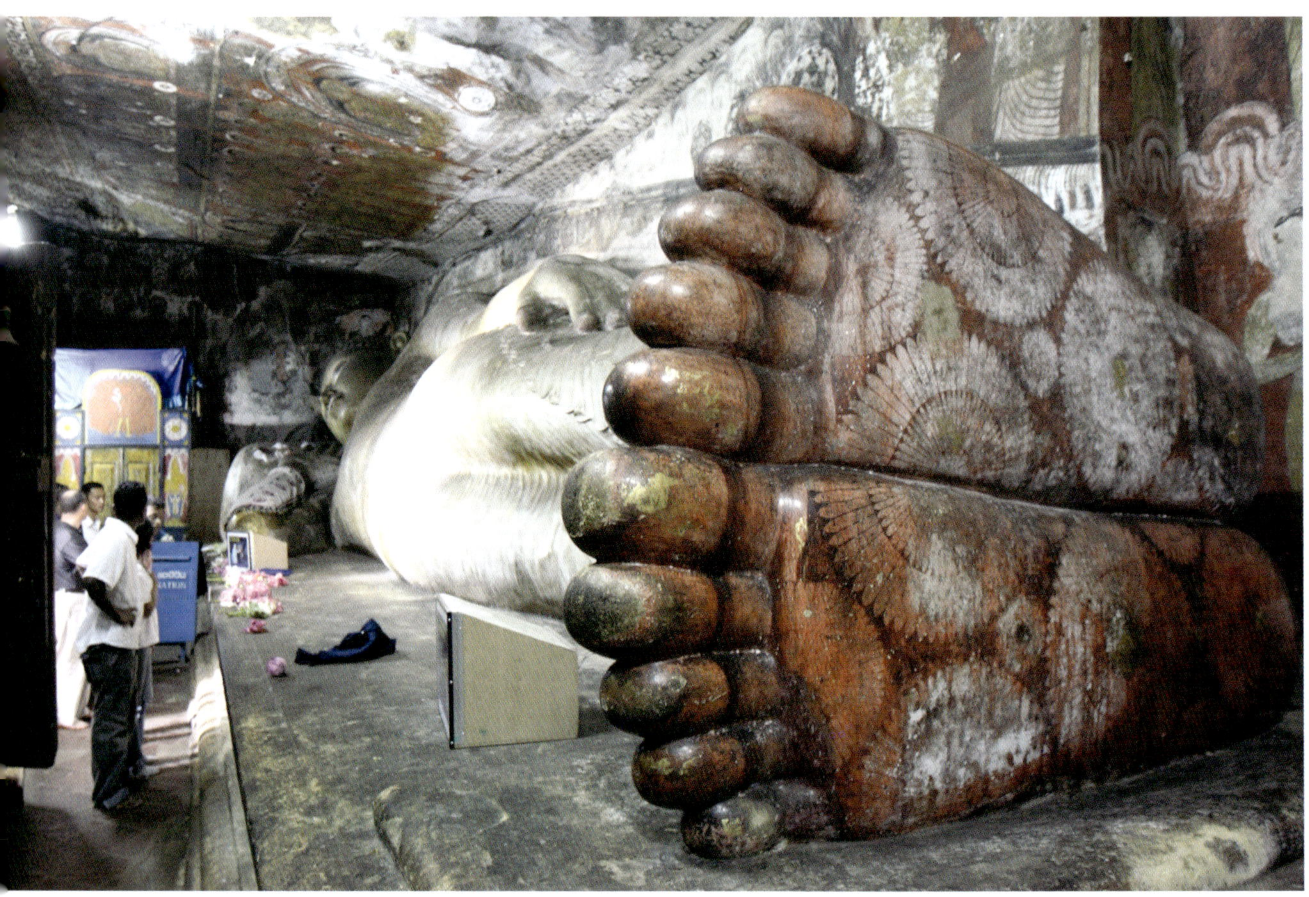

The reclining Buddha at the Golden Temple in Sri Lanka is characteristic of the Anuradhapura sculpture style.

immeasurable talent, producing forms in numerous hues and shades. New lines and shapes infuse the world every day. Beauty is its ultimate expression – seeking perfection in myriad forms and combinations.

Most of the world religions have influenced the art of painting, sculpture and architecture through construction and decoration of buildings dedicated to the divine. The beauty of such places has been emphasised as an element of great importance for a religious experience. Adornment of walls with paintings plays a fundamental role in portraying the lives and deeds of the divine, to benefit those who seek instruction from them. Temples stand as marked-out spaces to contemplate the ultimate realities of life. The divine structures contain a meaning, function and symbolism.

Astounding images of the divine were sculpted in metal, clay, stone, or wood to be enshrined and venerated. They symbolised the inexpressible spiritual qualities in the language of art expressing sublimity, grace and excellence, assimilating within such expressions the concepts of superhuman and supernatural energy, power and vision. The polytheistic worlds of the Greeks, Hindus and Buddhists have their own 'secretly potent pantheon of dreams'. Their worlds invented metaphors, concepts and categories of thought. There is no law of revelation, and no constraints of the monocentric supreme.

In Greece, gods represent the ideal perfection of human beauty, while in

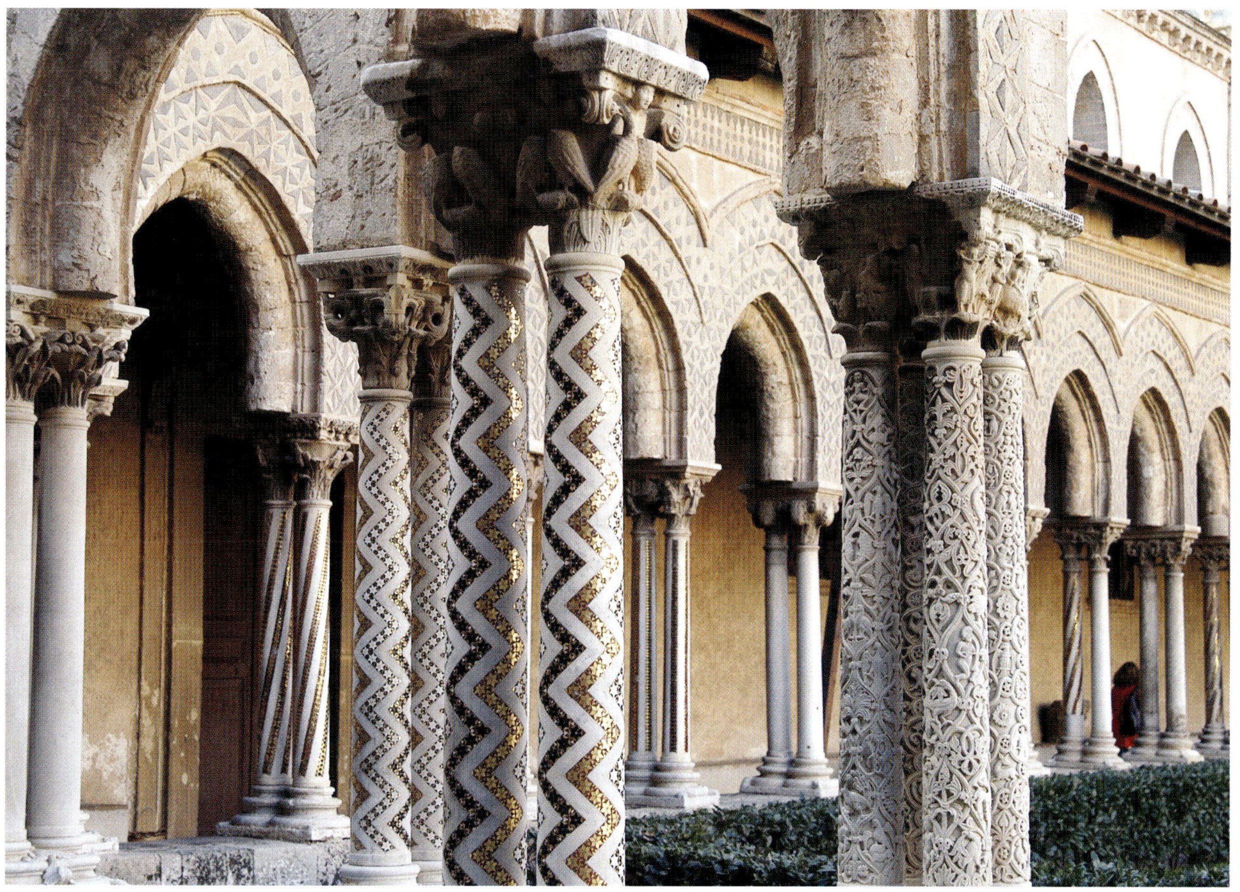

Mosaic decoration on pillars of Benedictine cloister at Monreale, near Palermo, Italy.

Buddhism and Hinduism divine representations are based on *dhyana*, a process of inner efforts to control the movement of mind culminating in *samadhi*. Thus, the divine is created from 'non-form'. Gods and goddesses enshrined in the temples are beyond measure, as immense as life itself. Divine images are not deliberately created as works of art. They enshrine devotion and dedication. The artists are skilful and well versed in philosophy, and they have a vision to create an inspiring effect and convey the message to the devotee. They follow the rules prescribed by the texts on iconography as guides.

Sacred literatures are the purest voice of the creator, reflecting the roots, the life, and the vision of the people. They contain words of wisdom and, hence, are objects of adoration. They have always been written in the best possible manner using the best available material. Hundreds of thousands of texts strewn in museums and monasteries were scribed, calligraphed or xylographed, illustrated or illuminated, and translated or copied to carry the divine word to the people.

Man shared his vision and his creative and aesthetic skills to decorate the interiors as well as exteriors of places of worship. Stained glasswork in the churches paid tribute to the glory of the outside, as the refulgence of the sun entered the divine interiors illuminating them with resplendent rays. It was actually identified with the prophets, the doctors of the

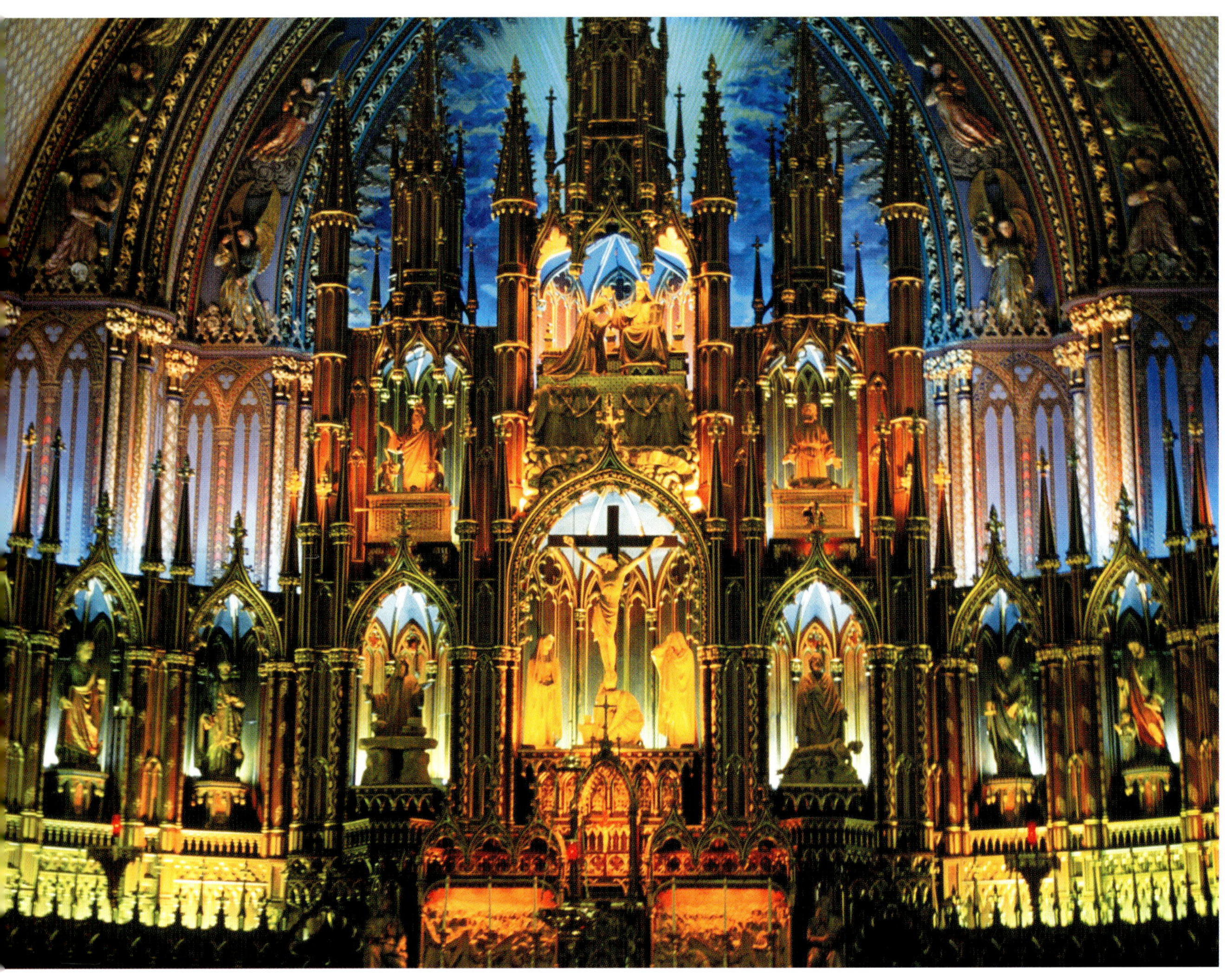

Cathedral of Notre Dame in Old Town, Quebec, Montreal, is a magnificent example of neo-Gothic architecture.

church, or the holy scriptures – in short, with all that enlightens the faithful and shields them from evil. The glass windows in the church are holy scriptures that keep out the wind and the rain, that is, all things hurtful, but transmit the light of the true sun, that is God, into the hearts of the faithful.

The feeling of extraordinary delight evoked by divine art is imbued with an element of transcendence; it is beyond personal joys and emotions. In India dance has been the enlivening movement of the absolute. It is poetry in motion combining worship, drama, play and art. Dance is integral to life, to passion, and to creation. Lord Shiva as Nataraja is the lord of dance. Angels dance on the heavenly musical instruments played by the *apsaras*, as painted in the *mandalas* in China and Japan.

Strolling minstrels perform the duty of transmitting the tenets of philosophy in an easy-to-understand manner to the unenlightened. Their art is known for its power of convincinq the audience of the basic principles and precepts conveyed by them. They have the power to please and enrapture

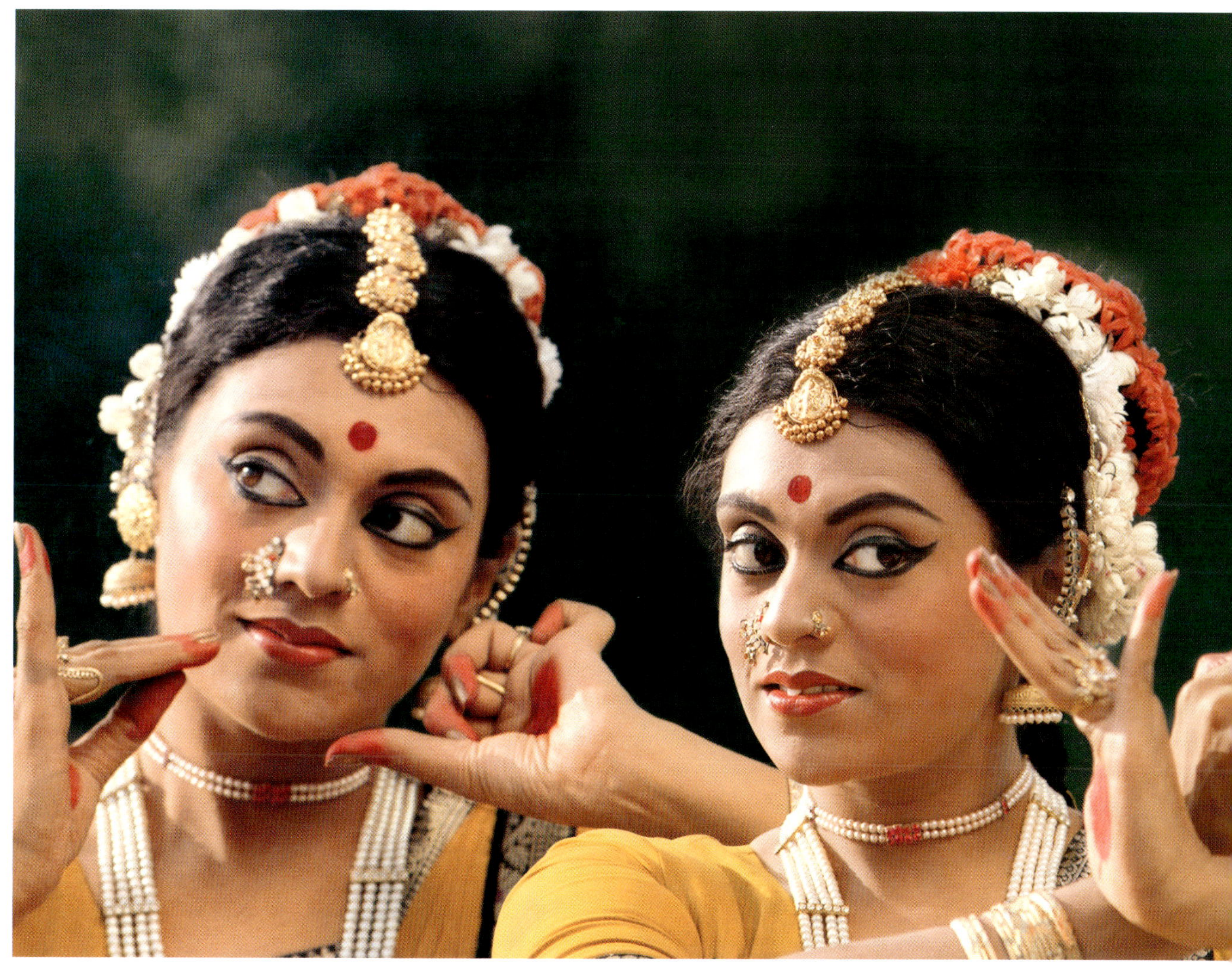

the audience while narrating stories in a loud and overwhelming voice, which vibrates through the mind and palpitates the heart. They try to make their language as attractive as possible, while being easily understandable. Normally, their narrations are a combination of poetry and prose.

Votive and liturgical objects are offerings made of free will, or are required during rituals and ceremonies. They are made from stone, metal, clay, wood and bamboo, and even grass, skins, butter and horns. Use of incense, rosary, candle and flowers is widely popular and often used by devotees in different religions. Prayer wheels and offering banners are often seen as Buddhist devotional objects.

Divine art objects embrace philosophical developments and various spheres of human activity – from the common to the elite. The forms may be serene or strong, but they fascinate the human mind by virtue of being part of a universal message. They portray a positive vision and offer spiritual delight.

Indian classical dance is a confluence of worship, drama and art. Here *abhinaya* comes to the fore as two dancers essay stylised poses.

Following pages 12-13:
A Tibetan Buddhist prayer is inscribed in rock along the pilgrimage route circling Mount Kailasha in western Tibet.

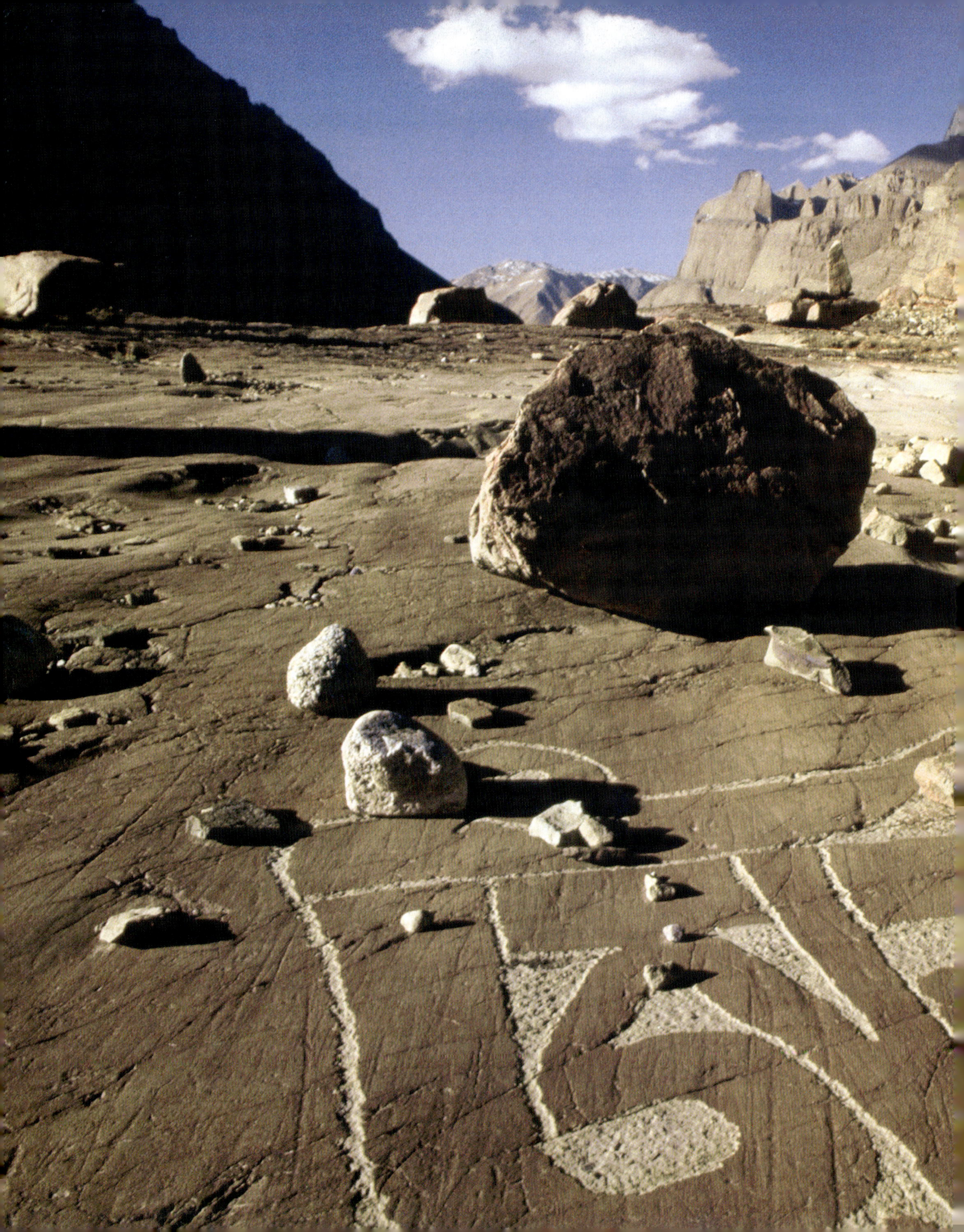

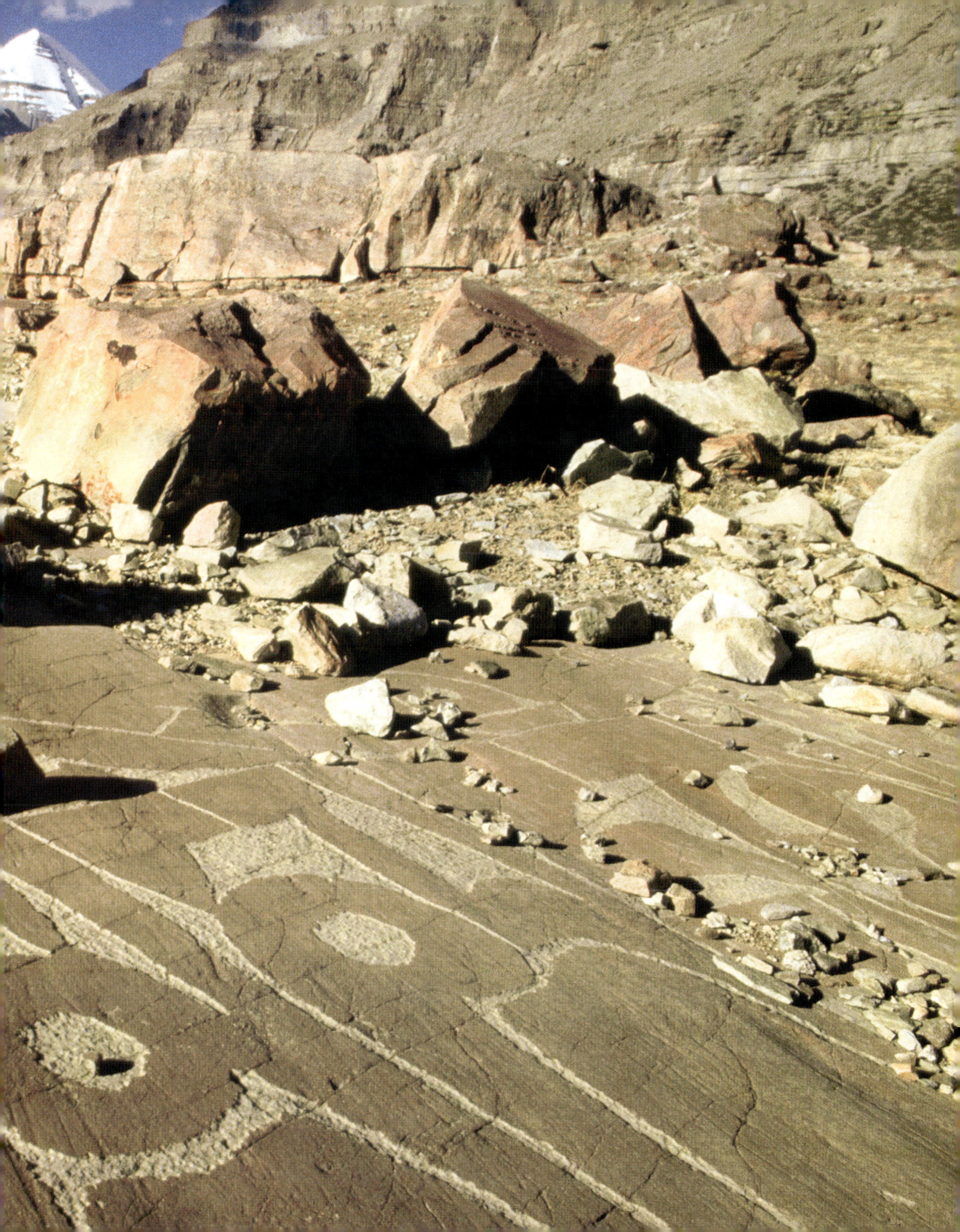

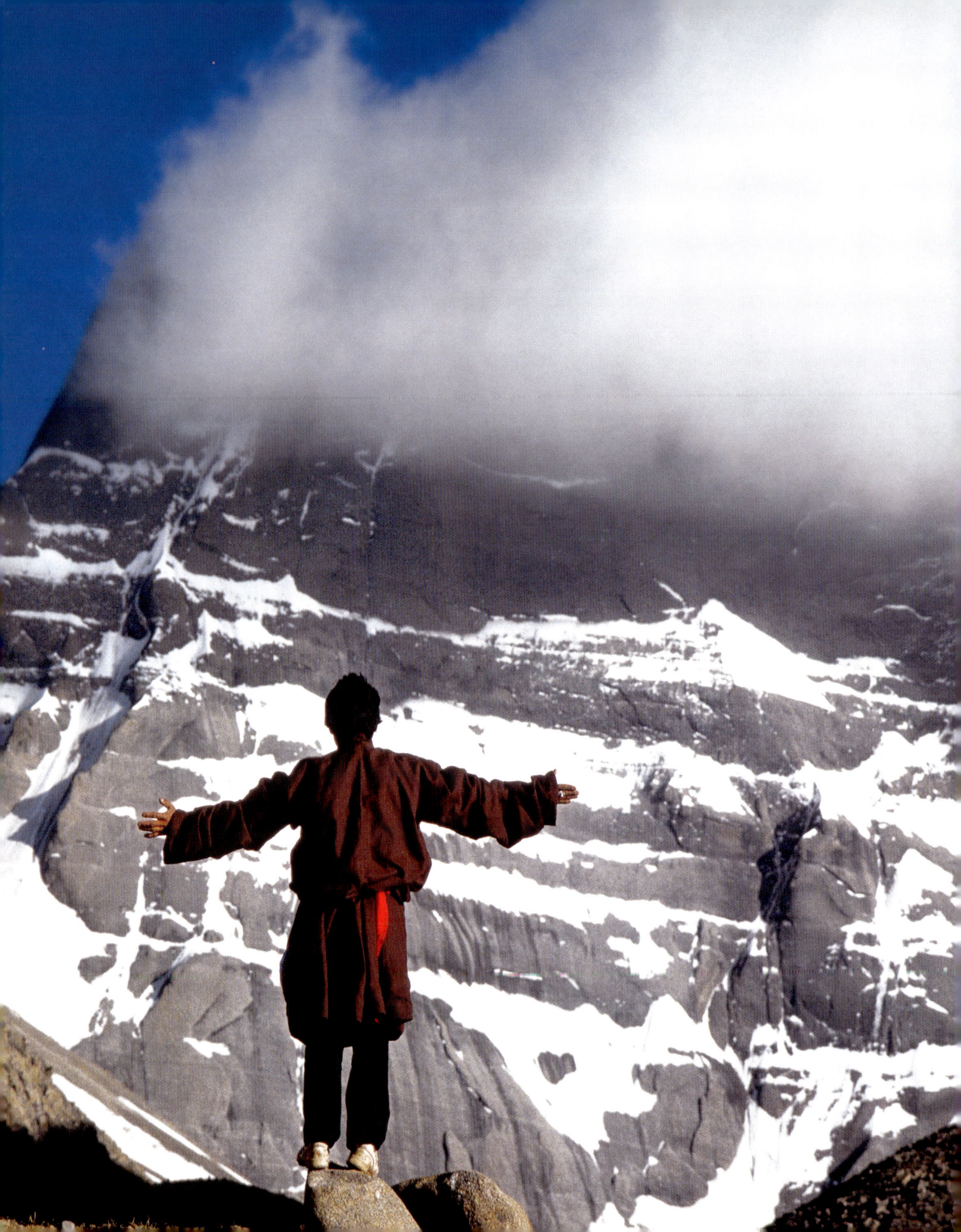

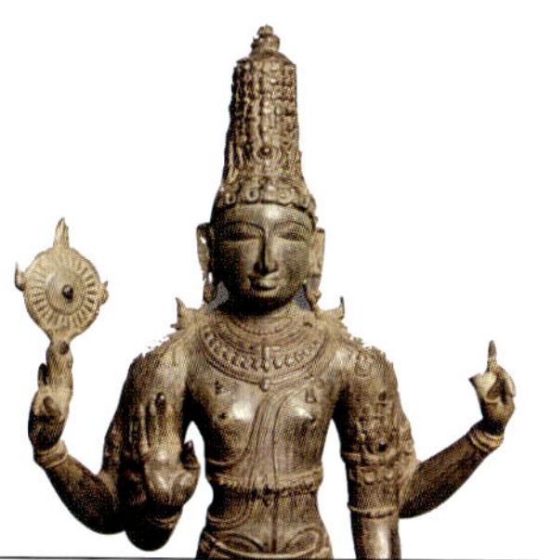

THE FIRST INSPIRATION: NATURE

Age-old traditions of preservation of nature recommend living in harmony with it, to live a life full of creativity. Religious thought is permeated with reverence for nature that is divine. Its relationship with man is not in opposition, but one of mutual dependence, keeping a dynamic equilibrium. Life begins with nature and man together. Their secret link is the purest. Thus, the texture of life exists in the symbiotic relationship of humanity, divinity and nature.

COSMOS

The entire cosmos fascinates, but the creator is unknown and invisible. Where is the architect, or the designer? When did he begin, and how? What was there before the creation of natural phenomena? No tangible answer is possible. The whole universe was, and is, unperceived, undistinguishable, undiscoverable and unknowable. There was total darkness that shrouded the primordial water. Out of chaos, order was born; and new forms emerged out of the formless.

Hindu mythology questions the identity of the cosmic architect. Is he Vishvakarma Prajapati, the lord of all creatures who created all phenomena, who is the sole king of the breathing world and who supports earth and the heavens? Or, is he Vishnu or Ishvara, who dwelt in the eggshell, lying lifeless on the waters of an ocean, from whose navel sprang a lotus splendid as a thousand suns, the abode of all living things, and where Brahma was born? Or, is it the non-manifest, the self-existent creator, who created the universe with five fundamental elements? He first created water to deposit a seed that became the golden egg, to give birth to Brahma.

Nature is ruled and controlled by the cosmic law that lies beyond human control. It controls the dual forces in nature which are opposite in every respect and unites them, so that creativity enters the primordial waters and the great mystery becomes a fact. The 'golden germ', *Hiranyagarbha*, the beginning and origin of all creation, is born.

To the religious consciousness, nature appears as a manifestation of the sacred in

Facing page: A Tibetan with arms spread praying at Mount Kailasha, the centre of the universe for Buddhists and Hindus.
Above: Vishnu, the protector and preserver of nature, acquires various forms to destroy evil.

material forms. It transcends its brute physicality. The sky is often revered as a manifestation of a divinity, or venerated as the locus of the gods. Prayers and sacrifices are offered to the divinities who dwell there, who welcome the soul of the dead into their dwelling place beside the flowing water of the Milky Way. Objects fallen from the sky come from the sacred locus of the heavens and often become objects of religious cults. Actual meteorites are seen as centres of cults associated with sky gods.

The sun shines in the sky as the most powerful creation in the cosmos. Worshipping it is a widespread phenomenon. Sacrifices are offered to its light at times of crisis – which may be in connection with the fertility of crops – as well as for the regenerative life of the cosmos. The sun's power extends to the human progeny. The Egyptian pharaohs reckoned that they were the children of the sun. Members of the imperial family in Japan believe that they are descendants of the sun goddess Amaterasu-no-omikami.

Age-old traditions treat natural forces and phenomena as divine personalities. Various natural features on earth are venerated to keep them pure and free from pollution. Rivers are invoked as flowing from the celestial ocean, full of the nectar of life, with an ever-renewing life force for the animate as well as human world. They are purifiers, and bestowers of wealth, vitality and immortality. We should befriend the water and the wind, the transient and the transcendental.

The concept has an inherent strength to restrict environmental pollution. The ancient values do not permit destroying the earth or polluting the sky; man is not given free rein to conquer nature, upsetting the basic rhythm and forcing it to rebel against humanity. Feelings of adoration for nature are reflected in beliefs such as circumambulation of Mount Kailasha and Lake Manasarovar, adding to the merits of the seven future generations of the devotee. Places of origin of the Ganga and Yamuna rivers are believed to be as divine as other places of pilgrimage.

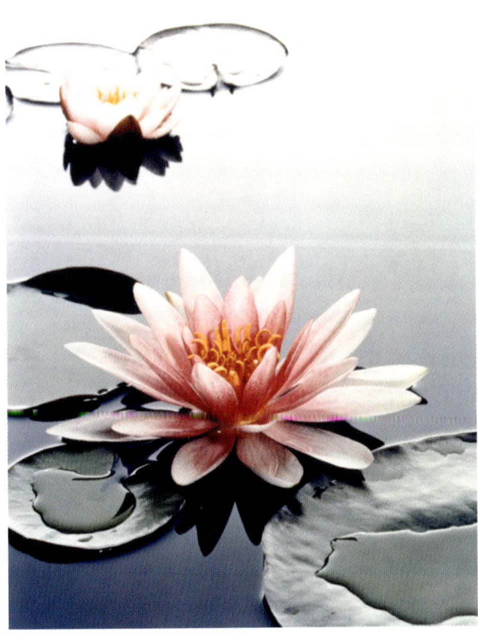

Water lilies are nature's manifestation of both the spiritual and the material universe contained in a single element.

PLANTS AND TREES

Plants and trees have been revered as divine from time immemorial because they are synonymous with life. Their planting and protection have been exalted. Herbal plants and trees are praised for their healing power. Peepal, the fruitless and flowerless tree, is sacred because it supplies oxygen and contains medicinal value. The forest as a whole is invoked as a goddess in the *Rigveda*. The lotus floating on water is a manifestation of divinity as also of the universe. Moments of sowing and reaping are marked by sacrifices. Many festivals are centred on vegetation and harvests. Picking the first fruits from the field is frequently an occasion for a religious festival and ceremony.

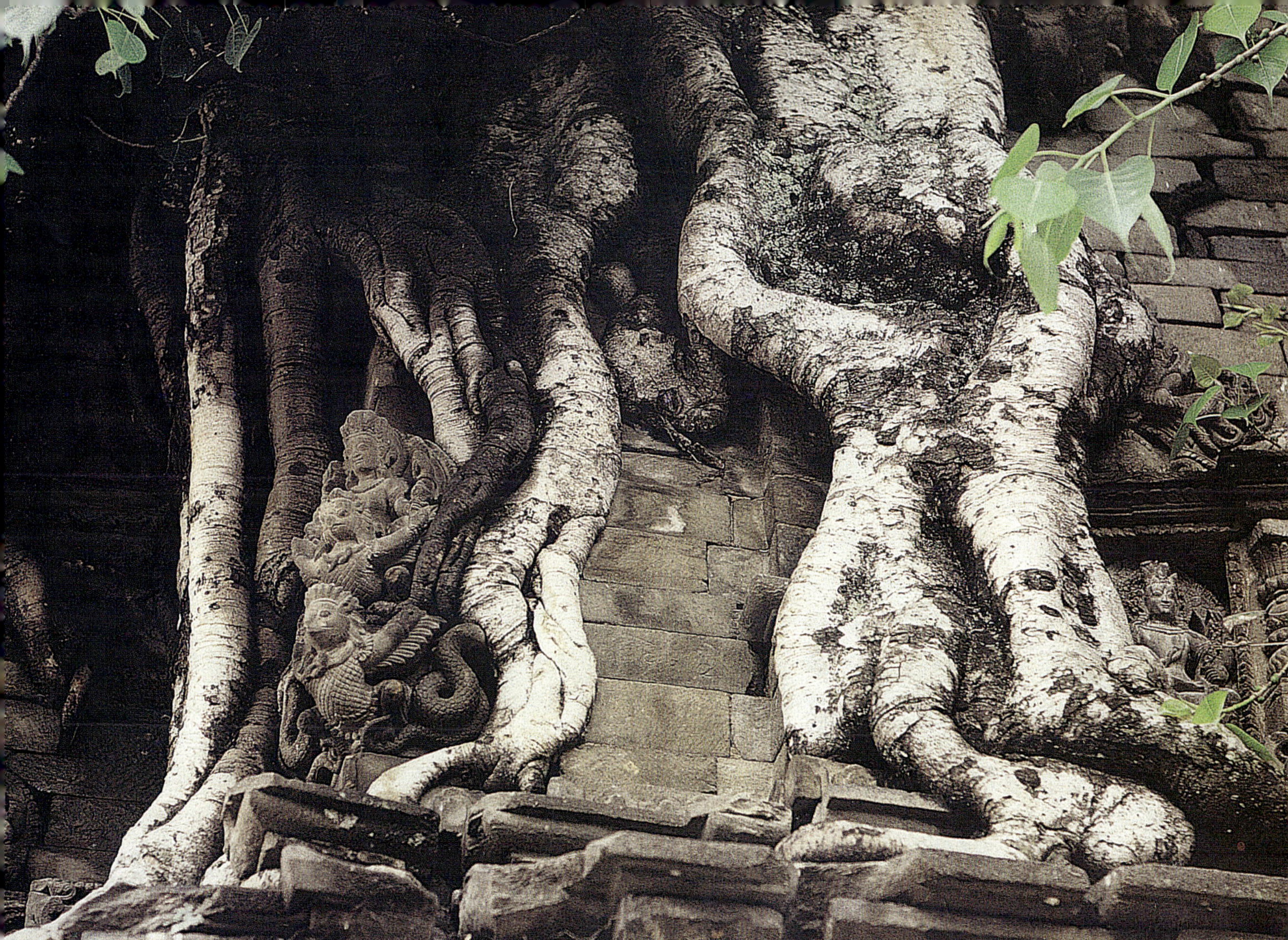

The earth is sacred in many traditions and is worshipped as an object of devotion containing the very source of life itself. It is a partner of the sky, and their marriage makes the cosmos fertile. Water, the second among the five fundamental elements and the source of primal life, was produced for preservation of all creatures. It washes away material and spiritual pollution. The running water of rivers is often used in rituals for purification. It is widely used in ceremonies for summoning the rain. Springs, rivers and irrigation waters are the centres of religious attention throughout the world. Fire is the third element and represented by the sun. Early morning, the mountains are set ablaze by its rays. But this fire is cool and refreshing. This is the fire to which homage is paid in the opening verse of the *Rigveda*. The bonfire on the ranges of mountains is seen as a creation of the sun; it summons the traveller of the world to toil and travel, to approach and experience the higher than the highest.

MOUNTAINS

Mountains have been conceived as divinely animate. They symbolise strength and permanence. They are divine creations and stand for the benefit of all. They give forth fluids that sustain life. These mountains are often a source of livelihood for many commmunities. They inspire reverence through

From ancient days Vedic Aryans have been worshiping trees, be it the Tulsi plant or the Banyan tree. Worshiping trees and believing in their divine powers is still prevalent in different parts of the world.

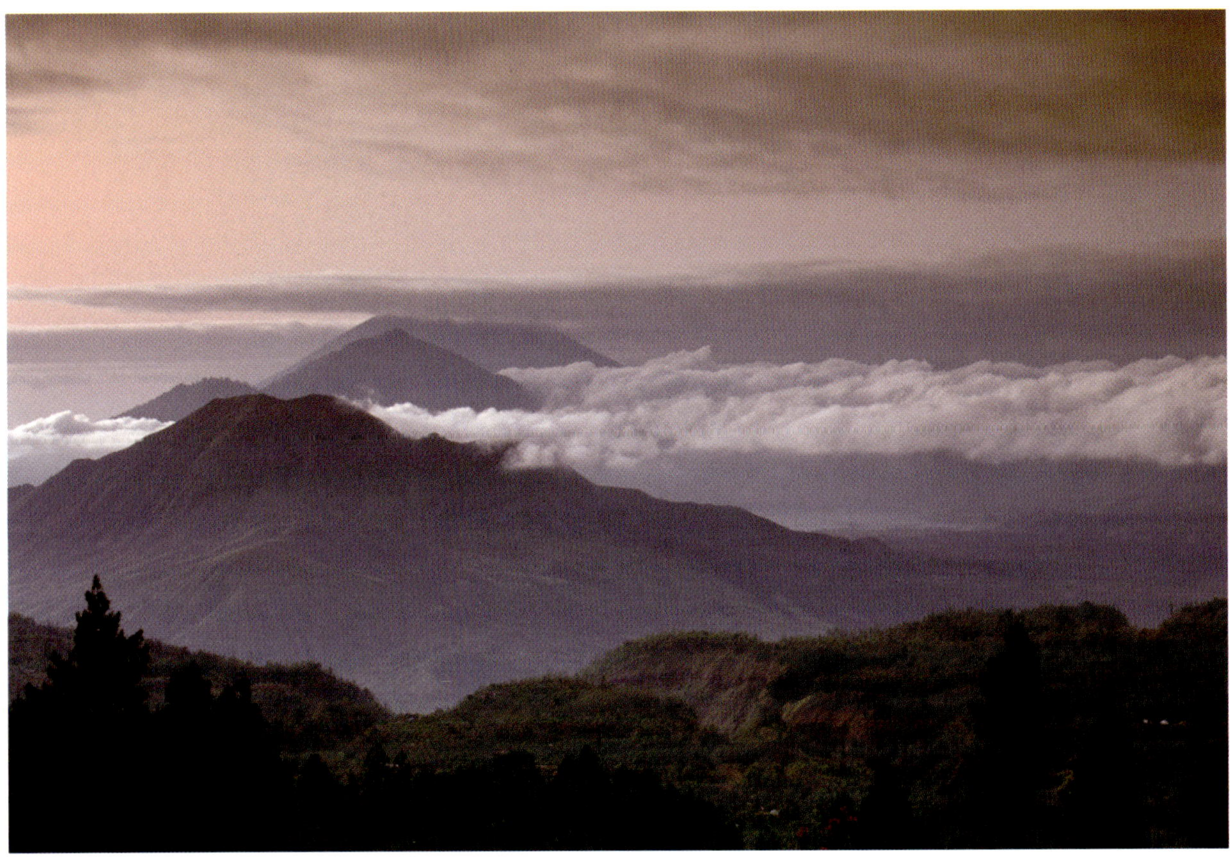

The holy mountain Gunung Agung Volcano in Bali, Indonesia is regarded as the navel of the world and as a source of well-being and fertility. It is believed to be the home of Lord Shiva and other deities.

their soaring heights and vastness, the mysteries of their recesses, and the clouds and mists playing on their slopes. Their summits are the abodes of the divine, merging into the sky.

Mountains often function as an *Exis Mundi* – the centre post of the world. They link heaven and earth, and anchor the cardinal directions. A cosmic mountain is central to the order and stability of the cosmos. Sumeru, a mythical mountain in Asia, has been repeatedly represented for centuries in art and literature. Superstructures of temples are often compared to mountains. Mountains are often engraved in stupas as well. In south-east Asia one of the many duplicates of Meru is Mount Gunung Agung, the great volcanic mountain that stands at the centre of the island of Bali. Mount Hara Berazaiti has a central place in the ancient mythology of the Zoroastrian tradition. In ancient Mesopotamia, the seven–storey ziggurat, with its high temple at the top and low temple at the bottom, allows the descent of the divine.

Mountains are given a persona of their own. Mexicans regarded all mountains as divine. In Korea, mountains are personified as divine guardians. In Japan, the term *Kami* for 'divine beings' is also applied to mountains because they possess great power. In China sacrifices are made to the mountains or to their spirits. Kanchenjunga is worshipped in Tibet. The Greeks adored divinities associated with mountains. In India they have been worshipped since Vedic times. The Himalayas are the king of mountains – and regarded as

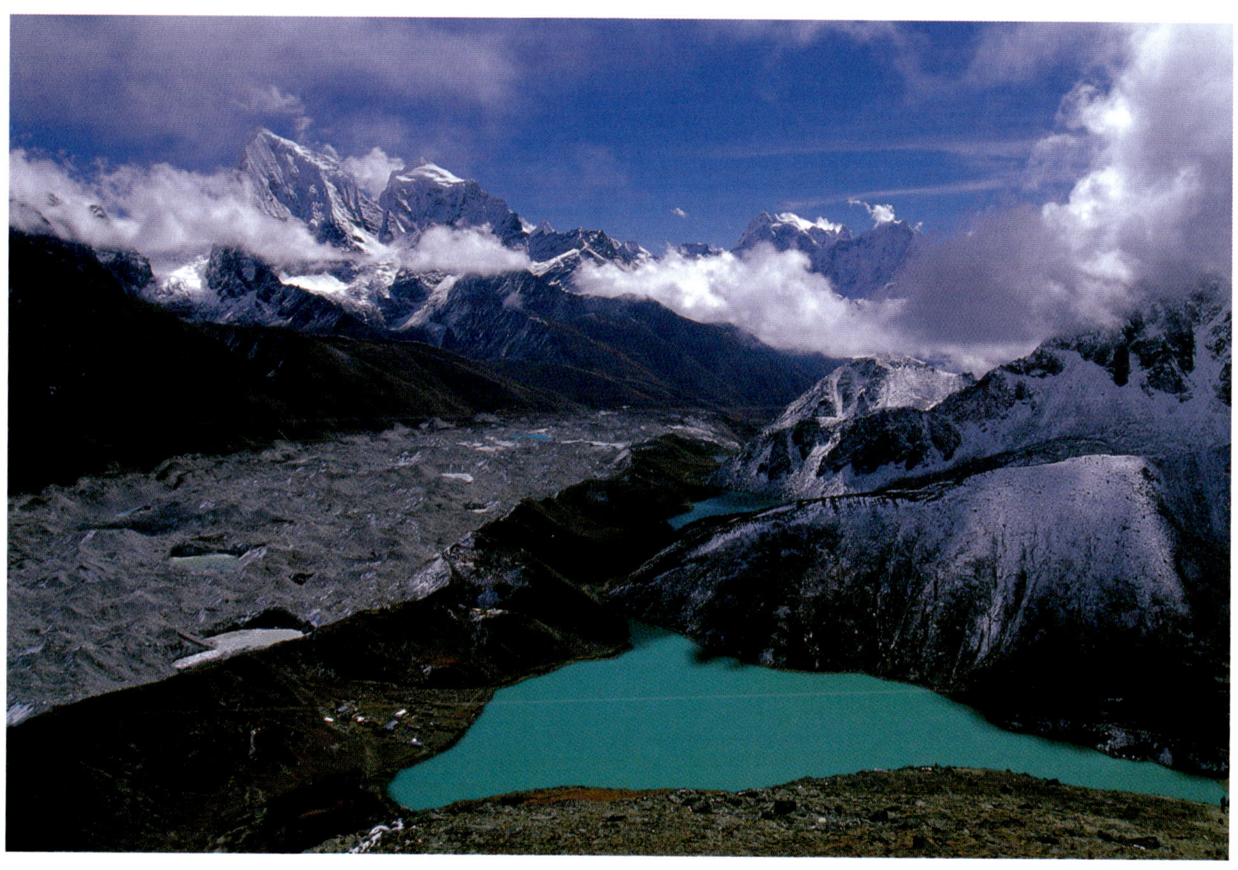

pre-eminently sacred. They are the abode of saints, and so mighty that nothing can shake them. The mountain range has been personified as Himavat, the father of Ganga and the mountain goddess Parvati.

The grandeur of the Himalayas is a wonder for the world. They are the abode of the divine and the cradle of holy places. The Himalayan ranges are also frequented by sages seeking wisdom. Kailasha, Manasarovar, Badrinatha and Kedarnath are its glorious gems. Ancient sanctuaries situated there are sites of pilgrimage and prayer. Many peaks are given very poetic and elaborate names – thus, Mount Everest is known as 'Snow White Queen'; Kanchenjunga is 'Five Treasures of the Great Snow'; and Kailasha is 'Precious Snow'. From Pamir to Lhasa, and from Kuenlun to Brahmaputra are scattered the legends of the Himalayas.

Whenever mountains are personified as gods or are considered as seats of cults, their sacredness is obvious. They are regarded as a great source of merit. Mount Olympus was believed to be the abode of the gods, with the palace of Zeus on its summit. Some Babylonian gods were called 'rulers of the mountain'. Mountains are associated with clearly defined gods. In Japan, Fujiyama is the sacred mountain regarded as a goddess of the same name. Pilgrims ascend its summit in large numbers every year. For artists and poets it serves as a major source of inspiration. The ranges of the Kwan-lun are sacred in Taoism and have given rise to numerous fanciful legends.

Top: The Mount Everest. Mountains are believed to be the *Exis Mundi* – the centre post of the world. They are considered a link between heaven and earth. Here the Everest overlooks the glaciated lakes at Ama Da Blam Himal, Nepal.
Below: Shivling stones from holy mountains are worshipped as divine objects.

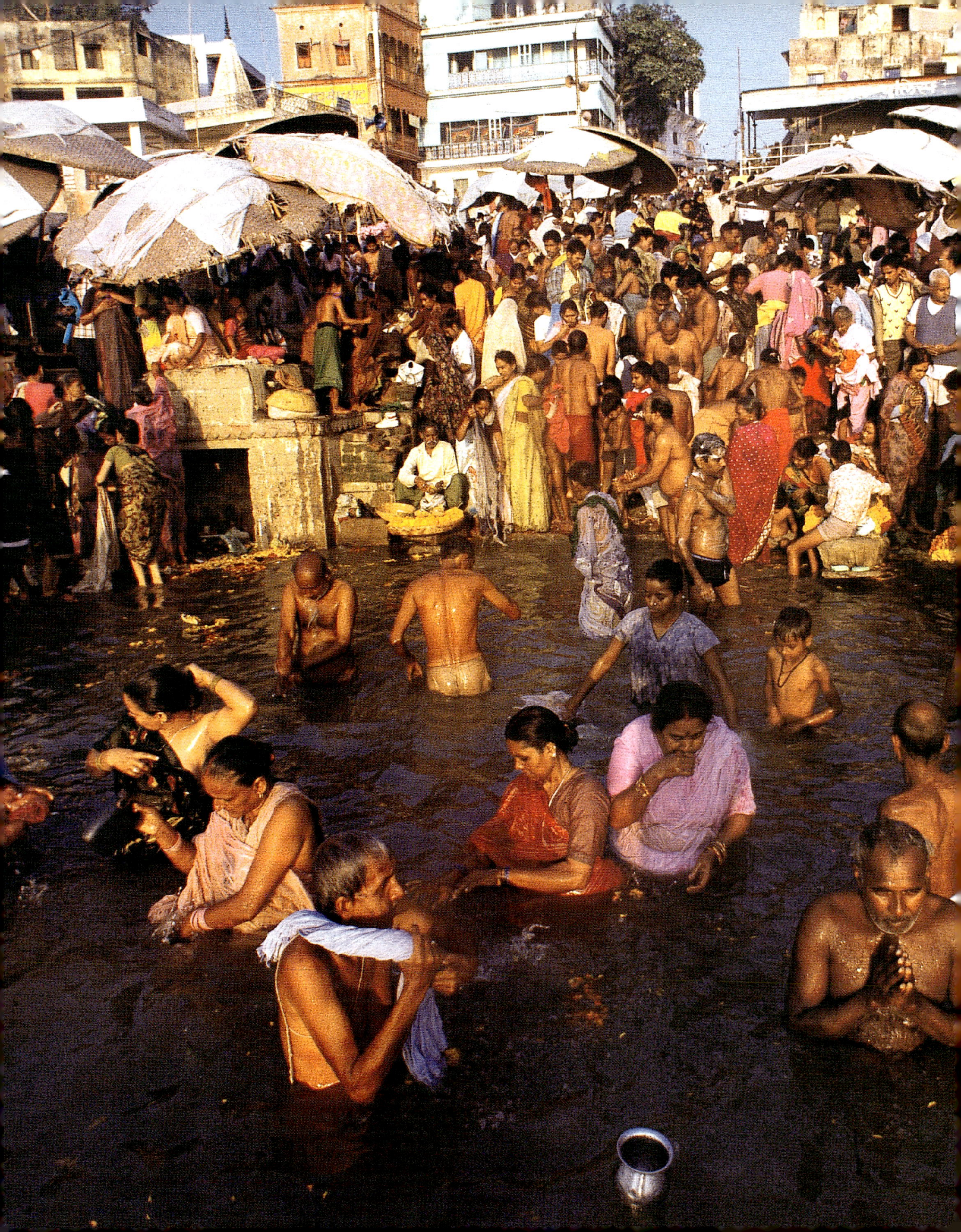

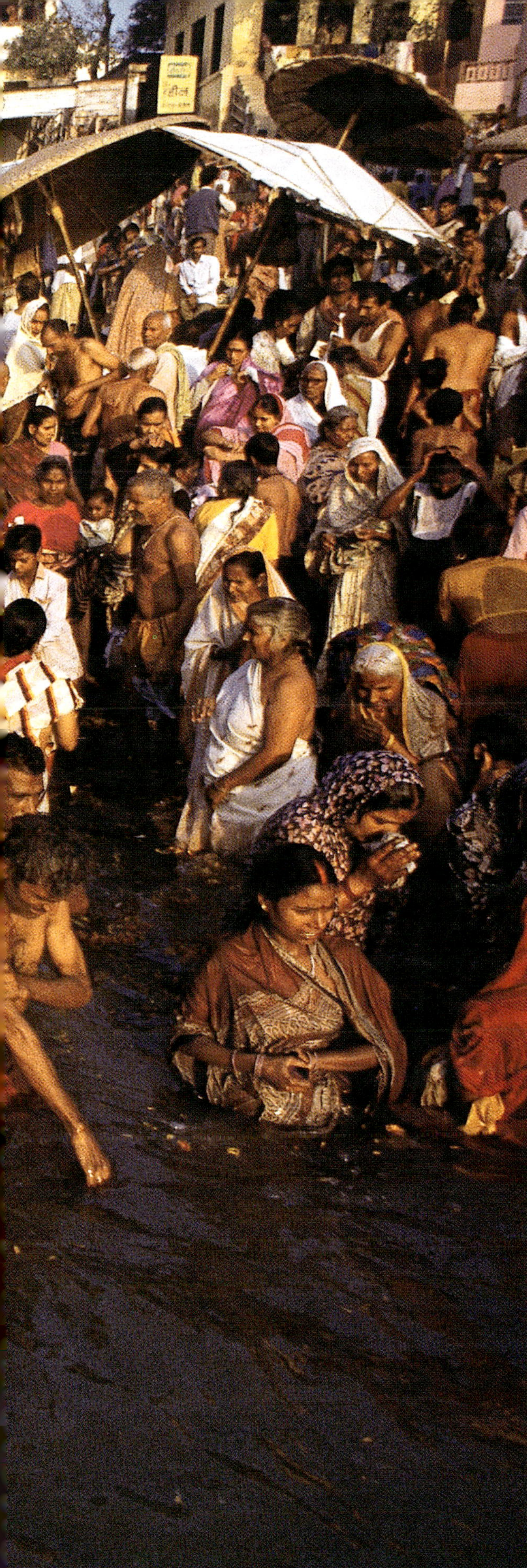

Some mountains are places of powerful contact between the divine and the human. For example, on the top of Adam's Peak, or Shri Pada, in Sri Lanka is a large indentation of a footprint. According to Buddhists, it is the footprint of the Buddha himself, matched by a similar imprint at Phra Sat in Thailand. For Hindus it is the imprint of Shiva; for Muslims, of Adam; and for Christians, of the apostle Thomas.

The Ganga is regarded as the river of heaven that came down to earth to wash off the sins of the suffering humanity.

Besides being an abode for the gods, mountains are also inhabited by spirits or haunted by fierce demons and ghosts. Mountains are lofty and seem to touch the clouds.

RIVERS

Life in most of the great civilisations was oriented towards rivers, and these came to be known subsequently as river civilisations: Mesopotamia along the Tigris and Euphrates, Egypt along the Nile, and the Indus Valley along the river Indus. Different divinities presided over the salt waters of chaos and creation, and the sweet waters under the earth that fill the rivers and the springs. Egyptians believed that fresh waters originated from the abyss beneath the earth. They believed in the existence of two rivers, both called Nile, one flowing on the earth and the other across the sky. Gods and goddesses are associated with rivers. The Sanzunokawa in Japan, for example, is said to divide the realms of the living and the dead. The dry riverbed of Sainokawara is believed to be the destination of the dead children.

Rivers are personified as goddesses. Sarasvati, Sarayu, Yamuna and others are invoked as they flow from the celestial ocean. Sarasvati is the mysterious river among the seven rivers mentioned in Vedic literature. In Puranic literature, the Ganga gained eminence.

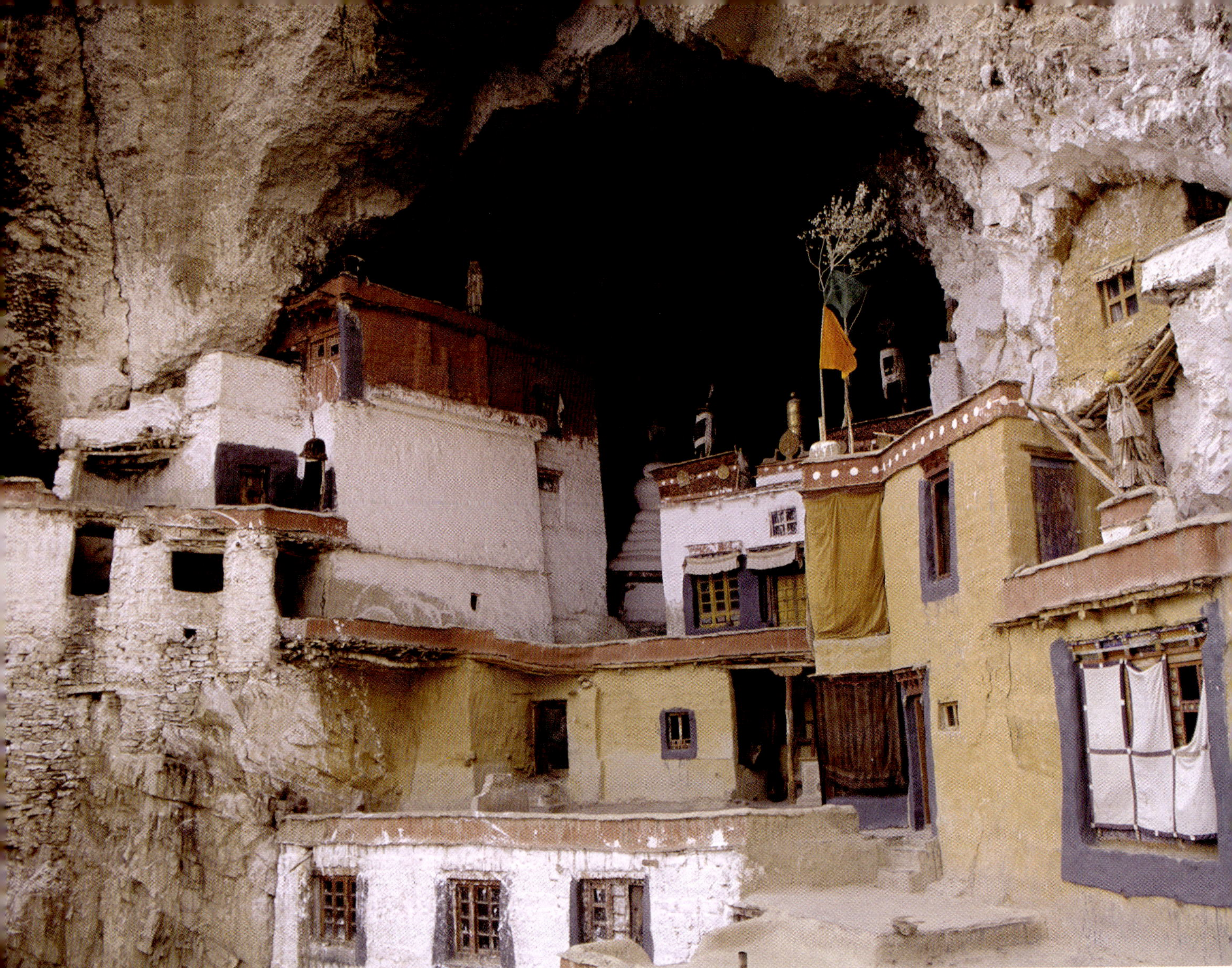

The Phuktal Monastery in Ladakh is built into a cave. Caves signify the very womb of the earth, a source of life and a passage from one cosmic world to another.

As a divine river, she accepted to flow from heaven to earth. The first gush fell upon the head of Lord Shiva, who broke the force of her cascade. The sanctity accorded to rivers attracts rituals; the water of these rivers is honoured as life-giving. People go for pilgrimages and holy dips on special occasions. Lamps are lit and prayers offered because they are worshipped as goddesses. The vision of Eden, presented briefly in Genesis II, also invokes a river issuing forth from the garden and splitting into four streams.

Ablutions with such waters prepare one for worship by removing impurities. Greek rituals also prescribed bathing in a river or a spring after an expiatory sacrifice. Similar rites of baptism are found in the Christian tradition, wherein they use the symbolic power of living water to wash away the sins of the past.

Rites of healing are meant for purification. The source of the Euphrates was famous for healing, and a bath there in springtime was believed to rid one of diseases all year long. The healing properties of the Ganga are also well known – its water is brought back home by the Hindus. The Hindus of Bali believe that the Tampak Springs are filled with healing waters.

Crossing a river at the time of death, as part of the journey to the other world, is common aspect of the symbolic passage. In Hindu mythology, the river Vaitarani marks the boundary between the living and the dead. In Japan, rivers are part of certain landscapes designated as realms of the dead in both Shinto and Buddhist traditions. In Christianity it is believed that the spiritual Promised Land is situated on the far shores. Similar symbolism lies behind the idea of the *tirtha* in Hinduism.

CAVES

Caves offering safe and permanent refuge for man are the earliest and natural abodes. Those who contemplate religious learning have also adopted these as dwellings. Caves show that the occupants possessed a striking variety of culture. In almost all cultures they are symbols of creation – a place for emergence of celestial bodies, and of ethnic groups and individuals. The cave is the great womb of earth, a symbol of life. It is a sacred place constituting a break in the homogeneity of space, an opening that is a passage from one cosmic region to another.

Gradually, caves acquired a sacred character and developed into places of worship. Thus began the tradition of creating cave temples, which reached a high state of development in India with the construction of thousands of cave temples cut out of rock. In ancient Egypt there were many such temples and these were divided into two sections – the true rock temples and those consisting partly of

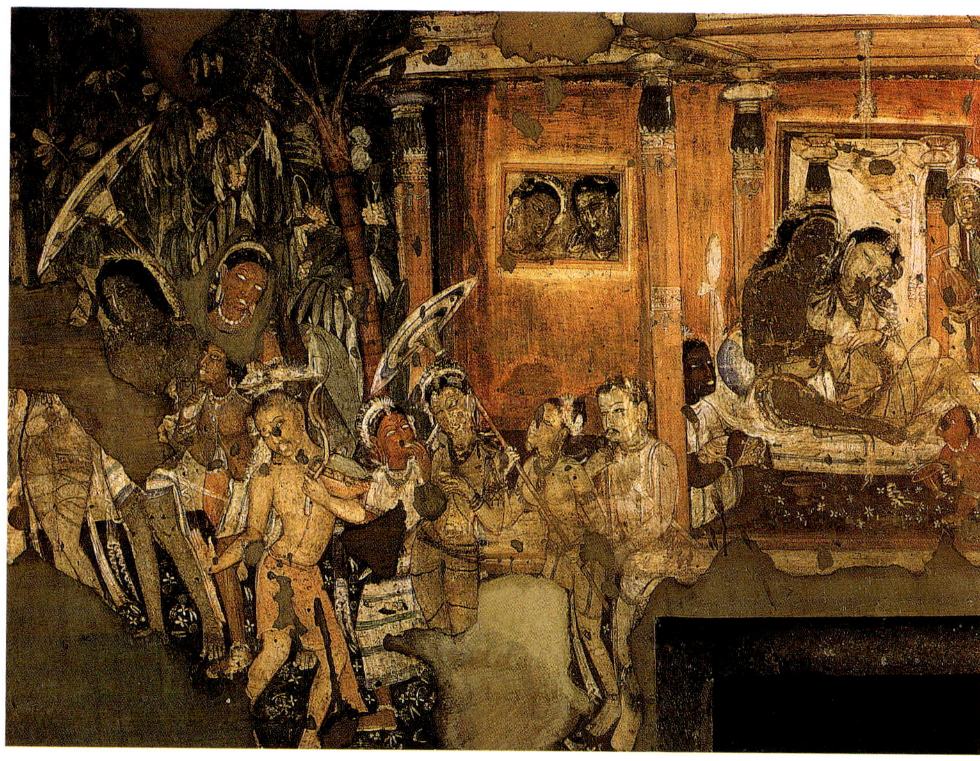

Above: The ceilings of Ajanta caves are decorated with motifs of flowers, animals or geometric patterns.
Left: The 17th century cave at Ajanta, depicting a scene in the harem coupled with the pageant of everyday life.

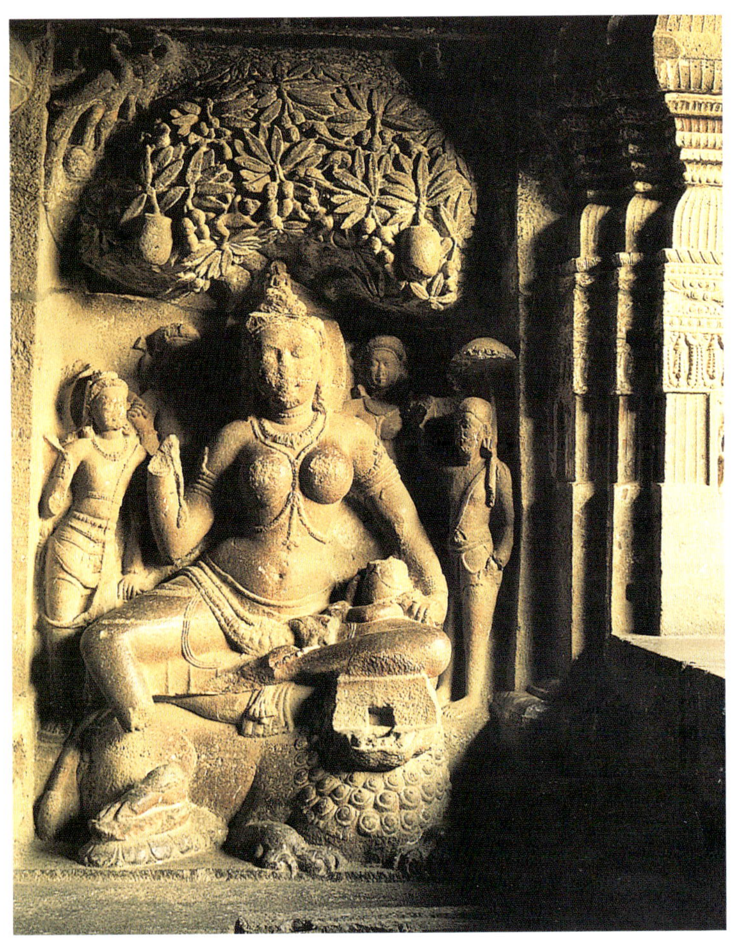

The statue of Ambika from the Indra Sabha cave, Ellora. The caves in Ellora, hewn in rocks, are considered sacred by Buddhists, Hindus and Jains alike.

an excavation in the rock, but with an exterior and an open-air building in front. The monastery of the great cave is situated in the Achaean mountains, about 3,000 feet above sea level. The monastery was originally tunnelled out of rock, above which buildings of ordinary character have been erected at later dates.

Art forms were created inside the caves for the initiated few and these did not need to be public. Some of the renowned works of art were created inside caves in Asia. The Buddhists were the first to carve caves and decorate their interiors. Cave paintings at Ajanta in India display the highest level of art of the 5th-6th centuries, through a careful depiction of scenes taken from the *Jataka* stories. Paintings on the walls of ancient caves or sculptures hewn out of rock within caverns, have been called 'invisible art' and likened to 'silent music'.

The caves at Ellora are an example of miracle in carving, hewn sometime between the 4th and 9th centuries. They are dedicated to three faiths: the early caves, built before AD 800, are Buddhist; the Hindu caves overlap (AD 600-900); and the Jain caves cover the period from AD 800 to AD 1000. At Ellora the great Hindu temple Kailasha is dedicated to Shiva, representing the mountain.

Caves are the oldest monuments in Sri Lanka. Natural rock shelters were improved by human effort. They contain early Brahmi inscriptions indicating that donating caves was a highly meritorious act that started as early as the 3rd century BC. The earliest surviving, and the most famous, example of Simhalese painting is at Sigirya. In the north-western frontiers of ancient India, at Bamiyan, there are scores of rock-cut caves, monastic cells and sanctuaries. The earliest goes back to the 3rd-4th century AD.

SEASONS

The number of seasons vary from country to country. In Thailand there are only three seasons – there is no term for 'autumn' in their language. Normally there are four in the rest of the world, but in India there are six seasons: spring, summer, rain, autumn, *hemanta* and winter. The Vedas recorded the names of six seasons for the first time. The various seasons have inspired poets and authors of a number of classical works in Sanskrit. The earliest references to seasons in literature are found in the *Rigveda*, the first literary work of the Indo-Europeans. Classical Sanskrit poetry gives a graphic description of spring, rain, winter and autumn. The later poets have dwelt upon the theme in their works, giving due importance to the description of seasons as being the catalyst in arousing romantic sentiments.

When spring arrives, the entire animal and vegetable world is awakened to a new life. It is the king of all seasons, a time when the air is full of promise, and when people are young, spirited and full of curiosity, and perhaps stirred by the growing pangs of adolescence. Grasses grow and trees blossom – they are full of charms and play a wonderful orchestra of colours. Nature is flushed with a new life and love at the advent of spring. While somewhere the pollen of mango blossoms falls, elsewhere a soft, cool and comforting, sandal-scented breeze blows from the Malaya mountain in the south of India.

Summer is a sweltering season in many parts of the world. It is a time when most people are relieved to find some shade beneath the trees, while swans close their eyes under cool lotus leaves. Blooming flowers and old wines are refreshing and invigorating. A fragrant breeze blows gently and causes a few trees to bloom.

When the earth is completely parched by the summer heat, there comes the rainy season to provide relief. The sky becomes overcast with dark, mountain-like clouds. They are the trumpet blowers and herald the advent of the rainy season with their ever-changing forms and gestures. They make the peacocks dance. They roar like the waves of the celestial ocean. Rains fall when the heavens overflow, inaugurating a musical concert in the forests. The showers shoot like meteors falling from the sky and the lightning flashes are much like the frowns of an ogress.

Autumn is known as *sharad* in Sanskrit. The season is refreshing; it brings the turbulent waters under control, and the paddy stalks are laden with rich harvest. The season is brilliant too, with a sky clear of clouds and the lustre of the sun spread in all directions. Lotuses and lilies bloom graciously, while peacocks shed their spangled plumage and discard all gaiety and courting. Nights are bathed in silvery moonlight, and stars twinkle joyfully in the soothing rays of the moon sailing through the sky.

Winter is the season of glittering frosts and bountiful harvests of golden grain. Stacks of ripe rice and sugarcane cover the earth. The dew falls thick, the chilled water of lakes shimmer under the mild sun, the blue lotuses open wide in beauty, the winds are chilly and people are ever shivering, and, finally, the sober

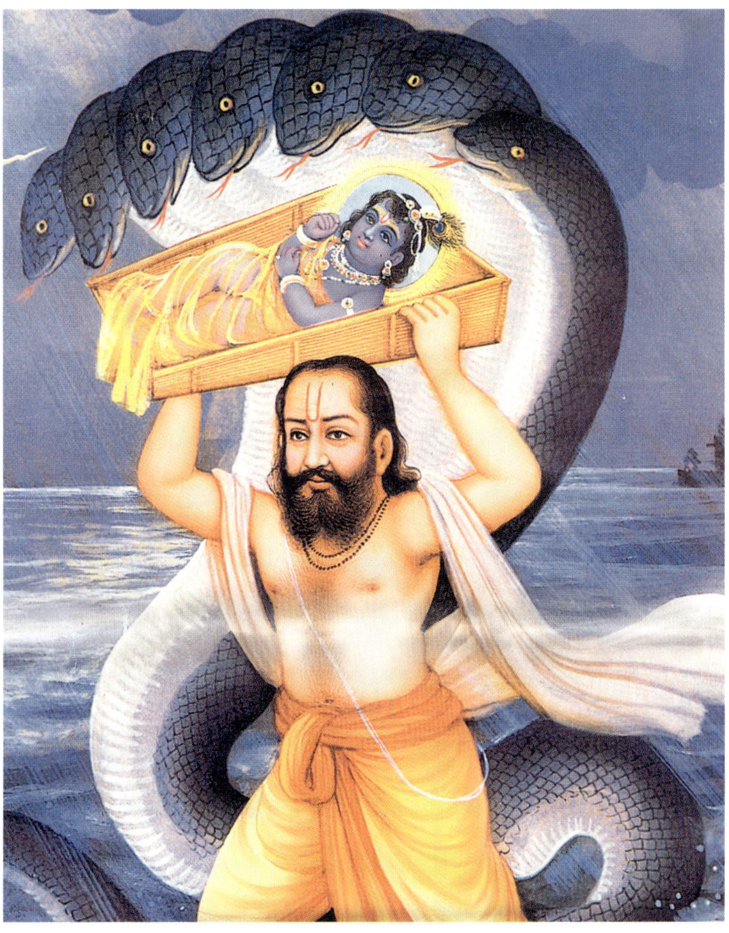

A scene where Vasudev carries the baby Krishna through the pouring rain. The rainy season brings relief to the earth parched by the summer heat.

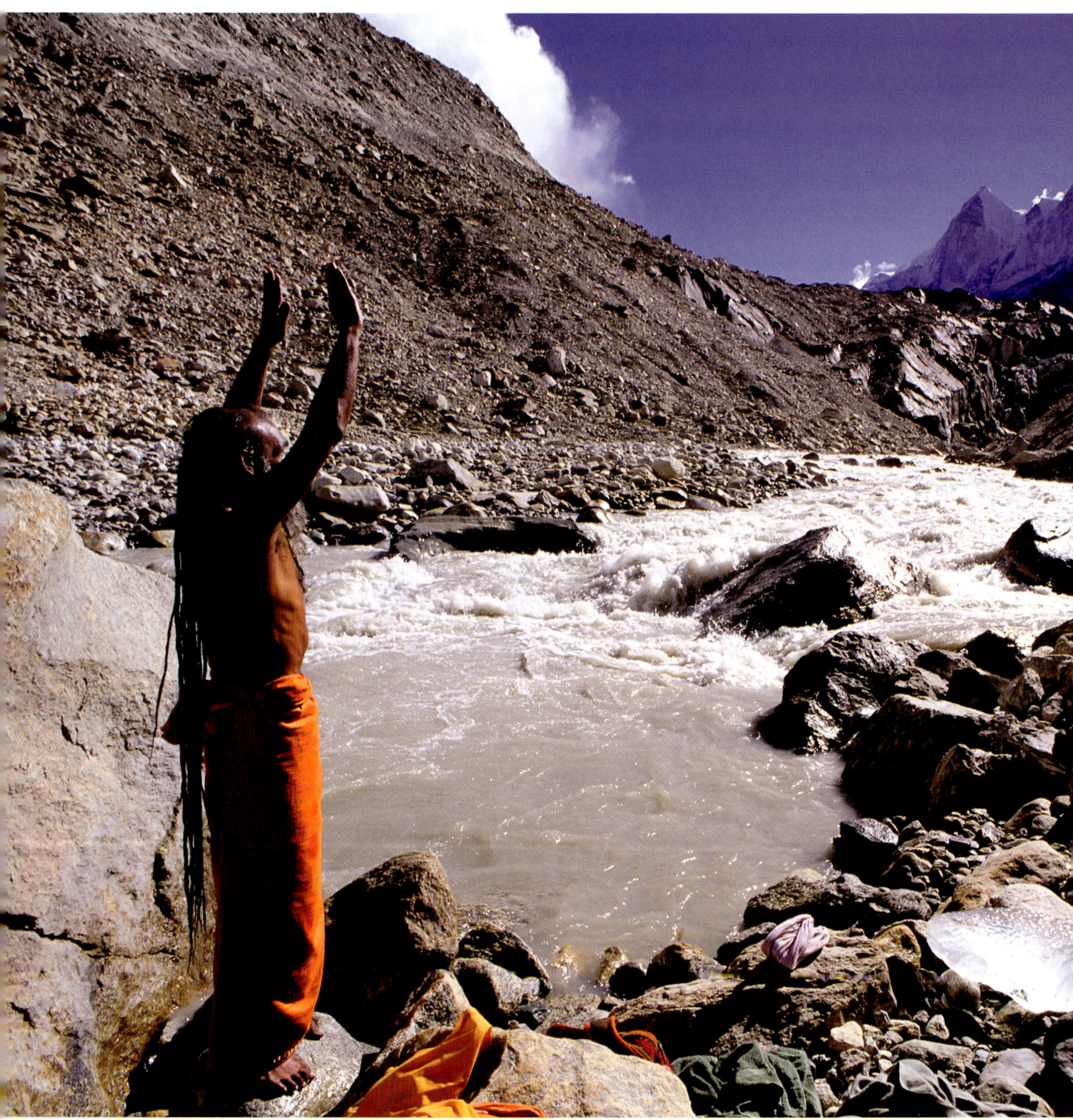

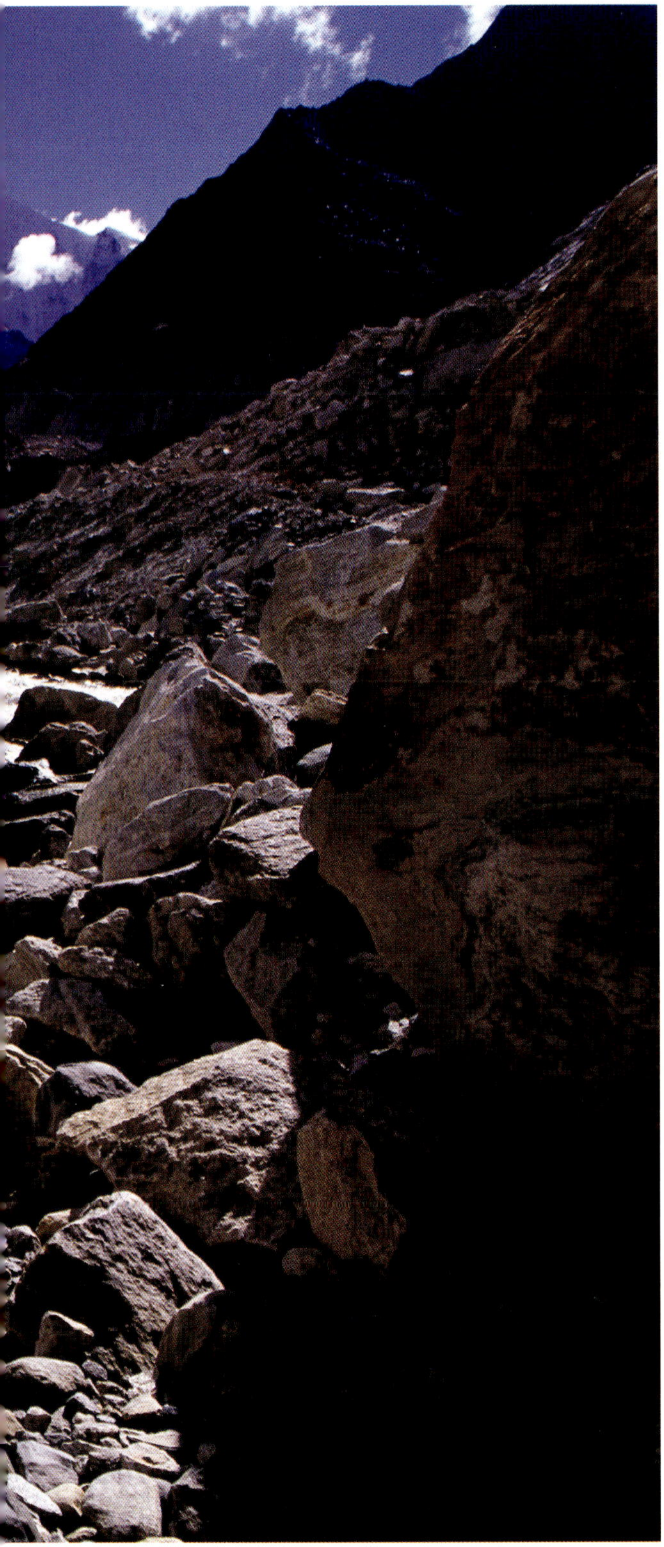

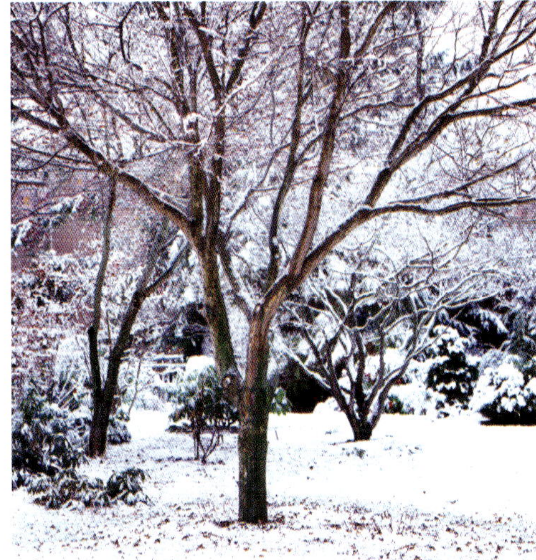

Left: A snowy winter. Many religions of the world deify seasons. Every season is reminiscent of a new birth.
Extreme left: A *swami* prays along the banks of the Ganga river in the town of Gaumukh, India. Gaumukh lies at the source of the holy river.

morning sun comes out for the people to bask in the gentle warmth of its rays.

In Tibetan Buddhism seasons are deified as goddesses. The queen of spring is dark blue in colour and holds a chopper in her right hand. She is dressed in human skin and rides a mule. The queen of summer is dark red. She holds a hook in her right hand, is dressed in silk, and rides a water buffalo. The queen of autumn is yellow in colour, holds a sickle in her right hand, wears a cloak of peacock feathers, and rides a stag. The queen of winter is dark blue and she holds a magic notched stick in her right hand and rides a camel that has a white spot on the forehead.

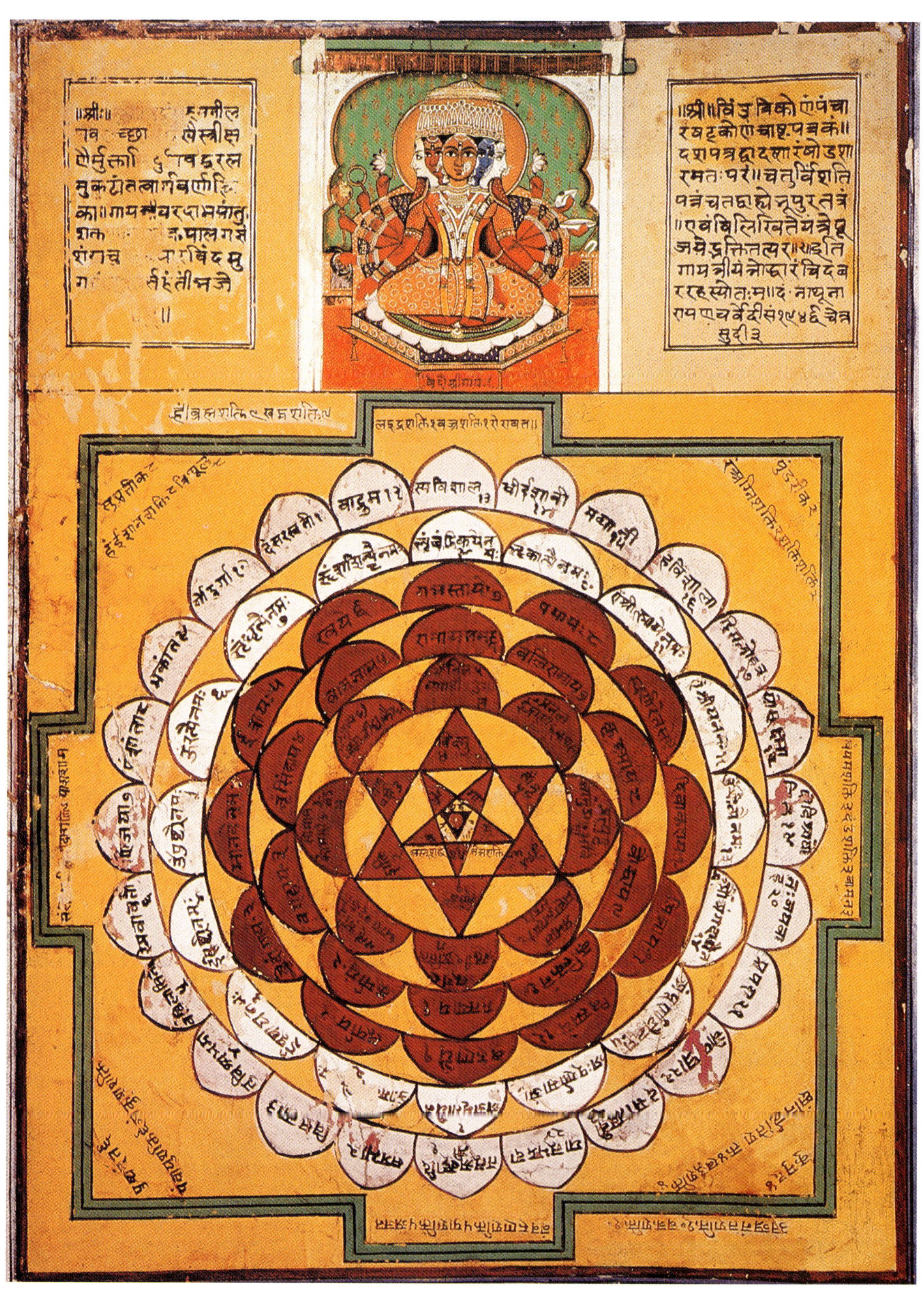

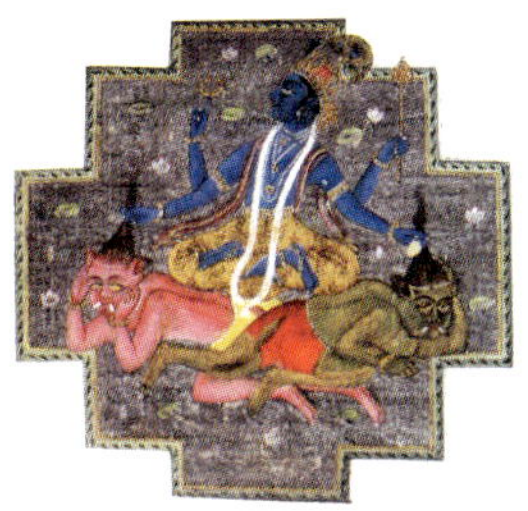

THE ART OF WRITING: SCRIPTURES

Writing is a system of signs to convey a meaning in an organised space. It runs, becomes functional, and looks cursive or current when used for commercial or secretarial purposes. Lapidary writing was meant for royal edicts, while donative inscriptions and legal charters evolved a well-proportioned epigraphic style. The symmetry of the book style is the literary style. The aesthetically modulated forms in Arabic are the hieratic style. The Chinese ideogram of pictographic origin transcends all these functions.

HINDU SCRIPTURES

Since the days of the Vedas in India, literature has been the purest voice of her deepest knowledge, of her life and vision, and of dreams and creation. The Rigvedic hymns were composed with a remarkable degree of metrical skill and command of language. Its poetry developed its own symbols, mainly ritualistic, but at times also aesthetic, metaphysical and physical, covering a wide spectrum of life. In those times every learned family cultivated the art of poetry, and the seers were great visionaries and intellectual leaders. They did not live in isolated places, but fully participated in the social, political and religious affairs.

Rigveda, the oldest sacred book, is a grand collection of prayers composed in Vedic Sanskrit sometime between 5000 BC and 1000 BC. It is divided into ten *mandalas* or sections of hymns (*suktas*) containing verses (*riks*) numbering 10,552. They were composed by such visionary seers as Atri, Vishvamitra, Bharadvaja and Vasishtha. The hymns are meant to invoke various deities in a language that has a distinctive accent of a musical nature. They are highly flexional and rich in an all-important morphological process – for example, affixation, suppletion, composition and reduplication. They are written in metres making them fit for chanting and singing. The smallest metrical unit in a hymn is called a *pada*, usually containing eight, eleven, or twelve syllables. Normally there are four *padas*

Facing page: Religious manuscripts. The art of religious writing dates back to the Vedas, when the written word was seen as the purest voice of wisdom.
Above: A miniature folio depicting Vishnu killing Kaitabha. It reflects the vigour and vitality of the Kota school of painting in Rajasthan.

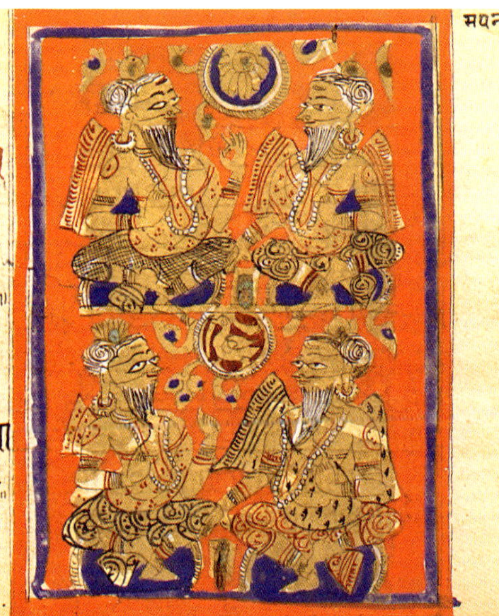

The *Guru Granth Sahib*, also known as the *Adi Granth*, is the supreme spiritual authority of Sikhism. It is a unique work containing writings by people belonging to other faiths as well.

in a verse. Some of the metres used are Gayatri, Anushtubh and Jagati.

Rigveda contains poetry that is lyrical, devotional, narrative, philosophical, dramatic and didactic. The seer's feelings are aroused by the grandeur of nature while composing the prayers to Ushas, Savitri and Surya. *Yajna*, the fire ritual, was the main religious practice of the Vedic period. There are hymns for *yajna* as well as for marriage and funeral ceremonies. They are also based on folk life and beliefs. Tales are written in the form of dialogues as an acceptance of the different shades of life.

The three other Vedas are *Sama*, *Yajur* and *Atharva*. *Yajurveda* contains sacrificial formulae in prose and verse to be pronounced by the priest who performs the sacrifice. It is related to performers of the sacrifice. Thus, the Vajpeyi is connected to the heroic deeds of a warrior. The Rajasuya sacrifice symbolises a military expedition. The Ashvamedha, or the horse sacrifice, was performed only by a powerful conqueror who wished to become a world ruler, *chakravarti*. The last 15 sections of *Yajurveda* contain prayers to sacrifices like the Pururshamedha, meant for everyone in society. Some of the outstanding prayers are Purushasukta and Shivasankalpa. The rhythmical prose of *Yajurveda* creates poetical imagery and symbolism. Stories like that of Pururavas and Urvashi became famous themes for Indian drama. Theological riddles like Brahmodaya preserve the primitive poetic heritage. The Vedas are an important read for a study of religions.

The last of the four Vedas is predominantly the Veda of domestic ceremonies and practices. It is a unique record of the day-to-day social life of the Vedic people. The hymns are composed in all the metres that are found in the *Rigveda*. Its language, though mostly archaic, contains some later forms also. Gods such as Indra and Agni are revered as killers of demons and bestowers of prosperity. There are hymns for achieving longevity and health, and are used during the ceremonies of tonsure, initiation, first shaving of the beard, etc. Some of the hymns meant to help gain prosperity are connected with activities like ploughing, sowing, growth of crop, irrigation, breeding cattle, trade, building a house, and travel. Prayers are offered for happiness, success and safe conduct; some are sung for achieving harmony in family and social life and also for overcoming rivals in debate. The oldest record of medical science can be traced in the hymns for curing diseases like fever, jaundice, dropsy, diarrhoea, constipation, retention of urine, rheumatism or colic, cough, and paralysis.

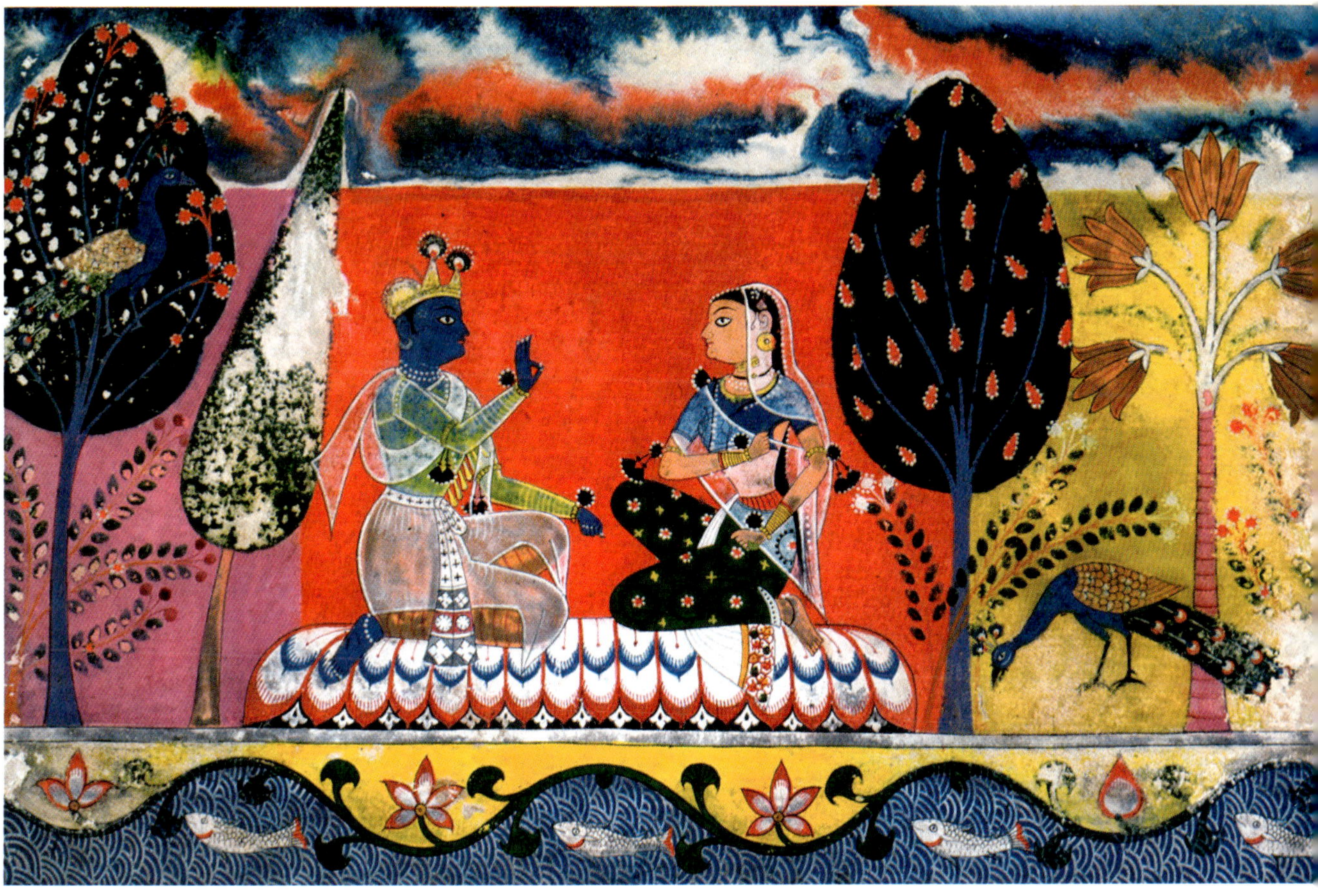

The *Puranas* and the epics are valuable sources of Indian history. The *Puranas* are classified as *smriti* – remembered, written and recorded literature – and not *shruti*, the revealed or heard literature as the Vedas, Upanishads and Brahmanas are. There are 18 Mahapuranas and many Upapuranas. The Mahapuranas are: Brahma, Padma, Vishnu, Vayu, Shiva, Matsya, Bhagavata, Naradiya, Markandeya, Bhavishya, Brahmanda, Brahma-vaivarta, Skanda, Garuda, Linga, Varaha, Vamana and Kurma. According to the *Puranas*, the duty of the chroniclers of history is to preserve and narrate the genealogies of the great sages and the glorious kings. Thus, they contain such voluminous details. However, the lists that they contain sometimes do not

Above: Krishna and Radha depicted in a scene from the poem *Gita Govinda* by Jayadeva.
Below: Illuminated manuscripts. Illuminating the scriptures was a way of dedicating one's time to god.

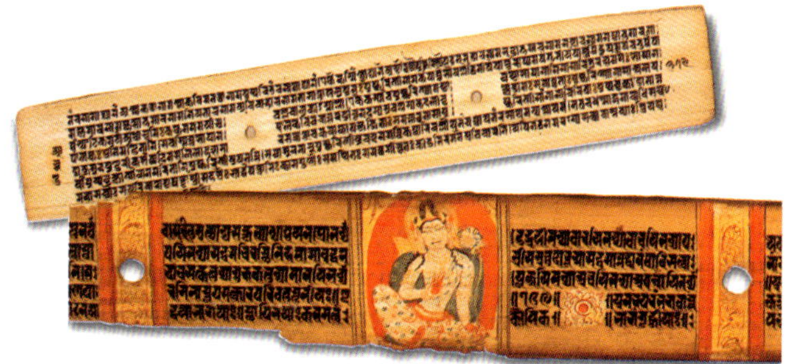

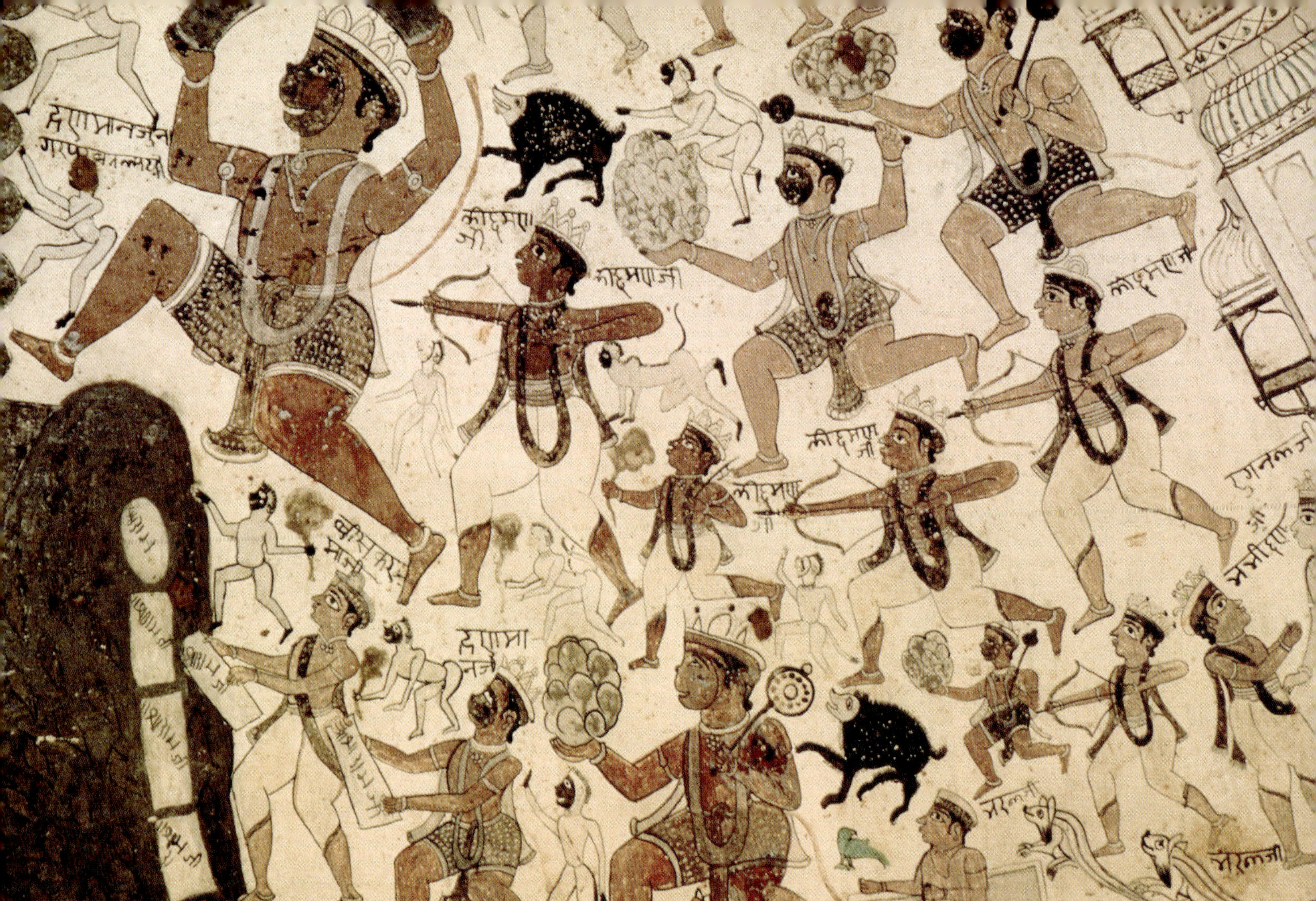

A detailed painting of the Ramayana battle scene. Hanuman, the monkey god, leads his army in a battle against the evil Ravana, to release Sita from captivity.

match. They cover various spheres of human activities including cultural, religious, philosophical and economic. They are written and preached by *sutas* (a *suta* is the son of a Brahmana by a Shudra woman) and not Brahmanas.

Upanishads are the utterances of the seers who spoke and put their illumined experiences together for the welfare of society. They are vehicles of individual, social and spiritual illumination. Their aim is practical rather than speculative. The knowledge contained therein is a means of spiritual freedom. The identity of the visionaries who wrote them is not known, but some of the doctrines of the *Upanishads* are associated with renowned sages like Aruni, Yajnavalkya, Shvetaketu and Shandilya. Possibly they were the early exponents of the doctrines attributed to them. The dates of the *Upanishads* are difficult to determine, though the early ones – Aitareya, Kaushitaki, Chhandogya, Kena, Taittariya, Isha and Katha – belong to the 7th-8th centuries BC. In all, there are over 200 *Upanishads*, but traditionally they are 101 in number. The great Vedantic philosopher Adi Shankara wrote commentaries on 11 *Upanishads*.

Vedic literature is followed by the two epics, *Ramayana* and *Mahabharata*. They were transmitted for thousands of years through oral tradition, which gave rise to the creation of a large number of recessions in different parts of India as well as abroad. The earliest manuscript of *Ramayana* was discovered in Nepal. It has been translated and transcreated in a number of countries in Asia.

BUDDHIST SCRIPTURES

Buddhism opened up an unfathomed universe of thought. Buddhist writings are enormous. The works of transcendental wisdom are so lofty that one cannot measure their height – and so profound that one cannot plumb their depths. Looking at Buddhist literature is like gazing at the sky or the sea. It covers hundreds of thousands of pages. In the Far East, Buddhist literature is regarded as a voice of unity of man, nature, art and the divine, where echoes of each are repeated at different levels of consciousness.

Buddhist scriptures were first collected and preserved orally. Immediately after the death of the Buddha, one of his senior disciples, Mahakashyapa, convened a council of five hundred Arhats. The monks, who had heard the Buddha recite all the discourses from memory, were later asked to transmit specific discourses verbatim to their students. For hundreds of years, the tradition of transmission of scriptures from teacher to student existed. In the 1st century AD they were first written and compiled in Sri Lanka.

The canon of Buddhist scriptures consists of three parts and is known as Tripitaka. They are Vinaya-pitaka, Sutra-pitaka and Abhidharma-pitaka. They were composed in Pali and have been preserved intact. The first two pitakas, Vinaya and Sutra, were written down at the first Buddhist council in 480 BCE, when Upali was questioned about discipline and Ananda about doctrine. The answers that they presented constitute the basis for these two pitakas.

Vinaya-pitaka, or the Ordinance Basket, contains the accounts of the Buddhist order and the rules laid down to discipline and regulate the lives of the monks and the nuns. Some of the oldest parts of the canon that originated in the first decade after the death of the Buddha are also contained in it.

Sutra-pitaka is composed of the discourses said to have been the words of the Buddha himself to his immediate disciples. The corpus of text is divided into five collections – Digha-nikaya, Majjhima-nikaya, Samyutta-nikaya, Anguttra-nikaya and Khuddaka-nikaya.

According to available sources, Abhidharma-pitaka originated at the time of the first council or in the period between the 3rd century BCE and the 3rd century CE. The final codification, though, was done in 400-450 CE. The Abhidharma-pitaka was added after a split into individual schools. The versions are of Theravada and Sarvastivada. The Abhidharma of Theravadis consists of seven books and was written in Pali, while that of the Sarvastivada school was written in

A monk deeply engrossed in the study of Buddhist scriptures in a monastery in Sikkim. The teachings of Buddha emphasise strict discipline.

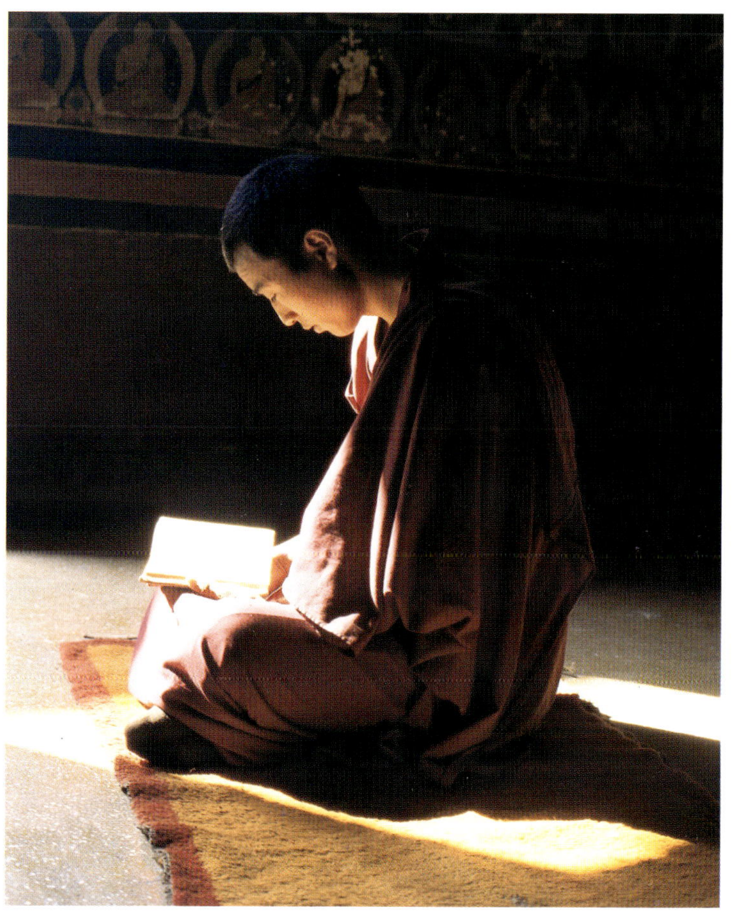

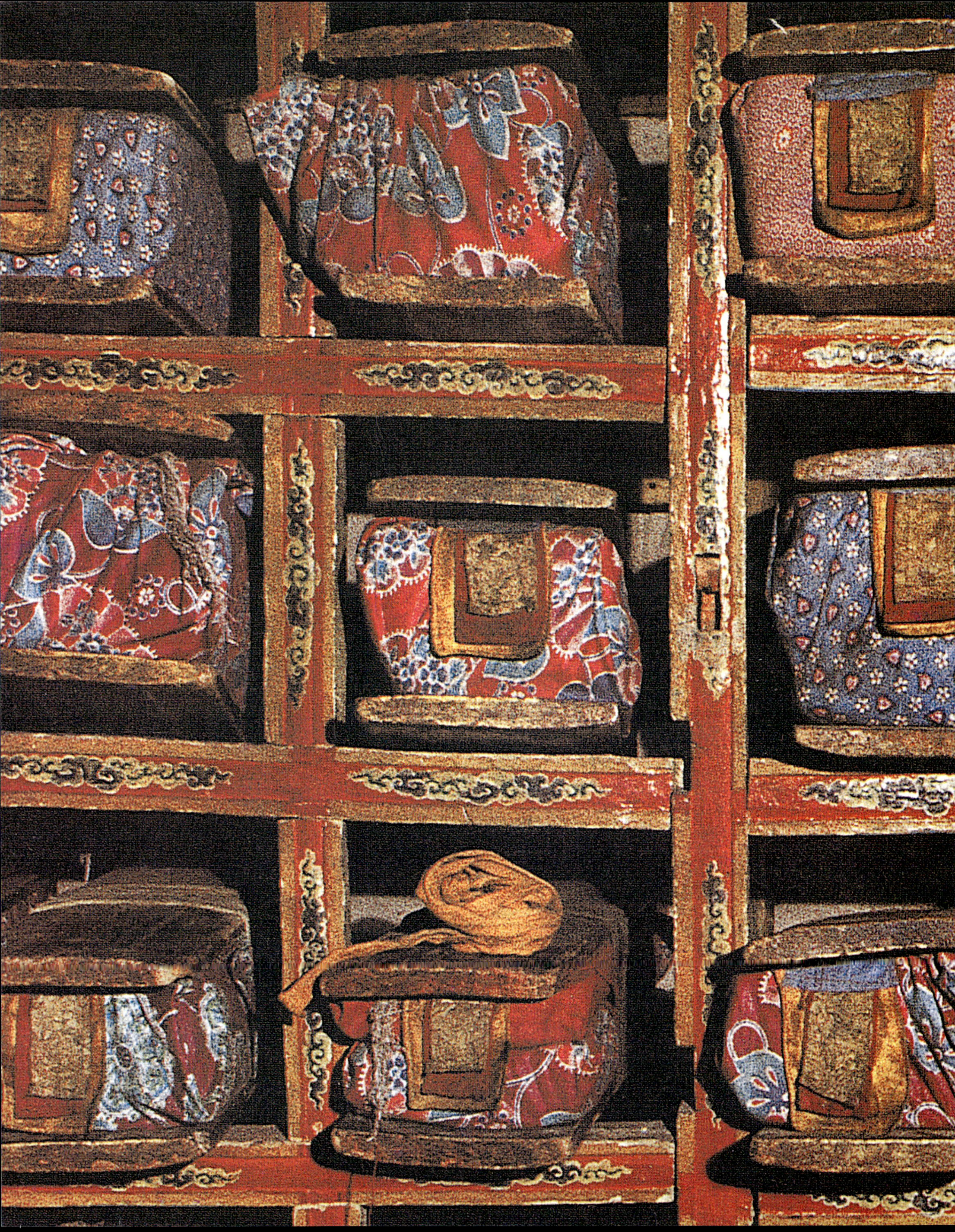

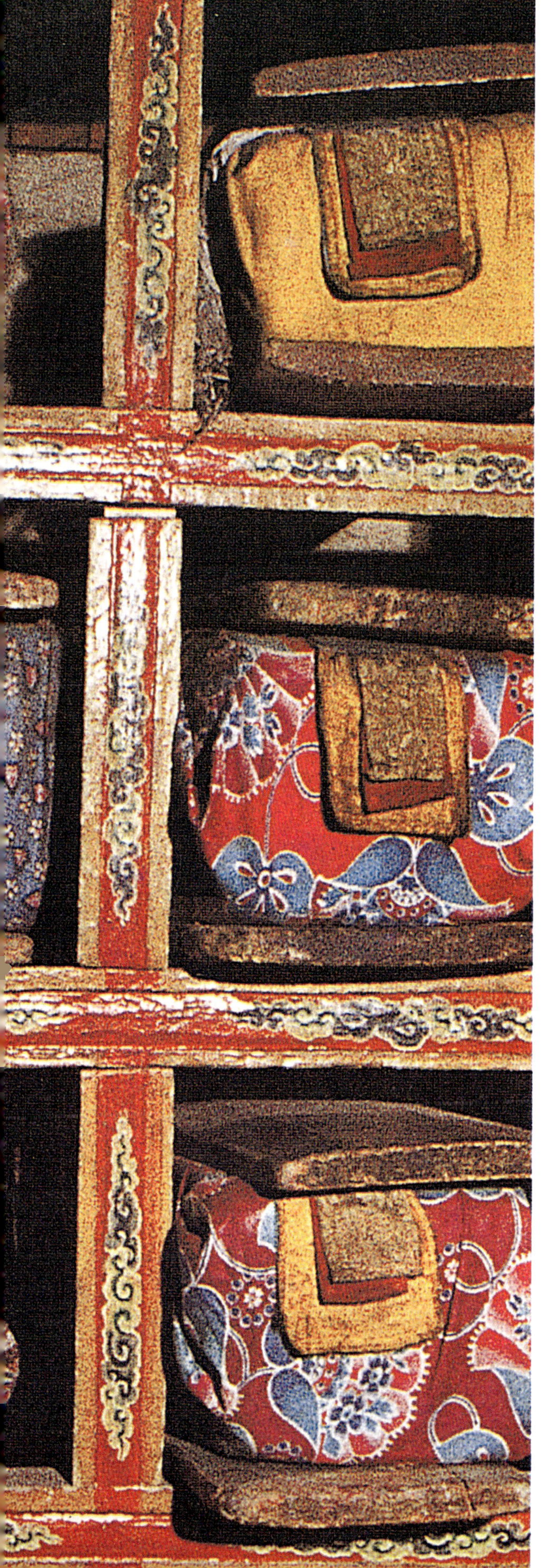

Manuscripts and scrolls in Thikse Monastery, Ladakh. They are sanctified and preserved in miniature caskets in libraries and are regarded as repositories of sacred objects.

Sanskrit and also consists of seven books. Abhidharmakosha is the most important compilation of the Sarvastivada teaching, composed in the 5th century in Kashmir. It was the fundamental work used by the Chinese. The Sthaviravada canon was authoritative in north-western India.

Buddhist literature in Sanskrit is a large and diverse category. It consists of both canonical and non-canonical materials. The latter, ranging from collections of anonymous narratives and ritual manuals to technical treatises, poetries and plays, are written by known individuals. Two distinct languages are used in this category: Sanskrit and the so-called Buddhist hybrid Sanskrit. The latter is the language of a text called Mahavastu and also of the Mahayana *sutras* (*sutras* are discourses attributed to the Buddha). These texts vary in character, particularly in the degree to which they employ vernacular grammatical forms. Later, such texts are identified largely through their vocabulary, their grammar being standard but simple.

Mahayana sutras form a diverse body of literature produced between the 1st century BCE and the 5th century CE. The earliest examples are thought to be perfect texts of wisdom. Many Mahayana sutras are now known only in Tibetan and Chinese translations. Among these scriptures are those of the Mahasanghika and Dharmaguptaka schools. Tantra in its wider connotation was applied to a large spectrum of texts, with several strands of thought and ritual. Their designations vary with time and space. The basic scheme, employed by Buddhaguhya and others in the mid 8th century AD, is that tantras emphasise external ritual activity or internal yogic practice.

Buddhist Sanskrit texts found their way across the boundaries of India when Buddhism

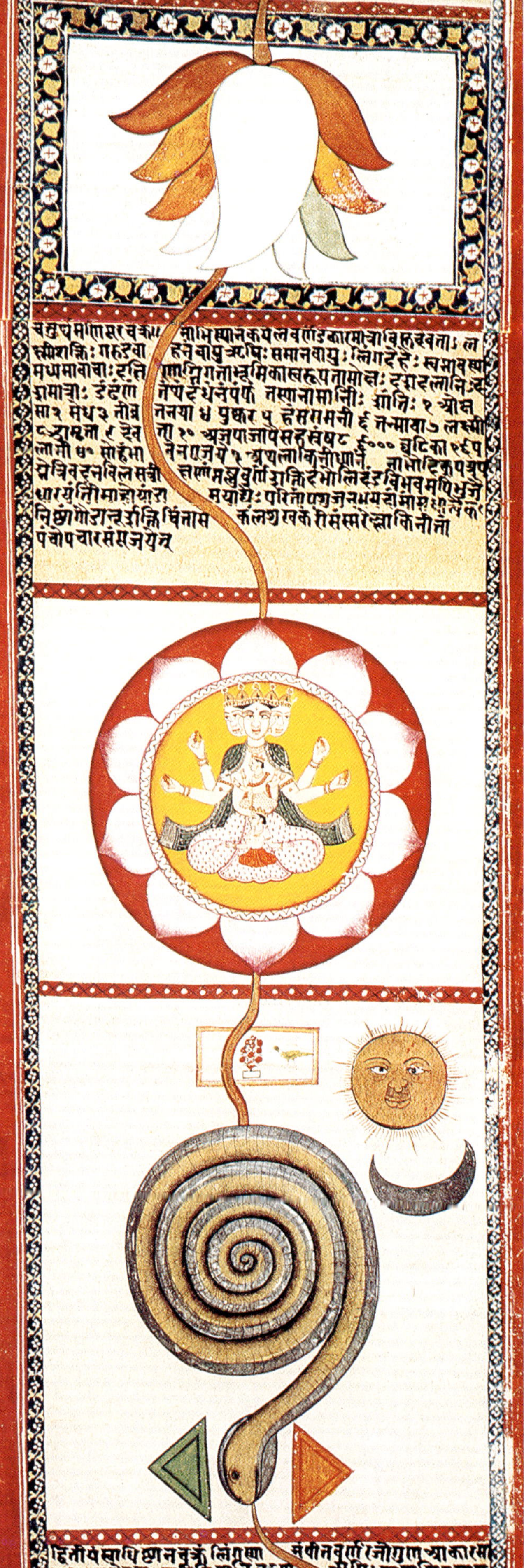

spread to countries in the East, the Southeast, and the Far East. They were translated into the languages of the people wherever they went. It was an order of the Buddha himself that his teachings should reach the people in their own languages. The widely accepted view is that the Chinese translations of the scriptures imported overland, and rendered from the 2nd century AD, seem to be the oldest – and those that came by sea are from the beginning of the 3rd century. However, a tradition holds that the first translation of Indian scriptures occurred in 246-219 BC, during the reign of the Chin Dynasty, when 18 wise men carried the scriptures from India to China.

The date of the official transmission of Buddhist scriptures into China, given on the basis of inscriptional evidence, is AD 67, when two Indian scholars, Kashyapa Matanga and Dharmaraksha, reached China on the invitation of King Ming Ti of the late Han Dynasty. The two scholars had settled in Loyang and first translated the 'Sutra of Forty-two Chapters'.

Fa-hsien was a renowned scholar pilgrim who came to India in AD 399 in search of knowledge. The best known among his translations are Maha-parinirvana-sutra and Mahasanghika-bhikshuni-vinaya. Kumarajiva, a descendant of a royal Indian family, was so famous for his wisdom that he was taken as a prisoner by the Chinese to propagate Buddhism. The king appointed more than 800 monks to assist him to translate. Kumarajiva retranslated a large number of *sutras* more accurately and completely, and more than 300 volumes were produced. To this date his translations are thought to be the best. Bodhidharma, the Indian monk from Kanchipuram, transmitted the philosophy of *dhyana* that became popular in China as Ch'an and in Japan as Zen.

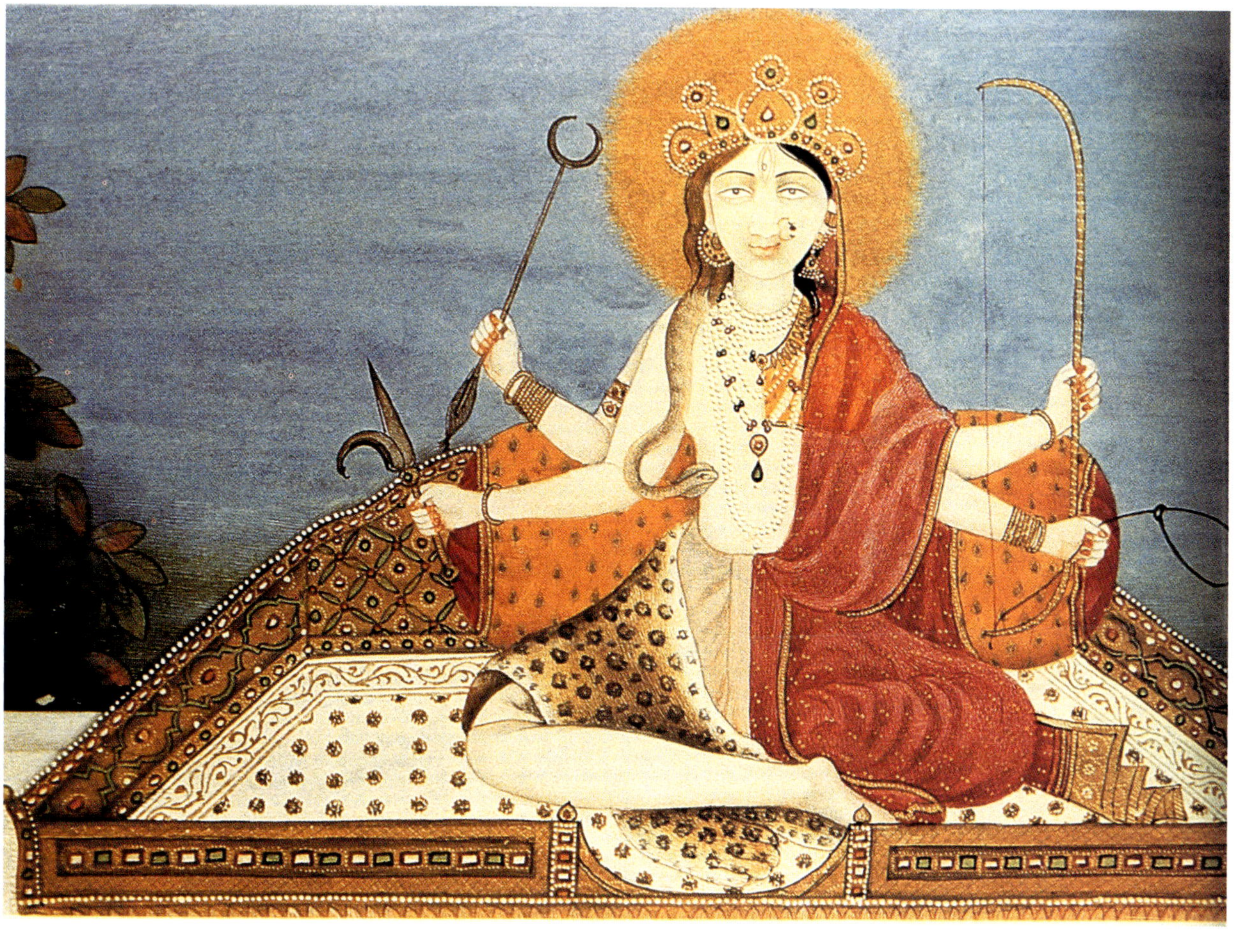

Tibetans have also preserved a rich heritage of Buddhist texts in translations. They are sacred to them and receive divine honour because they embody the word of the Buddha and contain knowledge emanating from his land. These Sanskrit texts reached Tibet, the 'land of snow', by virtue of the efforts and tenacity of scholarly missionaries from India and Tibet. The task was accomplished by ignoring the dangers and discomforts lying on their way. Tibetan scholars translated in collaboration with the Indian masters many Sanskrit books on various fields of knowledge for a perfect understanding of Indian theories. Temples and hermitages were no-disturbance zones and the most suitable places for them to undertake the momentous task. Indian and Tibetan scholars were assisted by Nepalese pandits including Shilamanju and Shantibhadra.

The Tibetan classification of Buddhist literature falls into *sutras* and *shastras*. Sutras are utterances of the Buddha, while shastras are written by the later teachers through interpretations. *Sutras* are collected in Kanjur in 108 volumes, whereas shastras are in Tanjur and consist of 225 volumes. In all, there are 1,108 works in Kanjur and 3,458 in Tanjur. The Buddhist *sutras* are texts that have the status of being considered as Buddha *vachana* – that is, 'words of the Buddha'.

Facing page: Tantras refer to religious Buddhist texts dealing with various strands of thought and ritual.
Above: Shiva, the mahayogi, manifests himself in Ardhanarishwara – a synthesis of both the masculine (Shiva) and feminine (Parvati) energies.

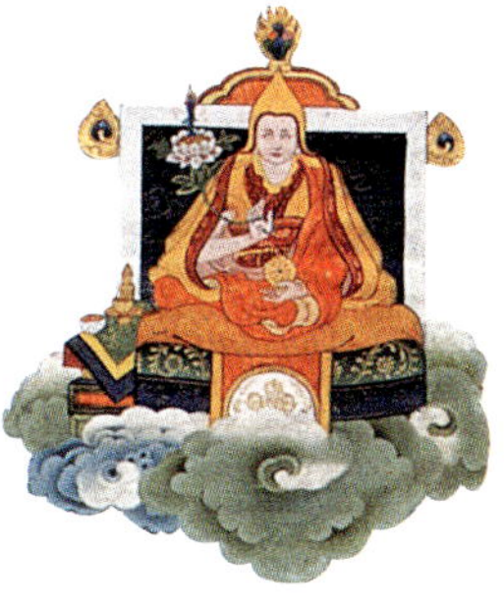

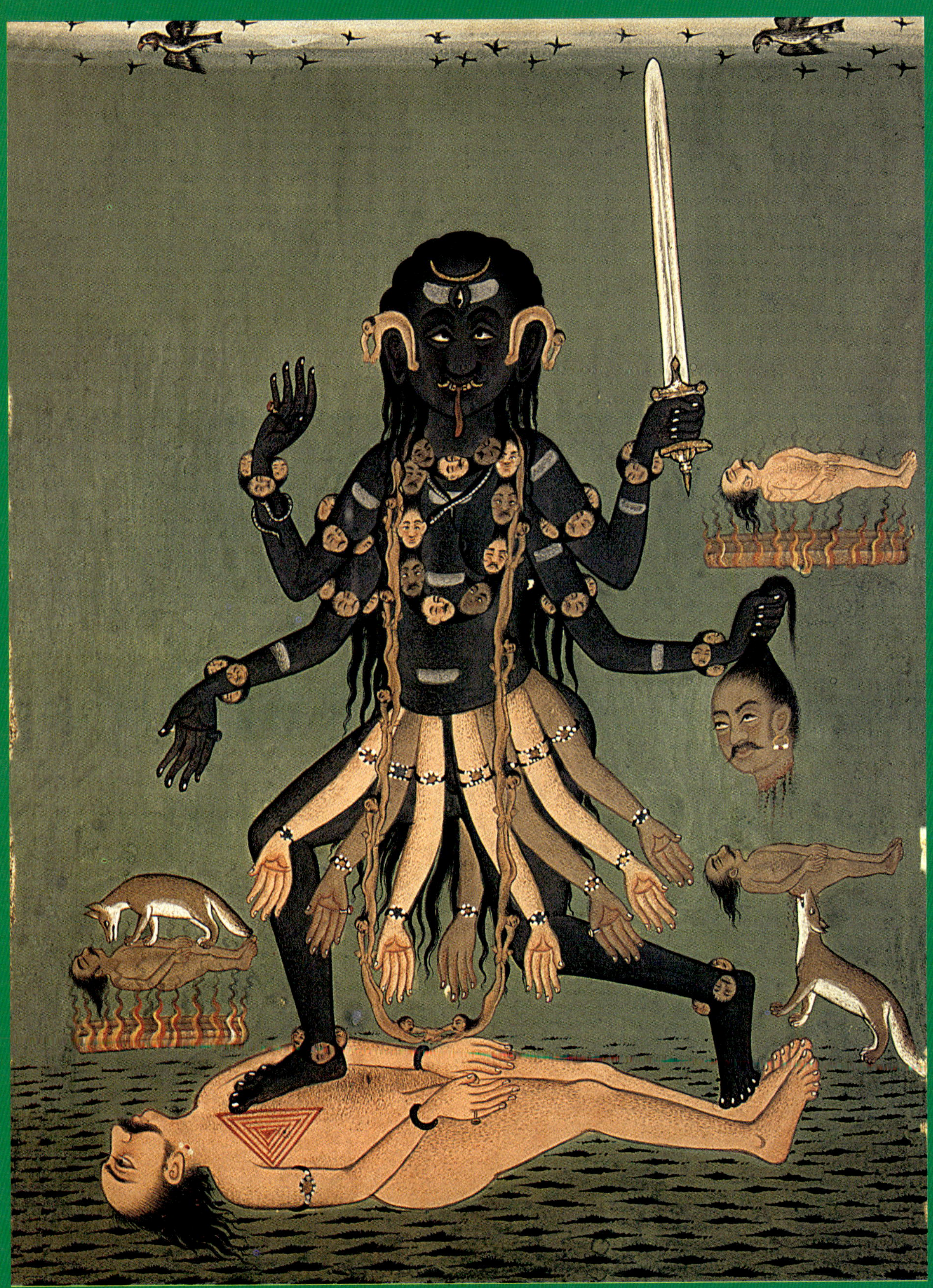

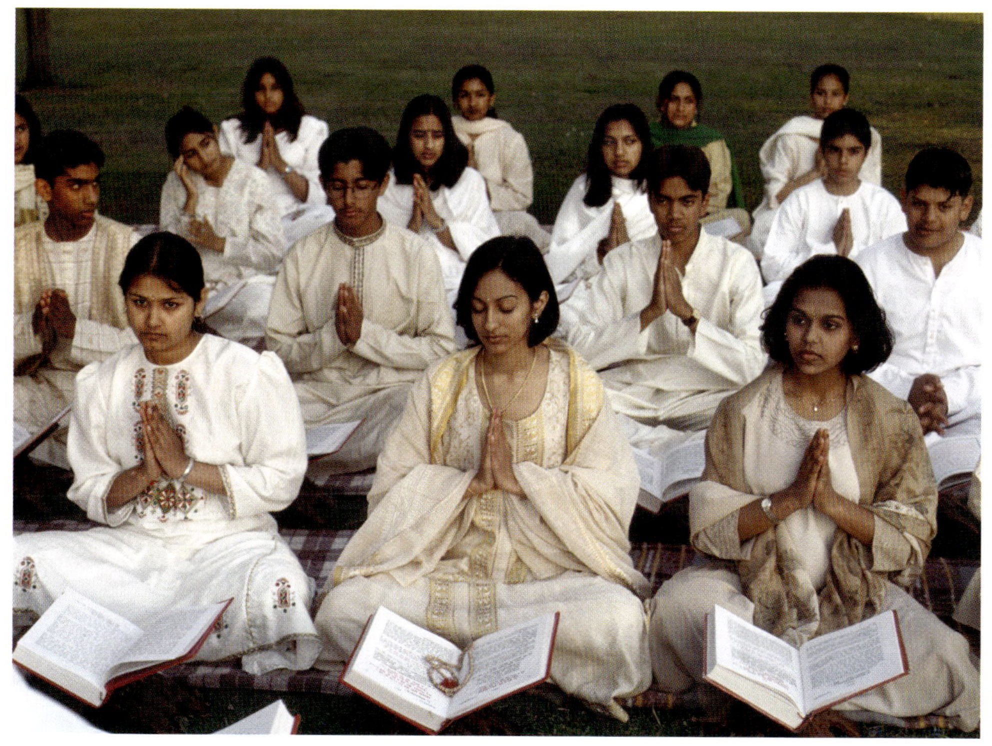

Facing page: Goddess Kalika, worshipped for gaining power to conquer enemies.
Left: Religious classes for Jain children where they study manuscripts on religion, poetics, astronomy, etc.
Below: Svetambara Jain man in traditional clothing.

JAINA SCRIPTURES

Since the time of the first Teerthankara, two kinds of sacred books have existed comprising the 14 purvas and the 11 angas. The fourteen *purvas* were reckoned to make up a 12th anga called Drishtivada. The 14 *purvas* are considered to be lost, but a substantial part of the material was incorporated into the later books. The Jain works were written in various languages to suit the audience. All the oldest works were written in varieties of Prakrits, more or less akin to the languages in use among the people of north India at the time of the first sermon. Later, the Jains turned to local vernaculars such as old Gujarati in the north and Tamil and Kannada in the south. In the Middle Ages, they adopted Sanskrit because it was the medium of all kinds of scholarly debates.

The earliest extant documents are the canonical scriptures of Shvetambaras and the systematic treatises of Digambaras. The Shvetambara canon, known as agama or siddhanta, is composed of 45 treatises grouped in six sections: Angas (limbs), Upangas (sub-angas), Prakirnas (miscellanea), Chedasutras (treatises on cutting, mostly concerning disciplinary technicalities), Chulikasutras (appendixes) and Mulasutras (basic texts). Thus, the canon is a compilation of texts of different origin, age and importance, focusing on a wide range of topics. Moreover, an enormous mass of scholastic exegesis was written in Prakrit and then in Sanskrit as traditional interpretations. Some of the works are chiefly in prose and some in verse, while others are a mix of prose and verse forms. Besides the sacred literature and the commentaries on

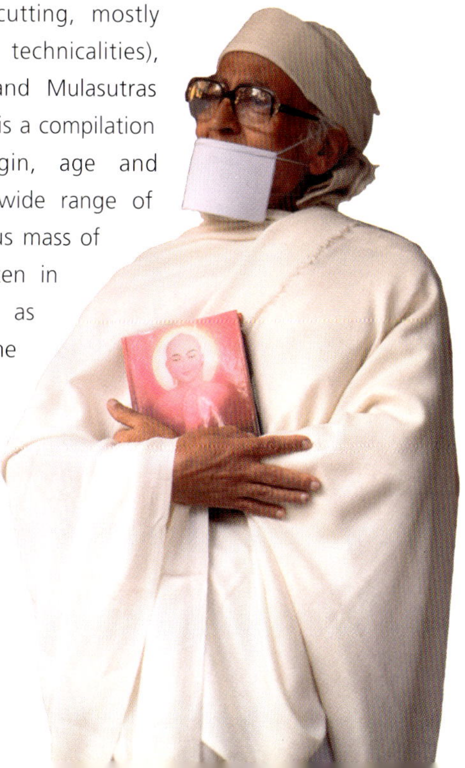

An embossed gold plate used to make offerings during Jewish festivals like Sabbath and Yom Kippur.

them, the Jains possess separate works also. One of the oldest is Umasvati's *Tattvarthadhigamasutra*, a Shvetambar work that is also claimed by the Digambaras. Another book also used by them is a sort of encyclopaedia called *Lokaprakasha*, by Tejapala's son Vinaya Vijaya.

The reduction of the texts took place under Devarddhigani in AD 454 according to common reckoning. Until then, the sacred texts were handed down without being embodied in written books. From the composition to the final reduction, they had undergone many alterations. The Jains believed that the original language was Ardhamagadhi, but probably it was modernised during the process of oral transmission.

The Jains also possess secular literature in poetry and prose, composed both in Sanskrit and Prakrit. There are numerous tales used by the authors to illustrate dogmatic or moral problems. They have also attempted more extensive narratives. Their oldest Prakrit poem, *Paumachariya*, is the Jain version of *Ramayana*. Poems in Sanskrit, both in purana and kavya style, and hymns in Prakrit and Sanskrit are popular among the Shvetambaras and the Digambaras.

Huge collections of Jain manuscripts, known as Jain Grantha Bhandars, were literary centres for many centuries. Rulers as well as masses had great interest in literary pursuits. Grantha Bhandars were established in Jaisalmer, Nagaur, Jaipur, Ajmer and Bikaner in Rajasthan. There are about 300,000 to 400,000 manuscripts in Prakrit, Sanskrit, Apabhransha and old western Rajasthani. The manuscripts in these collections include works on such branches of medieval poetry as *stotra*, *patha*, *sangraha*, *katha*, *rasa*, *puja*, *mangal*, *jaimala* and *mantra*.

There are manuscripts on religious texts, literature, poetics, astronomy, mathematics and medicine, and works also on the social, political and economic life of the times. Stories and dramas are also in abundance. There are six collections in the city of Bikaner. In Nagaur, the collection called Bharatiya Grantha Bhandar has 14,000 manuscripts written between the 14th and 18th centuries. Raja Sawai Jai Singh had founded the city of Jaipur in 1727 and established a Pothi Khana (House of Books) that preserves valuable manuscripts brought from various parts of India. There are a number of important collections attached to Digambara Jain temples. A number of illustrated manuscripts are part of these collections.

Jain literature in Gujarati connotes the literature produced with the sole aim of propagation of religious tenets and doctrines of rituals and practices of the Jain religion. There is an abundant variety in subject matter and manner of expression. Poems in some texts may depict a reaction of the human mind to the changing phases of nature, an eulogy to the deity, a place of pilgrimage, or a religious ceremony. Poems recited in Jain monasteries while atoning for one's sins or while attending a religious ceremony, are also included. Other subjects are those that would help to ward off evil and wash away sins so that life becomes pure and the soul is elevated. There are also devotional songs sung in the morning, while bathing a deity, or while worshipping.

CHRISTIAN SCRIPTURES

The sacred scripture of Judaism and Christianity is the Bible, which

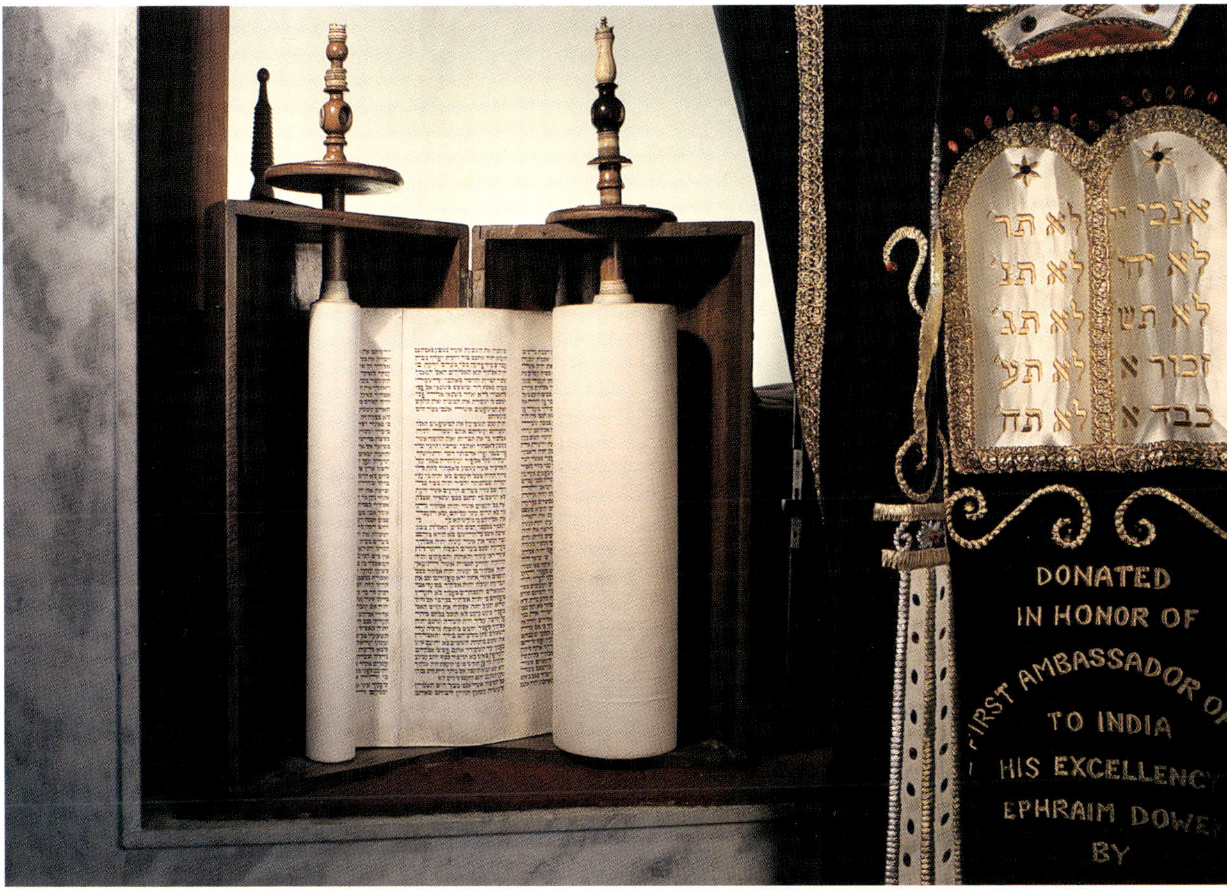

consists of the Old Testament and the New Testament. The Roman Catholic and Eastern Orthodox versions of the Old Testament are slightly larger because of their acceptance of certain books and parts of books considered apocryphal by Protestants. The Jewish Bible includes only the books known to Christians as the Old Testament. The arrangements of the Jewish and Christian canons differ considerably, while the Protestant and Roman Catholic arrangements nearly match one another.

The Jews have traditionally divided their scriptures into three parts. The first part, theLaw, is known as Torah or Pentateuch, and together with the Book of Joshua, can be seen as an account of how Israel became a nation and how it possessed the Promised Land.

Various types of literature are represented in the Apocrypha of the Old Testament. Its purpose apparently was to fill in some of the gaps left by the indisputably canonical books and to carry forth the history of Israel to the 2nd century BC.

The New Testament is the shorter portion of the Bible. It is a collection of books, including a variety of early Christian literature. The four Gospels deal with the life, the person, and the teachings of Jesus. The Book of Acts carries the story of Christianity from the resurrection of Christ to the end of the career of Paul. The letters or epistles are correspondences by various leaders of the early

Above: The holy book of the Jews preserved in special caskets with rich and elaborate decorations.
Following pages 42-43: The priests and rabbis cover their heads in prayer shawls, reciting the blessings from the Jewish Bible.

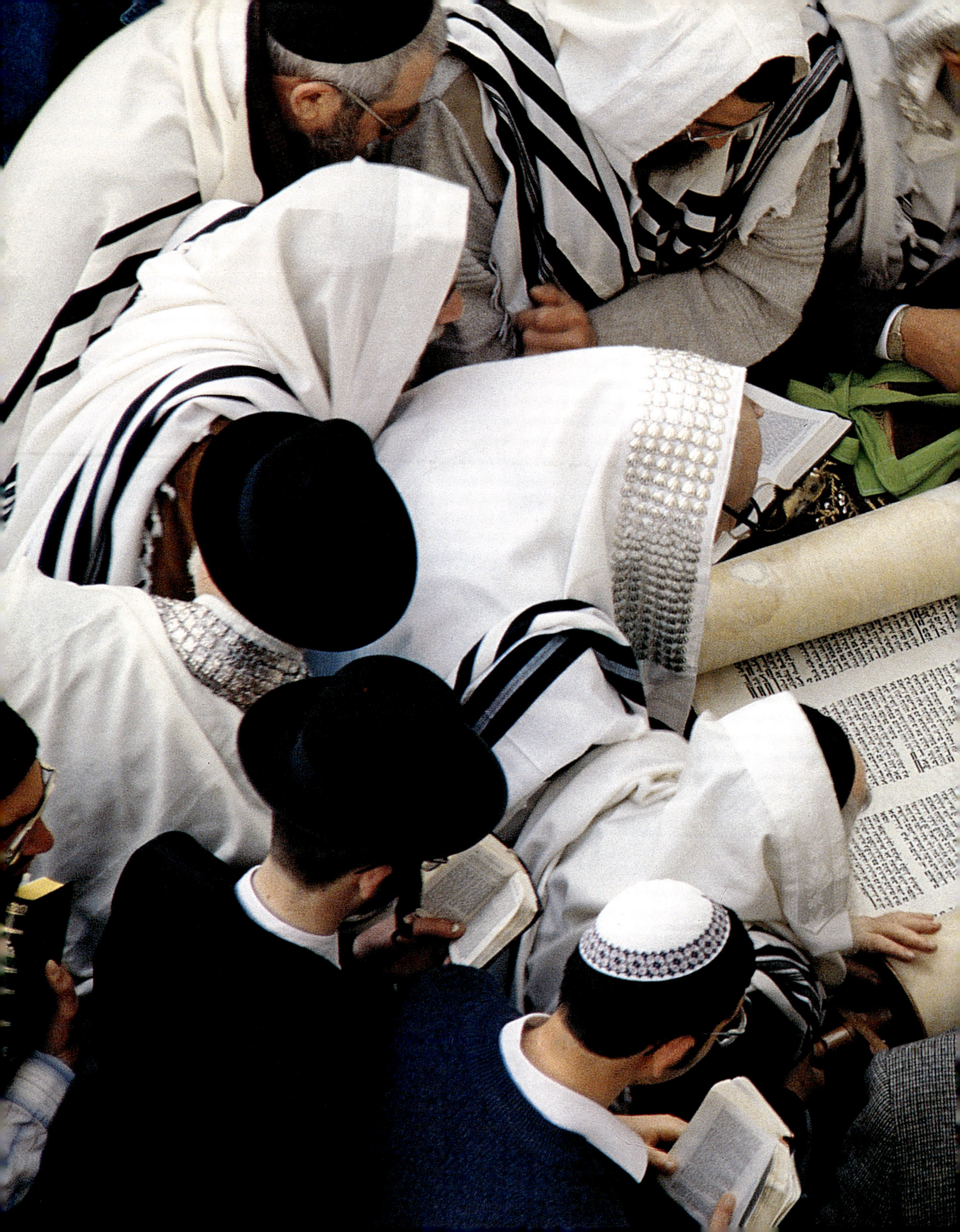

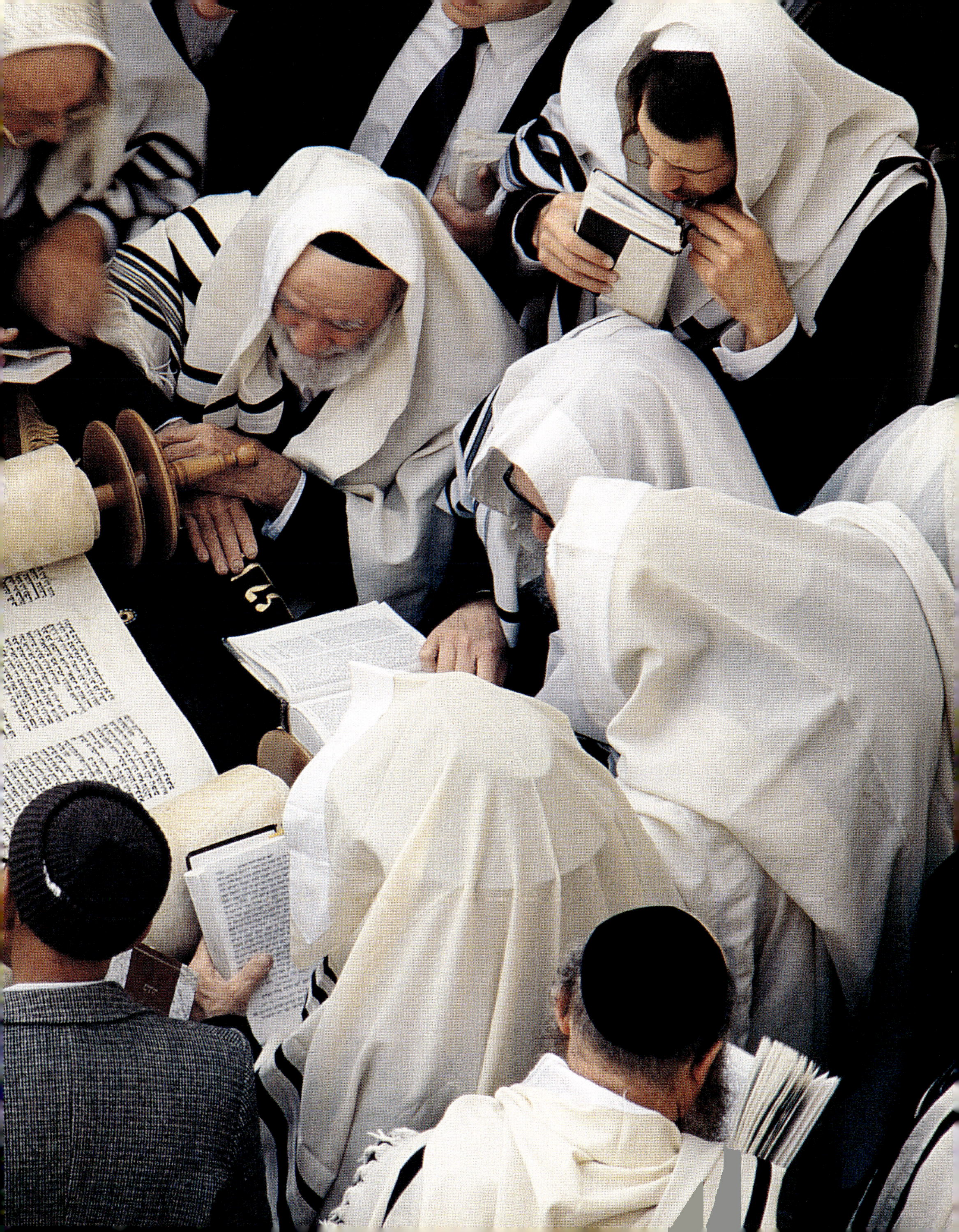

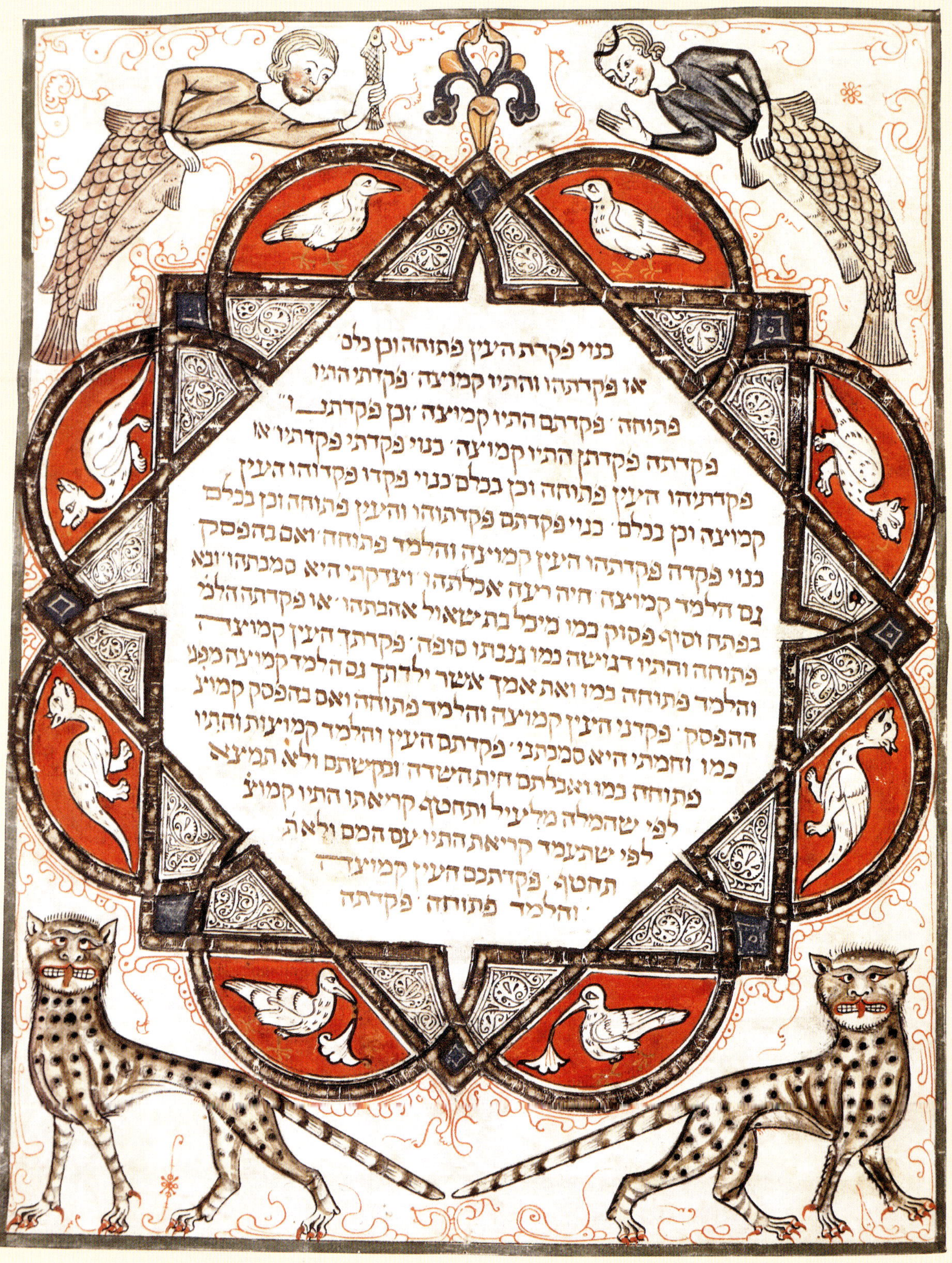

כנוי פקדת העין פתוחה וכן כלם
או פקדתהו והתיו קמוצה ׳ פקדתי הגוי
פתוחה ׳ פקדתם התיו קמוצה ׳ וכן פקדתנו
פקדתה פקדתן התיו קמוצה ׳ כנוי פקדתי פקדתיו או
פקדתיהו העין פתוחה וכן בכלם ׳ כנוי פקדו פקדוהו העין
קמוצה וכן בכלם ׳ כנוי פקדתם פקדתוהו והעין פתוחה וכן בכלם
כנוי פקדה פקדתהו העין קמוצה והלמד פתוחה ׳ ואם בהפסק
גם הלמד קמוצה ׳ חיה רעה אכלתהו ׳ וצדקתו היא סמכתהו ובא
בפתח וסוף פסוק כמו מיכל בת שאול אהבתהו ׳ או פקדתה הלמ׳
פתוחה והתיו דגושה כמו גנבתו סופה ׳ פקדתך העין קמוצה
והלמד פתוחה כמו ואת אמך אשר ילדתך גם הלמד קמוצה מפני
ההפסק ׳ פקדני העין קמוצה והלמד פתוחה ואם בהפסק קמוצ׳
כמו וחמתי היא סמכתני ׳ פקדתם העין והלמד קמוצות והתיו
פתוחה כמו ואכלתם חית השדה ובקשתם ולא תמצא
לפי שהמלה מלעיל ותחטף קריאתו התיו קמוצ׳
לפי שהעמיד קריאת התיו עם המם ולא ת׳
תחטף ׳ פקדתכם העין קמוצה
והלמד פתוחה ׳ פקדתה

Christian church, chief among them the apostle Paul, and these address the sundry needs and problems of the early Christian congregations. The Book of Revelation (the Apocalypse) is the only canonical representative of a large genre of apocalyptic literature that appeared in the early movement.

Most of the writings of the Old Testament are by anonymous writers and in many cases it is not known whether they were compiled by individuals or by groups. Numerous other sources for the Old Testament have been identified. The New Testament sources consist of the original writings that constitute the Christian scriptures, together with the oral tradition that precedes them. The first three gospels are referred to as synoptic, that is, they have a common source. The Gospel of John apparently represents an independent line of transmission. The major New Testament sources are known. The main sources of evidence are: the manuscripts of the New Testament in Greek dating from the 2nd to the 15th centuries; the early versions in other languages such as Syriac, Latin, Armenian and Georgian; and quotations from the New Testament by early Christian writers.

Biblical criticism lays the groundwork for meaningful interpretations of the Bible. It is a discipline that studies textual, compositional and historical questions surrounding the Old Testament. Textual criticism concerns itself with establishing the original or the most authoritative texts. Philological criticism is the study of the biblical languages for an accurate knowledge of vocabulary, grammar and style of the period. Literary criticism focuses on the various literary genres embedded in the text to uncover evidence concerning the date of composition, authorship and the original function of various types of writing that constitute the Bible. Traditional criticism attempts to trace the development of the oral traditions that preceded the written texts. Form criticism classifies the written material according to pre-literary forms such as parable or hymn.

The Bible was translated into several languages other than those in which it was written. The Jewish Bible was originally written entirely in Hebrew with a few short elements in Aramaic. By the mid 3rd century BC, Greek was the dominant lingua franca and the Jewish scholars began to translate the canon into the language. The spread of Christianity necessitated further translations of both the Old and New Testaments into Gothic, Ethiopian, Coptic and Latin. St Jerome finished the translation into Latin and this vulgate version became the standard of Western Christianity for a thousand years or more. The version served as the basis for translation of the Old and New Testaments into Syriac, Arabic, Spanish and many other languages including English. The vulgate provided the basis for the Douai-Reims version, which

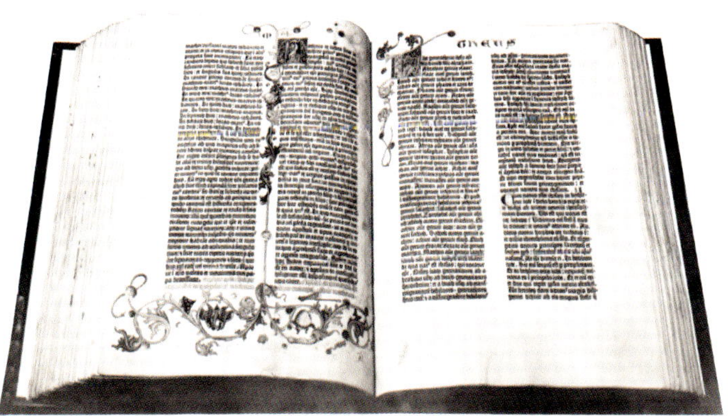

Facing page: The Jewish Bible is traditionally divided into three parts: the Law (Torah), the Old Testament and the New Testament.
Left: Ornate initial letter 'B', from the Book of Hours of Ferdinand I.
Below: A richly illuminated copy of the Gutenberg Bible showing the page with the beginning of the New Testament.

A Persian illuminated fragment of the Quran. It is the Muslim holy scripture containing revelations recited by prophet Muhammad.

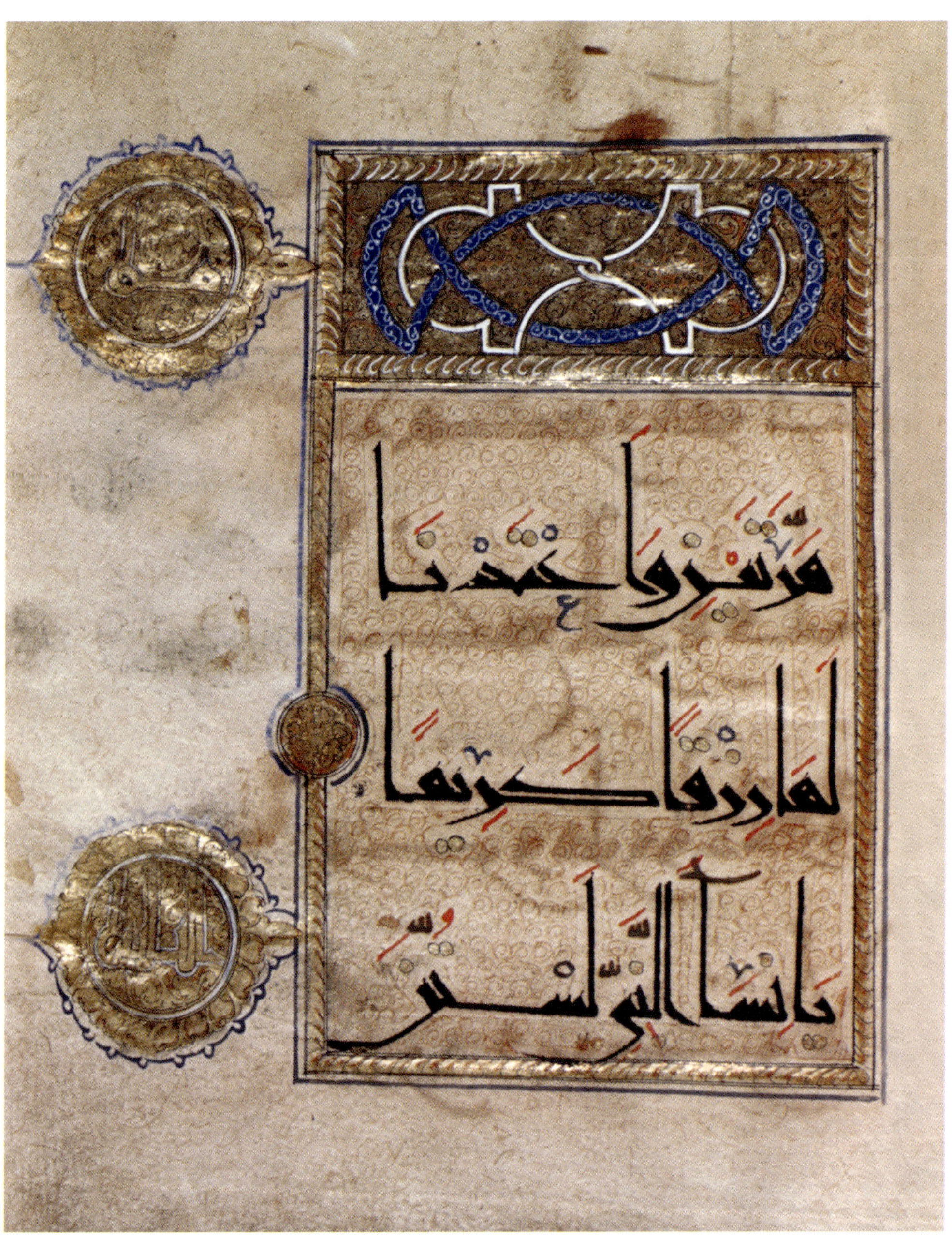

remained the authorised Bible in English for Roman Catholics.

A Dutch scholar, Desiderius Erasmus, published his translation in 1516. In Germany, meanwhile, Martin Luther produced the first complete translation from the original Greek and Hebrew into a modern European language. His German translation of the New Testament was published in 1522, and that of the complete Bible in 1534, the latter remaining the official Bible for German Protestants and becoming the basis for Danish, Swedish and some other European translations. The first complete English version dates from 1382, credited to John Wycliff and his followers. Nevertheless, the work by William Tyndale accomplished in 1525-35 became the model for a series of subsequent English translations. The King James I version appeared in 1611, prepared by 54 scholars appointed by the king. By the time printing was invented, there were 33 different translations. By about 1800 the number had risen to 71, and by the late 20th century the entire Bible had been translated into more than 250 languages and portions of the Bible published in over 1,300 of the world's languages.

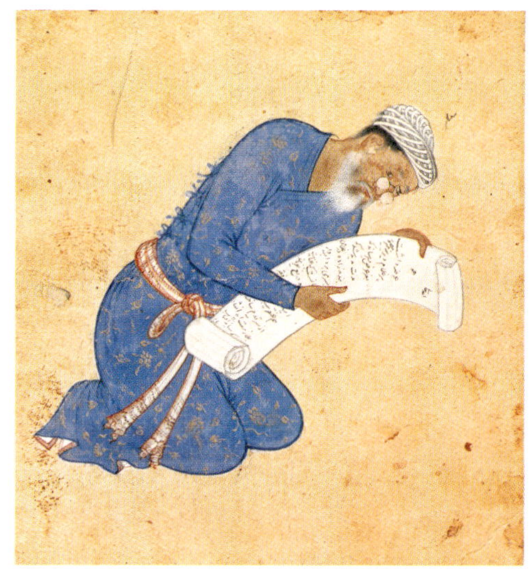

Left: *Mir Mussavir* – by Mir Sayyid Ali. This is an example of Islamic art that accompanied numerous Islamic manuscripts as well as religious scriptures. **Below:** Writing the Quran.

ISLAMIC SCRIPTURES

The Quran is the Muslim scripture containing the revelations recited by Muhammad and preserved in a fixed, written form. It reflects constantly and often explicitly on Muhammad's historical situation – answering questions from his followers and opponents, giving encouragement in times of persecution, commenting on current events, and so on. The major doctrines and regulations for the Muslim community are introduced gradually and in stages. Chronological studies of the text play an important role because there are apparent contradictions and inconsistencies in the presentation of the beliefs and regulations, and the latter are sometimes adapted to fit new situations. It is essential to know the approximate date or historical settings of some passages, and the chronological order of others. Muslim scholars devoted much attention to establish a fairly rigid system of dating. The Quran gives the Muslims a code of conduct that not only applied to the time in which it was written, but could also be adapted and interpreted for modern times.

The term 'Quran' itself has been used in the Quran 70 times. Most Western scholars accept that the word Quran is derived from the Syriac *keryana*, which means 'scripture reading' – as used in Christian liturgy. The verb *kara'a* occurs in the Quran 17 times, usually meaning 'recite' but occasionally also 'read aloud'. The Muslim scripture and Muhammad's prophetic experience are so closely linked that one cannot be fully understood without the other. The orthodox view of the dramatic form of the Quran is that God is the speaker throughout, Muhammad is the recipient, and angel Gabriel is the

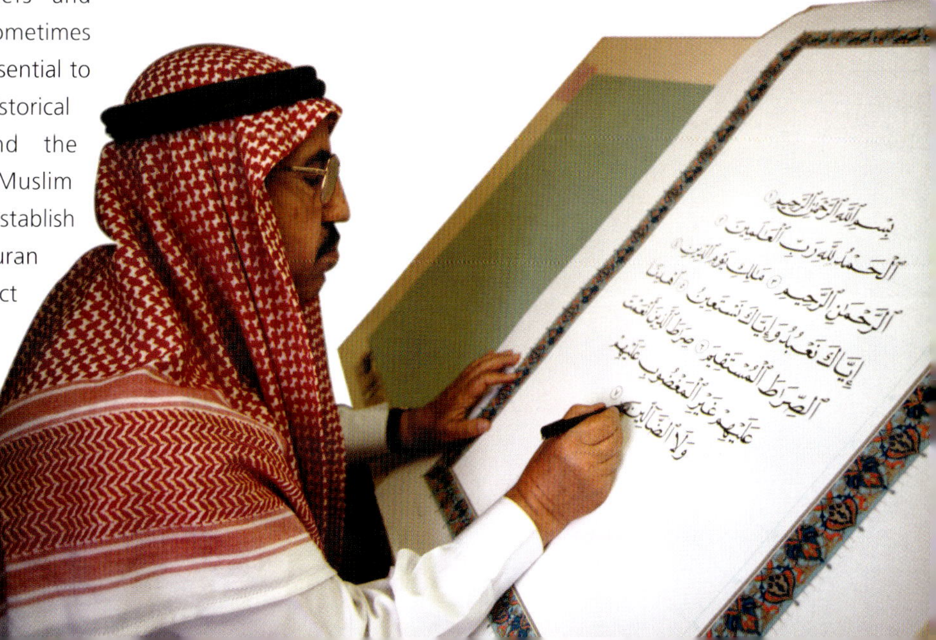

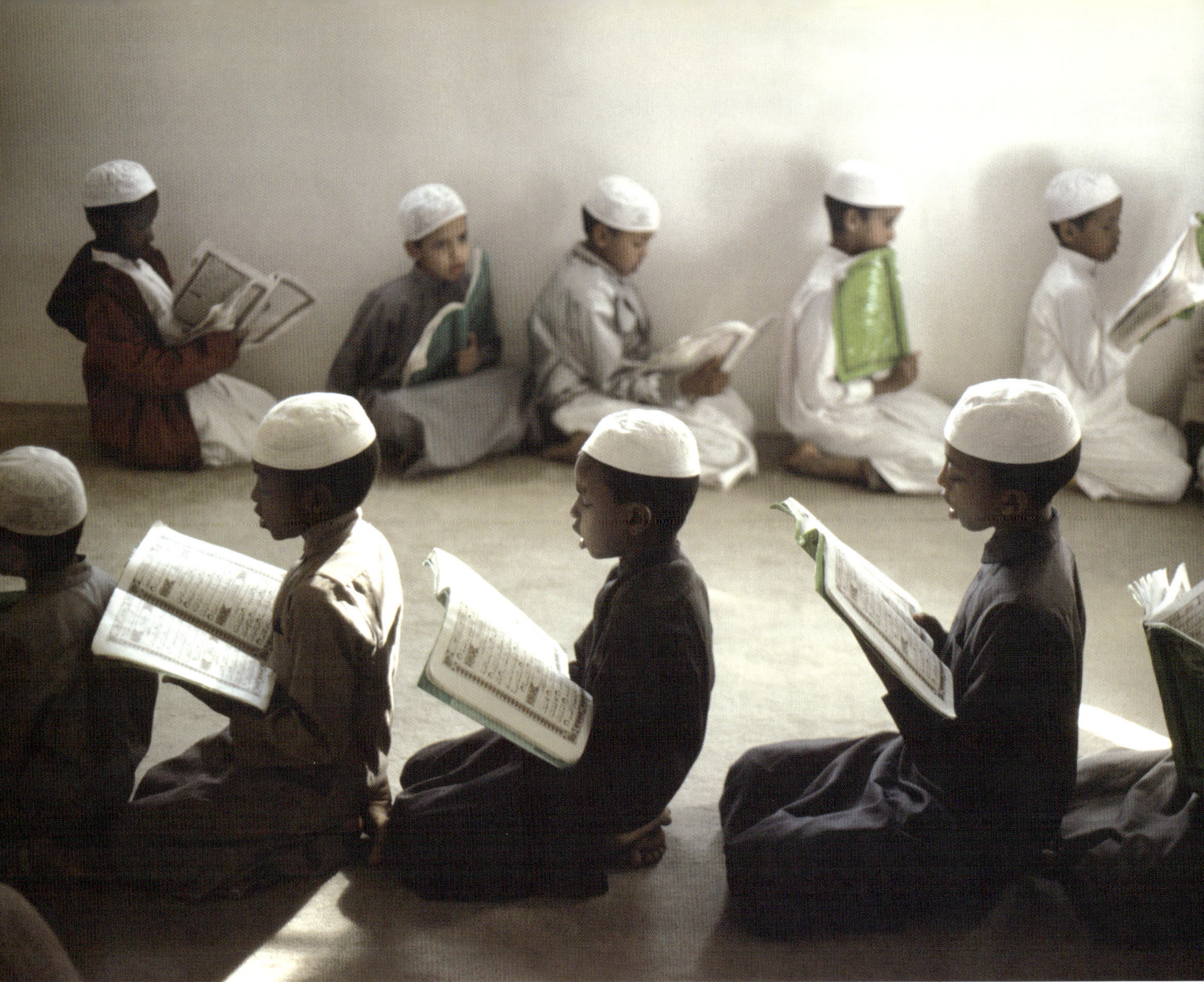

intermediary agent of revelation – regardless of who may appear to be the speaker and the addressee. In the oldest parts of the Quran, the speaker and the source of revelation are not indicated, and in some, Muhammad seems to be the speaker. In the earliest passages that mention Muhammad's God, he is not named but is spoken of in the third person, usually as 'my Lord' or 'your Lord'. In some verses it is clear that Muhammad had visions of God, and at least in the Mecca years it was the voice of God himself, and not of some intermediary.

The Quran consists of 114 *sura*s of widely varying length and forms, and these in turn are divided into a number of verses, *ayatas*, ranging from 3 to 286. *Sura* is sometimes translated as 'chapter', but the first *sura* is a prayer and the last two are chants or incantations. Only a few of the *sura*s appear to be structured entities, since most consist of several segments that are loosely connected. Some short *sura*s seem to be isolated fragments, and it is not unlikely that some of the present *sura*s were once joined with others.

After the *fatiha* ('opening' of the book), the *suras* are arranged roughly in order of descending length. Finally, they end with just two or three lines. Muslim writers normally refer to the *suras* by their names rather than their numbers. The *sura* names used in the Egyptian standard edition can be classified as follows: just over half take their names from the key words at or near the beginning of the *suras*; some are named after key words in the first or the second verse; and others take their name from a catchword that occurs elsewhere in the *sura*.

Like the *suras*, the verses vary considerably in length and style. Some of the verses are rhythmic, and sometimes there seems to be an element of metre, though not by any effort to carry through a strict metre of either syllables or stresses. Symbolism, metaphors and other poetic features have made the verses difficult to be translated.

The nature and arrangement of the Quran make it difficult to classify its literary forms or systematise its main themes. Any attempt to classify the parts of the Quran according to the standard literary types – myth, legend, saga, short story, parable – very soon flounders. It seems best to discuss the literary forms of the Quran in terms of its own distinctive types of material. Usually, at the beginning of the *suras*, an interesting variety of oaths and related forms occur. Some of those oaths are cryptic and difficult to interpret or translate, and are generally thought to be typical utterances of an ancient Arabic soothsayer. In other cases the oath form has simply been used to convey Quranic themes. Some of the stories in the Quran are called punishment stories. They illustrate features of the Quran: the complex development of its multiple accounts and their changing relationships with other accounts. Many stories are repeated in different versions in two or more *suras*, and these multiple accounts of the same story differ not only in length and details, but also in their purpose and their relationship to other stories.

Most medieval Muslim scholars believed that the Quran was composed in the spoken language of the Prophet – the dialect of the Kuraysh and also the language of classical Arabic poetry of Muhammad's time. According to the German scholar Karl Vollers, the Quran was first recited by Muhammad without case endings and in colloquial Arabic. However, his theory found little support outside Germany. Some scholars argued that the language of the Quran was not the spoken language of any tribe. On the other side, it has come to be generally agreed that the classical Arabic of the poetry of Muhammad's time was neither the spoken language of the poets nor the dialect of any tribe, but a literary language that was understood by all the tribes. This language has come to be called the 'poetic koine', or the *arabiyya*.

***Facing page**:* Young boys learn to read the Quran in a madrasa in Rawalpindi, Pakistan.

Below: The Quran at Kairouan's Great Mosque, Tunisia. The term 'Quran' is derived from the Syriac word 'Keryana', which means 'scripture reading'.

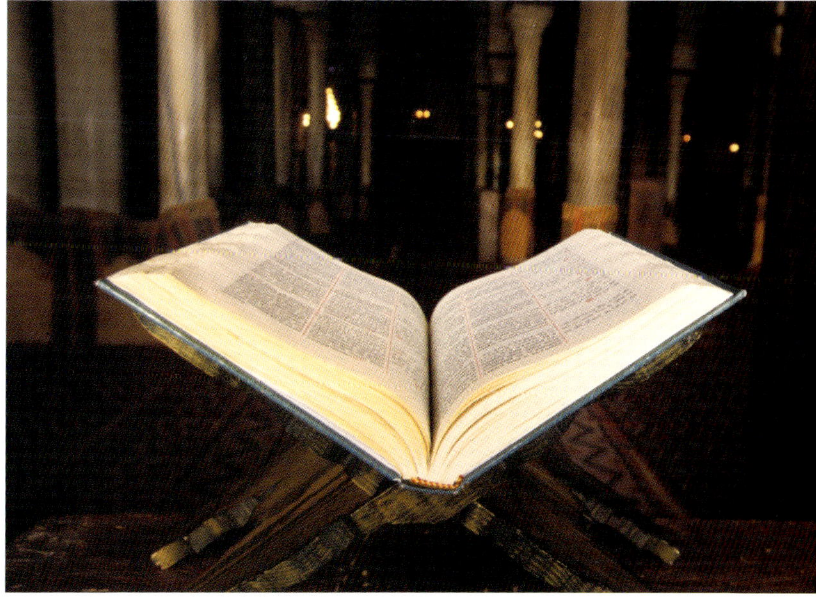

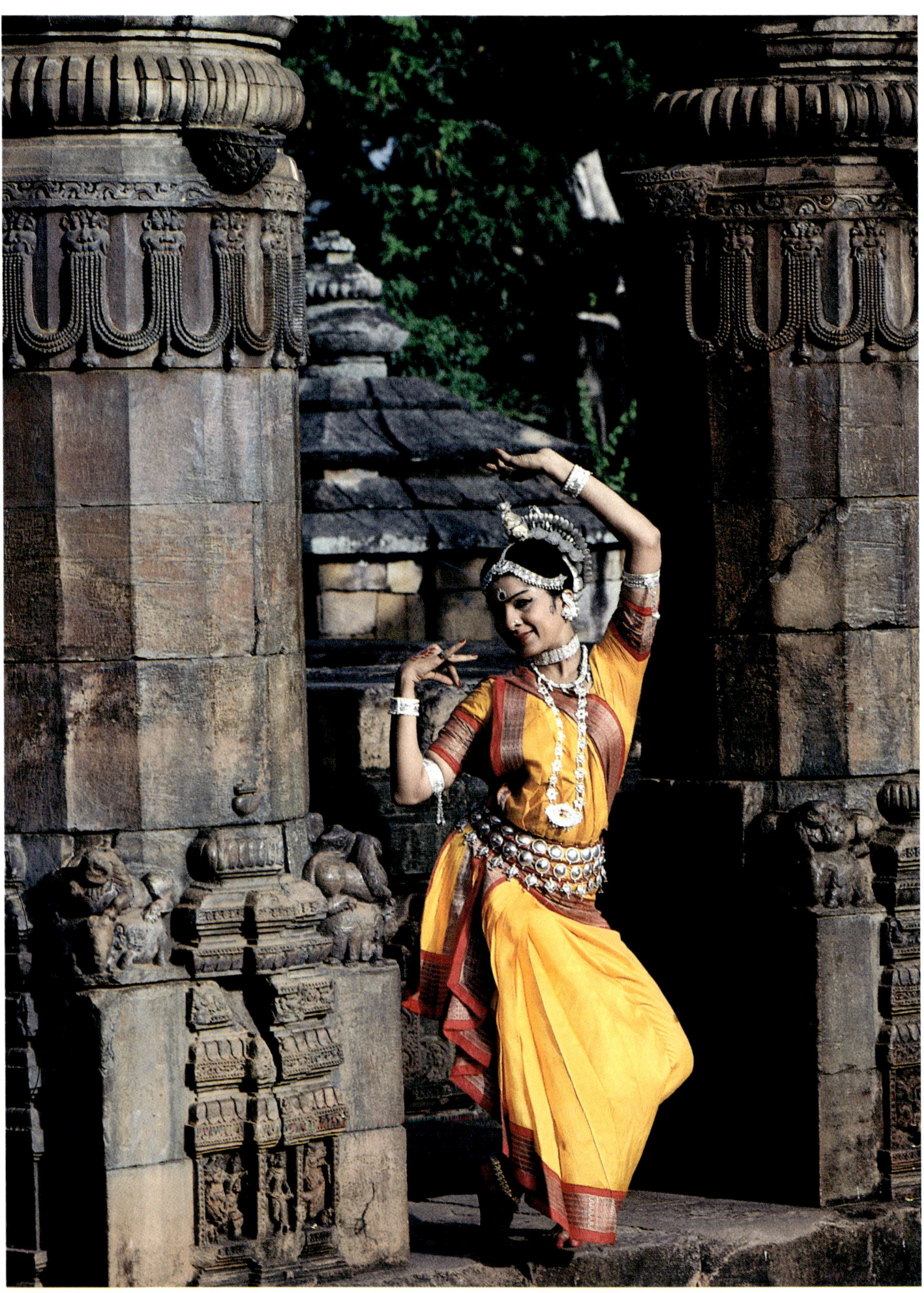

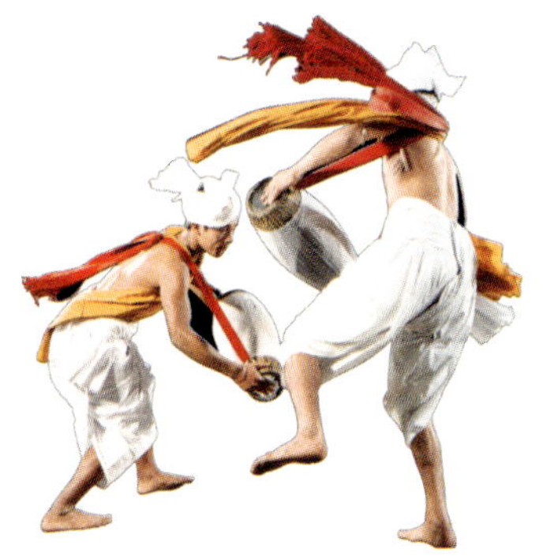

DANCE, MUSIC AND DRAMA: PERFORMING FOR THE GODS

Dance, music and drama elevate the human spirit and put it in an ecstatic state. As has been said in Sanskrit, 'A man without any interest in literature, music, dance and the allied arts is in essence a beast without tail and horns.' Shakespeare wrote: 'The man that hath no music in himself nor is he moved with concord of sweet sounds, is fit for treason, stratagems and spoils; let no such man be trusted.' In olden times the intention behind performing music, dance and drama was to inspire people to follow the principles of good living, besides providing the main source of pleasure and diversion for people weary of the strains and stresses of life.

In India, the term *sangeeta* is used to encompass music, musical instruments and dance since they are intertwined in such a way that one cannot exist without the other. The patron deity of music, dance and drama is Shiva, in the form of Nataraja – the king of dancers and performers. *Sangeeta* is thus a divine art.

MUSIC

Music brings bliss and supreme joy; it allays grief, expels diseases, softens every pain, and subdues the rage of poison and plague. Hence, the wise of ancient days used the power of melody and song. Music is seen to work even on cattle and birds. Musical arts are the soul of a happy and contented life.

Music is different from ordinary speech – it is the sequence of sounds produced artistically and impregnated with aesthetic sentiment and mood. It constitutes the art of combining and regulating sounds of various pitches. The idea behind it is to produce compositions expressive of various ideas and emotions. It is a sweet, pleasing and harmonious sound. The word 'music' is derived from the French *muse*. Muse, the daughter of the Greek god Zeus, presides over various arts, particularly music. Zeus is the counterpart of the Indian mythological god Indra.

Facing page: An Odissi dancer posing outside a temple: it is a highly lyrical and sensual dance form. ***Above:*** Manipuri dancers performing the Pung Cholom dance. During the stage performance, the dancers play the drums and twirl in the air. ***Below:*** Traditional Rajasthani musicians.

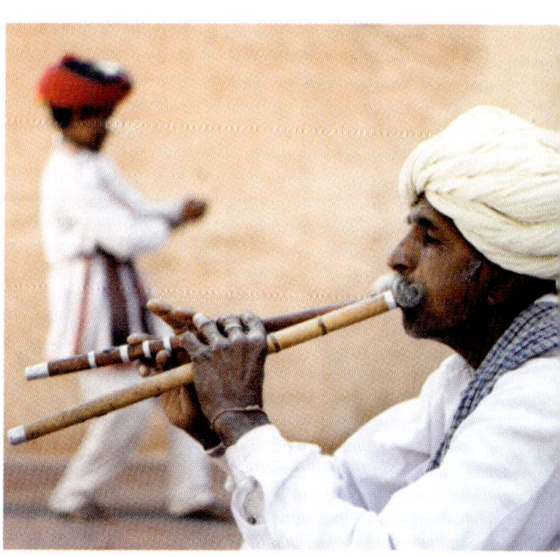

Radong, an ornate long horn trumpet, is an important accompaniment to Tibetan Buddhist chants and rituals. ***Facing page***: Dancer Shobha Naidu depicts the Viswaroopa, the cosmic dimenson of Lord Vishnu. ***Folowing pages 54-55:*** A dance production choreographed by Geeta Chandran focusing on the theme of peace and harmony.

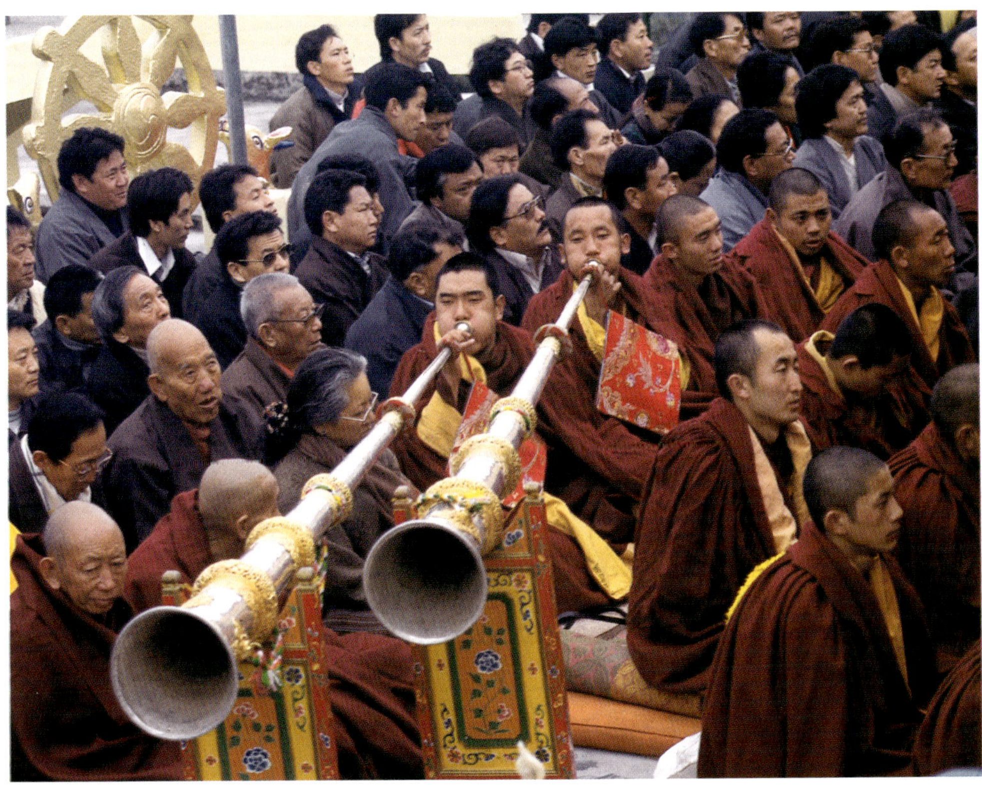

In India famous temples kept their own musicians and patronised them. Music could even be a part of bloody battles or funeral ceremonies.

Indian music is built on *nada*, or the primal causal sound. The notes or *svara*s emanate from different parts of the human body – nose, throat, chest, palate, tongue and teeth, and they evolve into seven basic notes from the vibrations of the air that one breathes. These seven notes are known by their initial letters and are the foundational structure of Indian music. This was passed on to Persians as Hindu musicians used to grace the courts of kings abroad.

Music must be in complete harmony with high, medium and low tones when played successively. Metres, stanzas and letters of a song regulate the tones. Adornments are manifested in the tonal sounds between high and low sounds of an instrument. The atmosphere should be conducive to enjoy the music being played. Facial expressions should be pleasing and the presentation, lucid. Words, metres, notes and melodies have to be clear and unambiguous. Presentation of notes in different octaves – low, medium and high – should be easy and graceful. The beauty of music lies in its easy grace and expressions.

Rhythm is the soul of good music. The secret of music lies in rhythmic movements, in determinate intervals in the *taala*s, and in ratios between notes which give rise to the harmonic impact of the sounds in various sequences and shades. Rhythm gives aesthetic beauty to the expression of sounds.

DANCE

Dance, or *nritya*, is an inborn art that denotes youthful exuberance. It is poetry of motion – a

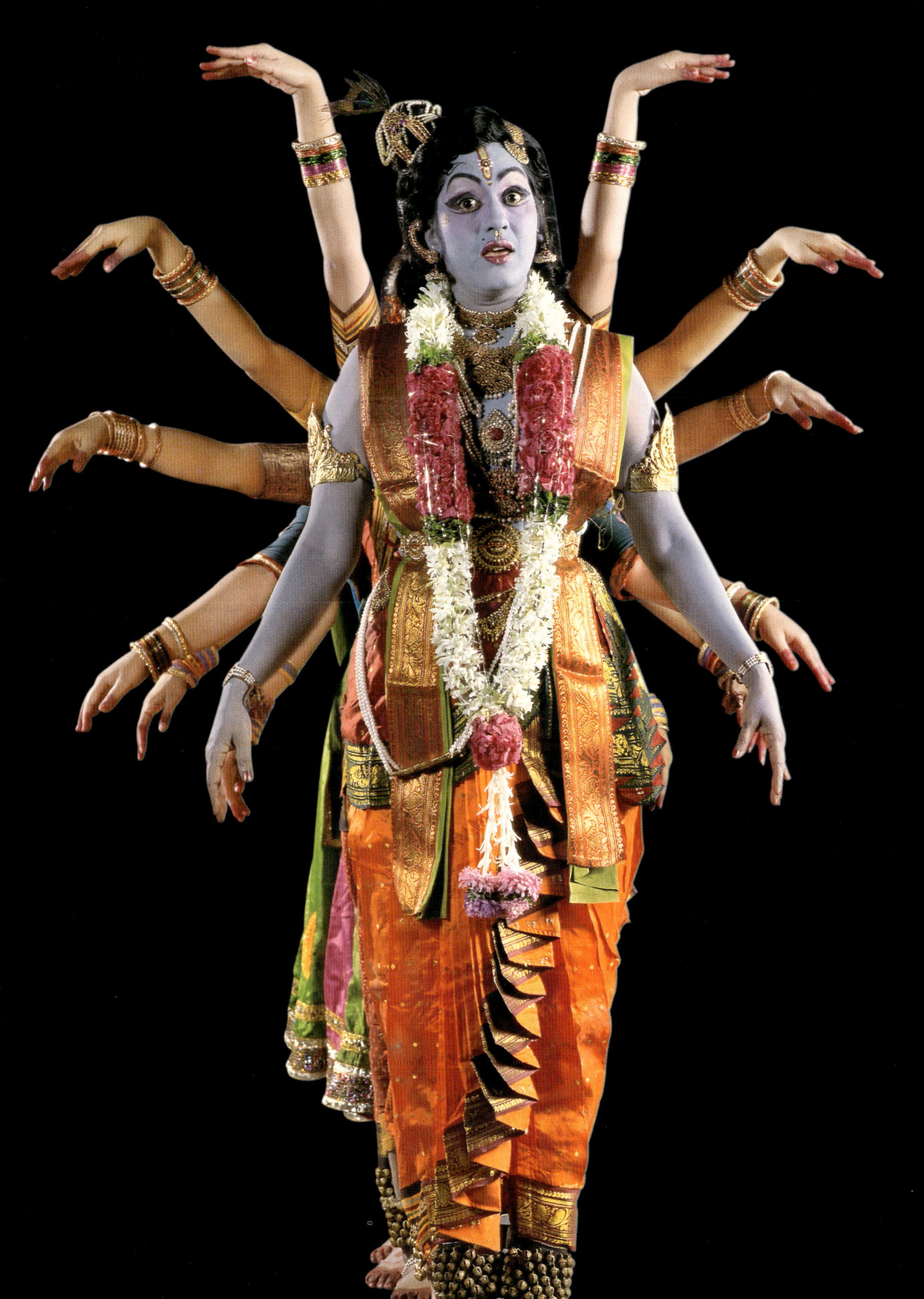

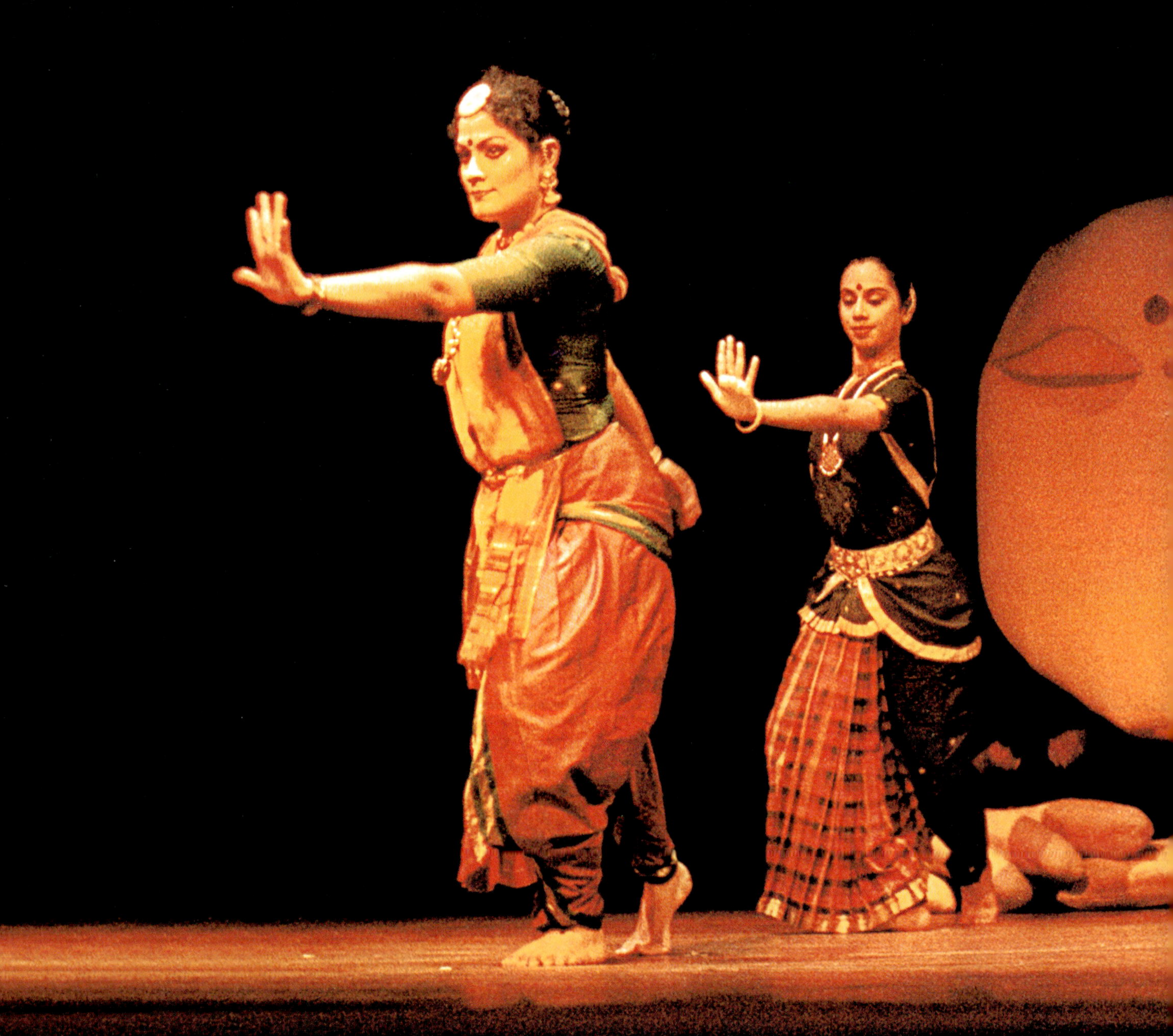

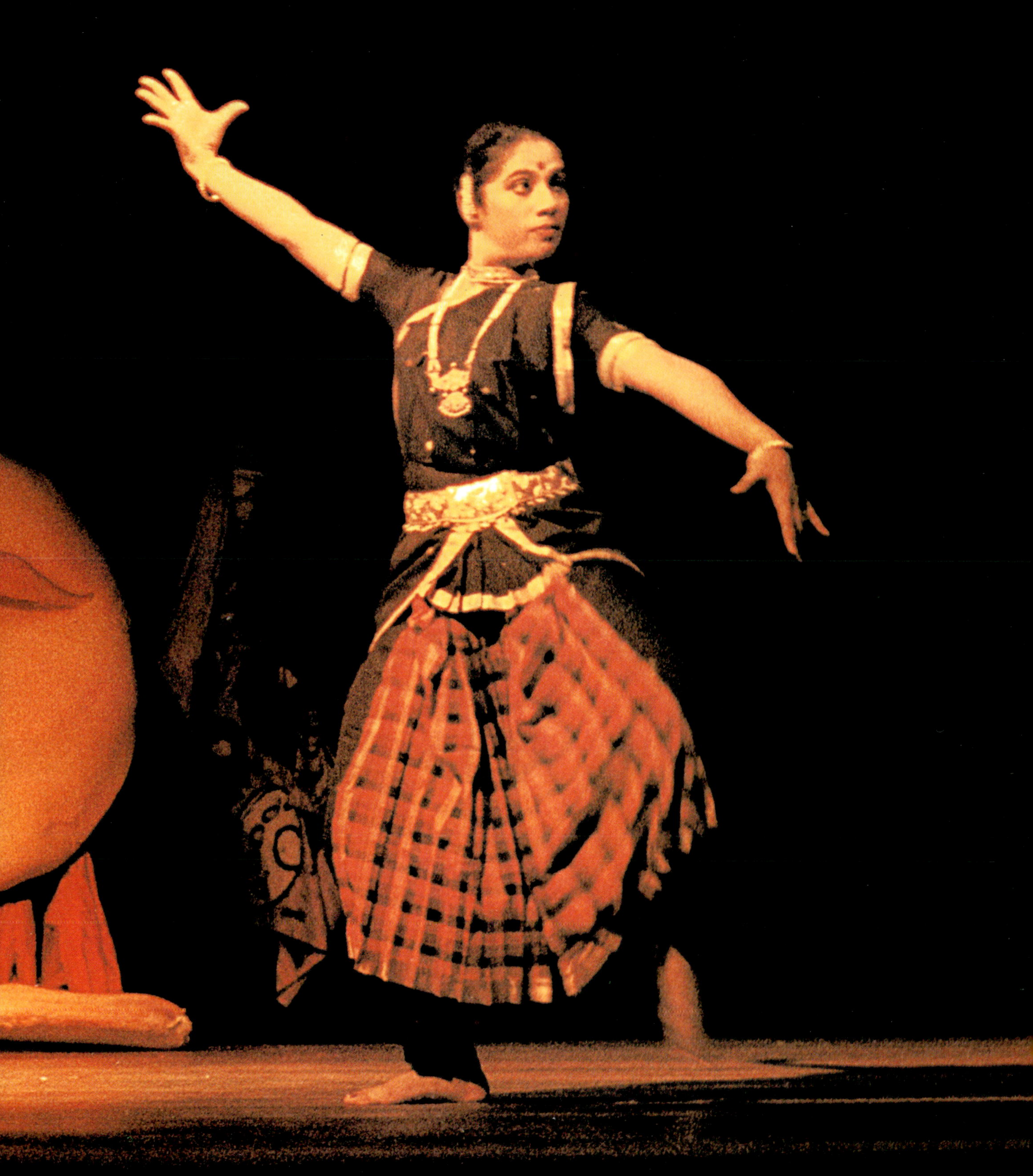

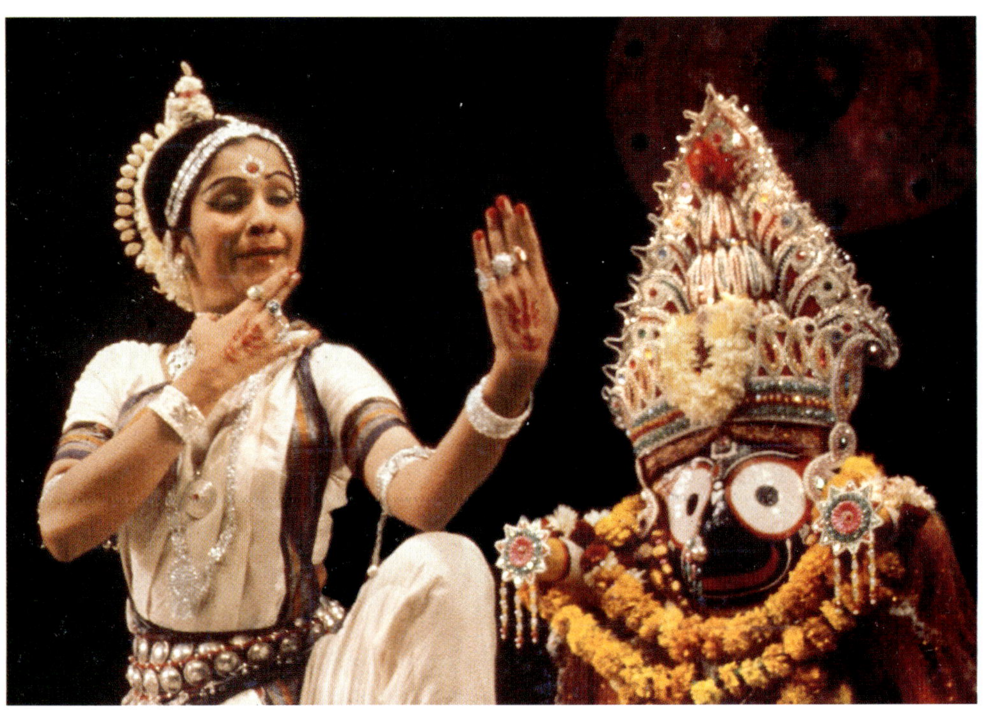

Right: Lord Jagannath is a powerful presence on the Odissi stage; the dancer here, the late Sanjukta Panigrahi, offers her art to him.
Below: Dancer Rama Vaidyanathan depicts the pure beauty of dance movements through the rich *abhinaya* of Bharatnatyam.

combination of worship, drama, play and art – and an expression of the most solemn human emotions. Music and dance elevate man's consciousness and provide immense pleasure and happiness. Manifestations of Hindu gods and goddesess are integral to Indian dances because they embody the higher states of vitality. Ganapati, the lord of Ganas or 'categories', brings everybody joy as Nritya - Ganapati, the eight-armed dance manifestation. Shiva as Nataraja, the lord of dance, is the manifestation of primal rhythmic energy. The dancing Shiva is the symbol of physical and emotional beauty, capable of creating similar feelings in the heart of the viewer. Nataraja sustains the phenomenal world.

The *nritya murti* of Krishna, Nritya Gopala, 'the dancing cowherd,' is well known in Indian art. Krishna as Gopala represents agrarian tradition. His dance with his friends is known as Rasalila. Men and women of any age can enact it. They dance in a circle with Krishna, the leader, standing at the centre.

While dancing, the arms move gracefully in harmony with the motion of the body, especially the legs. The rhythmic motion expresses the feelings of pleasure and pain through brightening eyes or smiles, gestures and contractions of the body. A persistent pain can be expressed by making the body swing to and fro, or by clinching fists. Shedding tears, sighing, wringing hands, or tearing clothes, hair or ornaments, is an expression of grief. Anger is shown in frowns, in distended nostrils, or by stamping the ground.

TEMPLE DANCES

Temple dances flourished in Tamil Nadu, mostly at Tanjaur and Mahabalipuram. The Chola and Chalukyan kings of Karnataka also patronised such arts. Devadasis and Rajadasis enjoyed

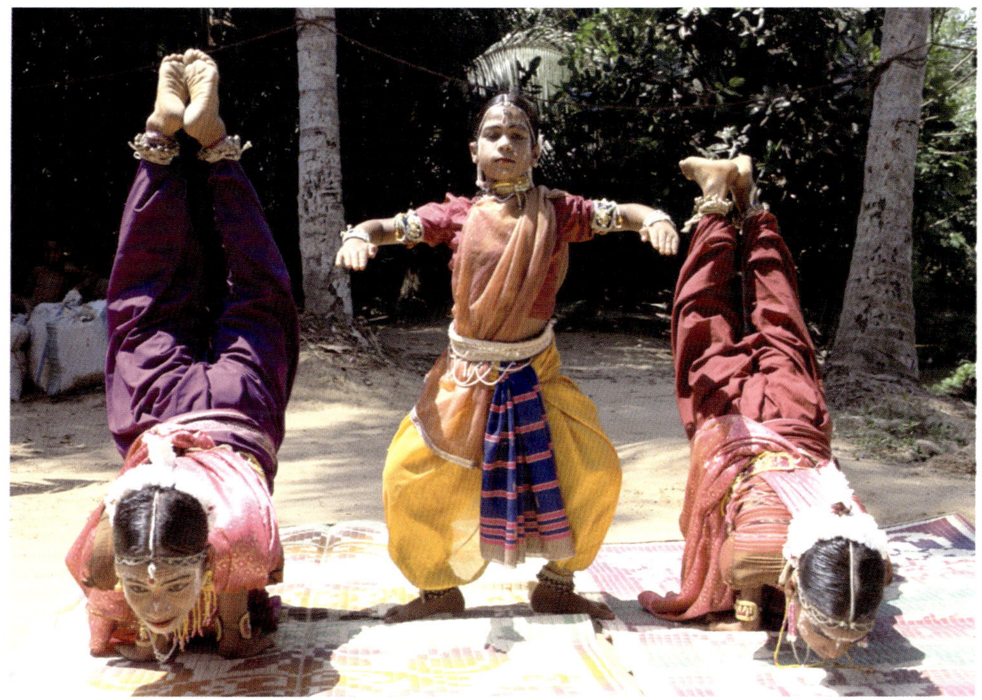

Three boys dressed in brightly coloured, traditional female attire, perform sacred acrobatic moves during the Gotipua dance in Raghurajpur, Orissa.

a respectable status under the rule of Krishnadevaraya of Vijayanagara. Special halls for music and dance were built, and beautiful statues of dancers were installed therein. The dance of Devadasis was an inherent component of worship in India and exists in some form even today.

Bharatanatyam was encouraged by the Vijayanagara emperors. Kuchipudi was developed in Andhra Pradesh. Kathakali was patronised in Kerala and Odissi in Orissa. Chaitanya Mahaprabhu developed street dances in honour of Krishna, while his disciple Shankaradeva introduced Ankiya Nritya – a variety of Chaitanya Mahaprabhu's street dance – in Assam. In Manipur a variety of Rasa dances were performed in honour of the Govinda Deva temple. With the coming of the Muslims, though, these arts received a setback. Under the Mughals, Devadasis became prostitutes, singing and dancing for the king and the nobles. The Sufis, however, were not averse to music or dance. They had spread far and wide in most of India before Muslim rule was established firmly.

Bharatanatyam originated in South India and is based on Bharata Muni's *Natya-shastra*. It remains mainly a woman's art that, in Indian mythology, was said to have been first taught by Lord Shiva. Gestures, facial expressions, *mudra*s and *karana*s play an important role in conveying feeling and notions.

Musical instruments accompany the dance, while someone recites and explains the theme. The dancer comes to the stage and first offers flowers and prayers to the statue of the deity for a successful dance. The performance opens with the dancer impersonating a lotus opening its petals. Recitation and instrumental music begins, maintaining perfect rhythm with the dancer's footwork, movement of eyes and neck, and other actions. Themes are often derived from divine stories. Dancers are draped in traditional silk saris or dhotis, with a

Below: The tradition of highly stylised Rasa dances of Krishna in Manipuri style. One of the oldest dance forms of India, it is performed to please the deities and is often called a folk dance. **Facing page:** The challenging hero as portrayed by dancer Navtej Singh Johar. **Following pages 60-61:** A performance of the urban, sophisticated form of Kuchipuddi, developed by Vempati Chinna Satyam, in his academy at Chennai.

shining border made of *zari*. Brilliantly shining ornaments and garlands of flowers add to the dancer's persona.

Kathakali, a male dance that originated in Kerala, was devised by the Nambudiri Brahmanas. It is based on the stories of Rama and Krishna. The faces of the dancers are painted in different styles, and different colours denote different things. If the faces are painted green, the colour symbolises ethical behaviour and indicates that the character hails from a high and noble family. A strip of white colour extends from one ear to the other covering the chin; lips are painted deep red, and eyes and eyebrows are black. If red and white colours are added to the green, then the character is a powerful person like Ravana and Duryodhana. Faces of evil personalities are painted black, while mild colours indicate sages and women of high rank imbued with spiritual temperament. Their jewelled crowns and ornaments sparkle on stage. An oil lamp keeps burning on the side of the stage.

Odissi is lyrical and sensuous in its *tribhanga* and *atibhanga* postures. The earliest reference to the dance in Orissa is found in an inscription in Kharavela dating to the 2nd century BC. The tradition continued and Choda Gangadeva (1077-1147) constructed the temple of Jagannatha at Puri, and employed Maharis in the Nata-mandira for propitiation of the lord. The rich temple sculpture of Orissa depicts and conserves the dance poses of Odissi. A great part of the vocabulary of Odissi dance has been inspired by Konark and other visual representations.

Kathak is another popular dance form and is performed by both men and women. The artist tells the story verbally as well as through acting, accompanied by appropriate dance techniques. Its origin lies in the cult of Vasudev Krishna or of Bhagavata. Swami Haridas

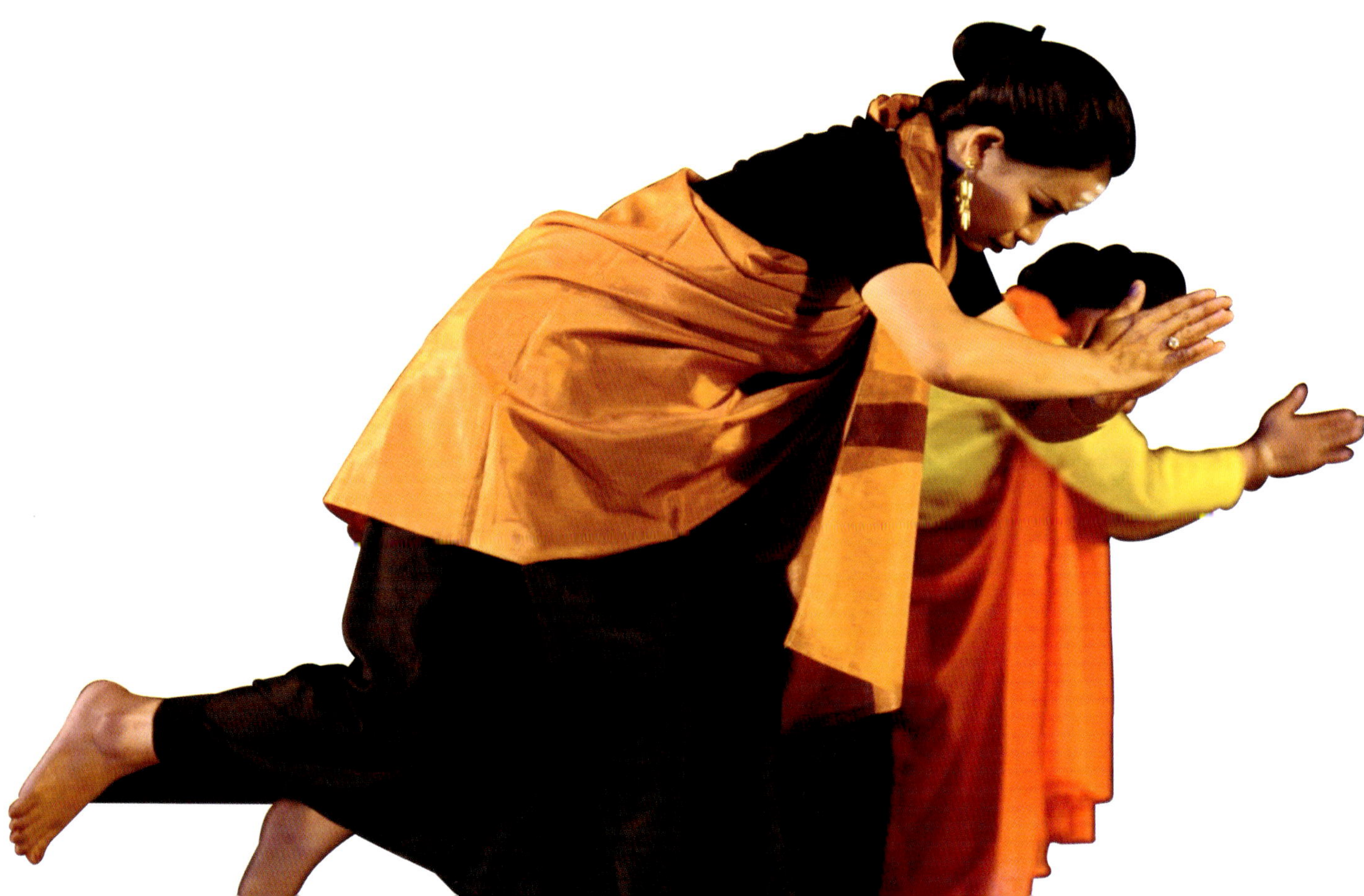

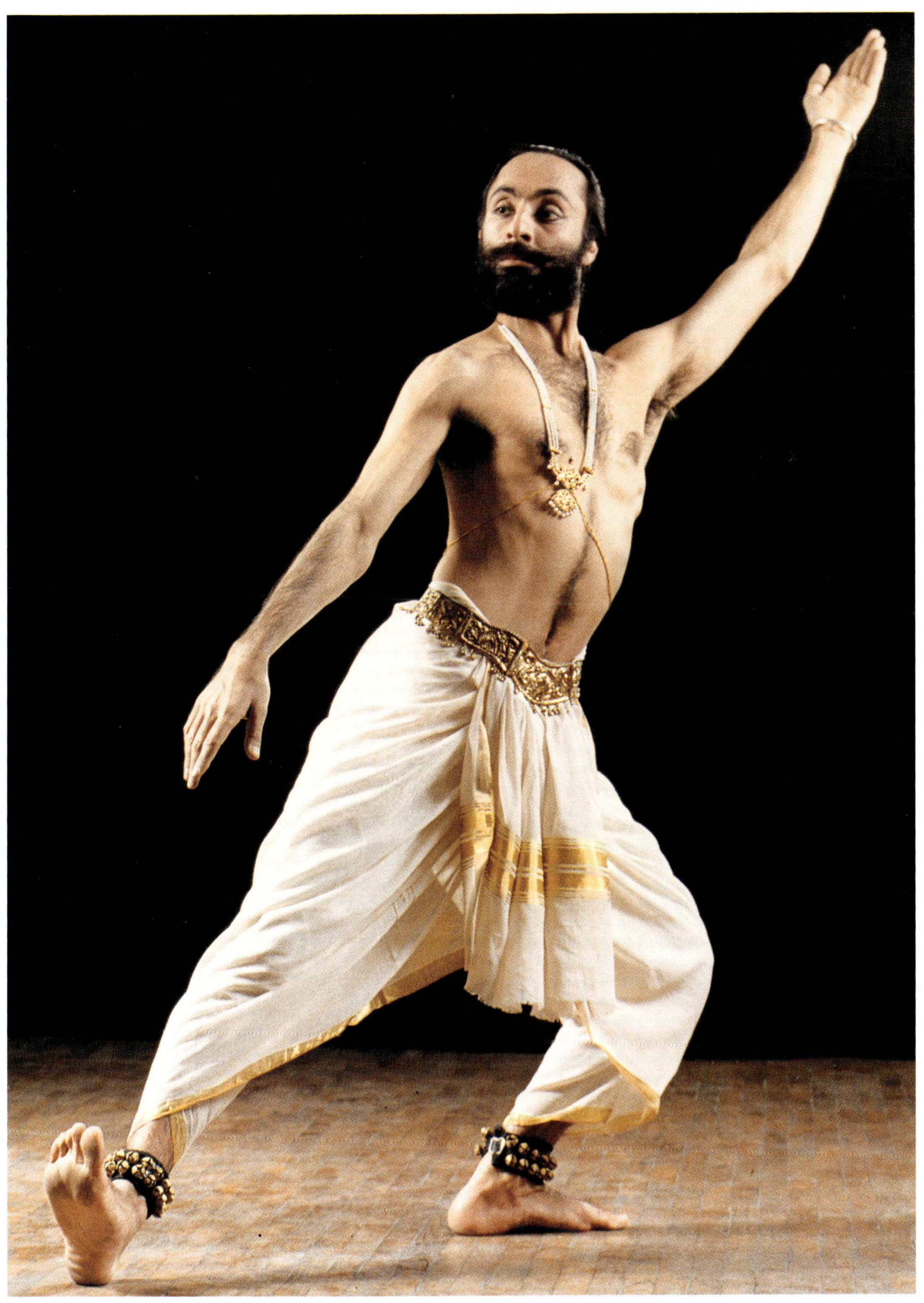

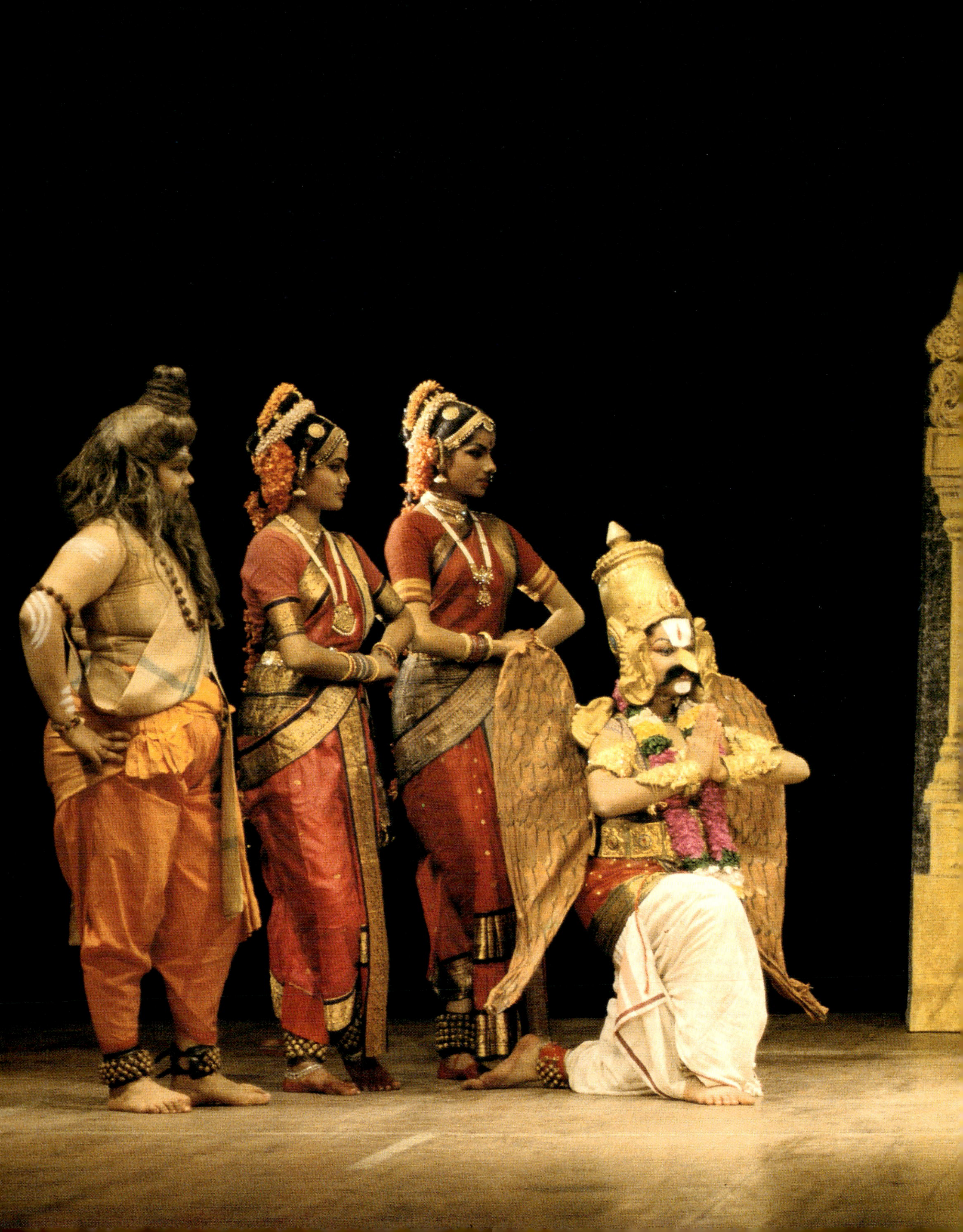

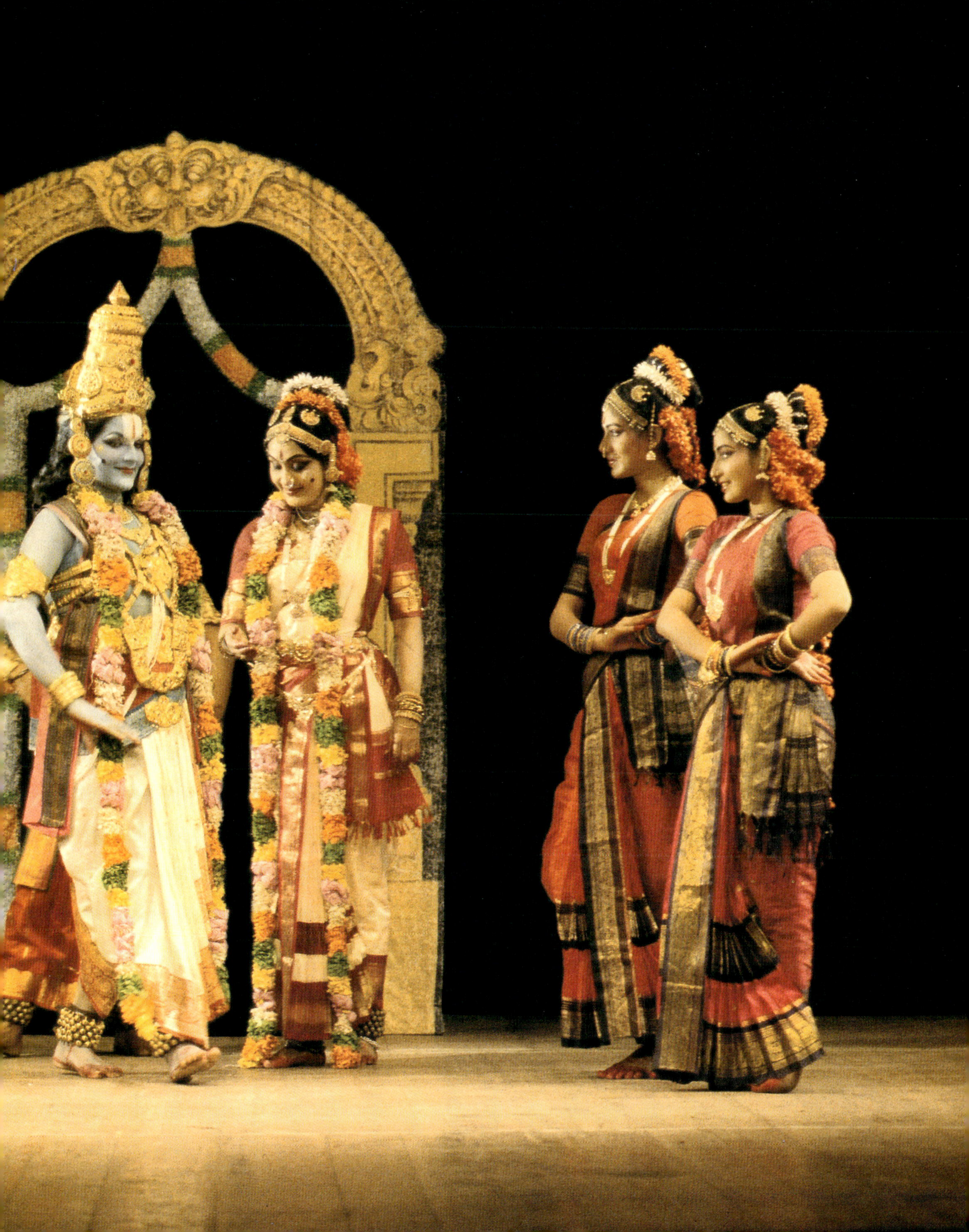

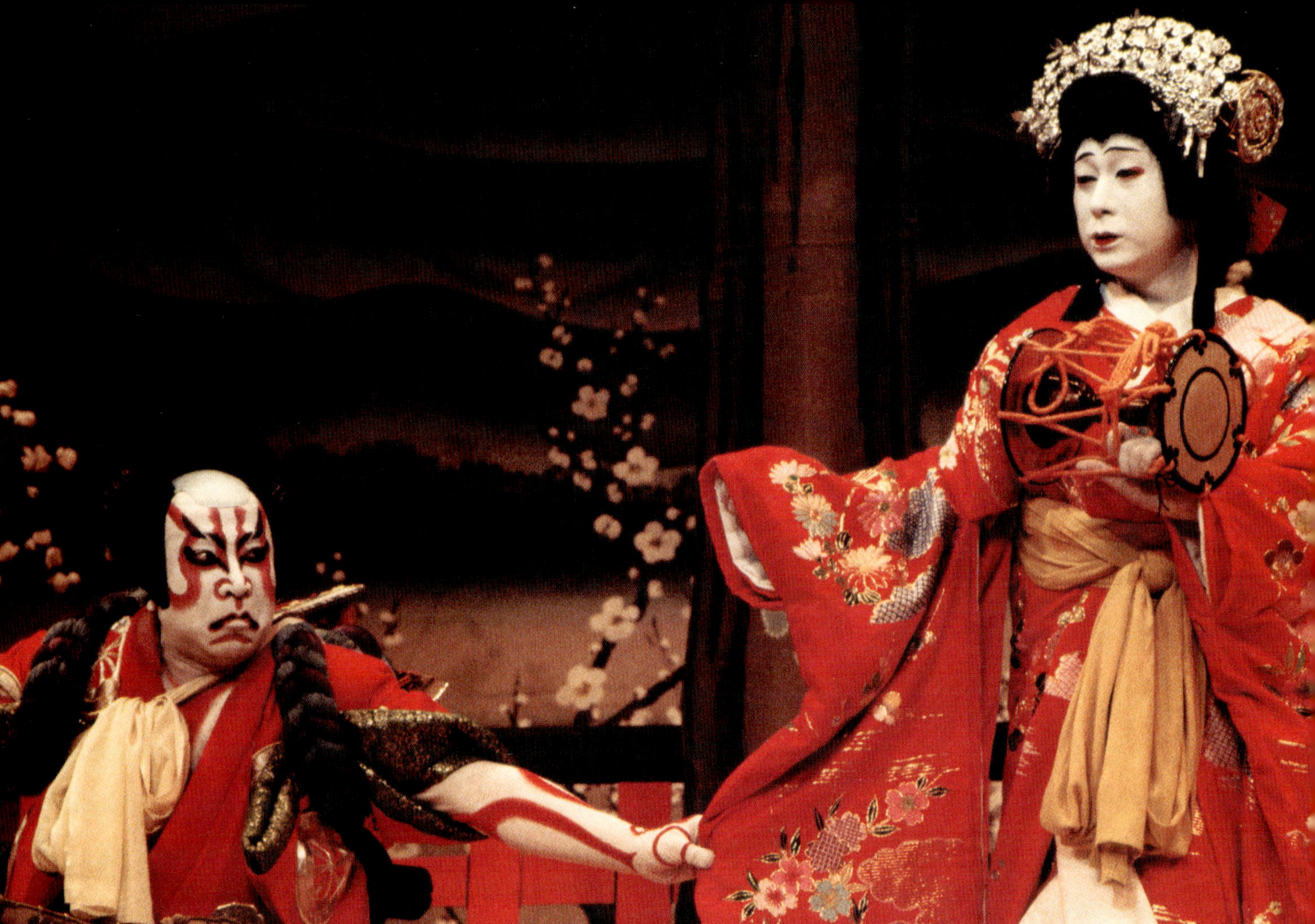

founded this dance style, an embodiment of the ultimate relationship between the dancer and his beloved lord. Tabla, sarangi, flute and mridanga are the major accompanying instruments. Long skirts and jackets, with *churidar pyjama*, or a sari with a blouse, and a shawl-like upper garment for male dancers, are worn by the artists. In Jaipur this style has remained true to its ancient tradition, but in Lucknow it changed under Mughal influence.

The Manipuri style comes from the east Indian states and is a Rasa style dance performed by a group of male and female dancers to worship Lord Rama. It is a rendering of song in dance. In Manipur, every village has a temple dedicated to Krishna with an attached hall for dancing. The dance is also performed to please the deities guarding farms and fields, and is sometimes looked upon as a folk dance. Boys and girls gather in the temple premises and dance on themes derived from various philosophies, and offer prayers to god.

Angels dance in heavens, while heavenly musical instruments are played for them. Sukhavati, the paradise of Amitabha, has been depicted in monasteries and cave temples in Central and East Asia for the last two millennia. Some of the finest examples are from the Dunhuang caves in China, where goddesses are shown dancing in the joyous tenderness of their vibrant movements.

A ritual dance called *Tsam* was performed in monasteries in Tibet and Mongolia to exorcise the enemies of religion – to destroy demonic forces or, on a subtle level, to obliterate ego, the enemy of enlightenment. It is a day-long ritual, usually held at every monastery once a year. It requires both physical and mental preparation. Actors enter followed by two *acharya*s, Indian pundits, who present a copy of the tales of Vikramaditya to a dancer. A series of figures then enter the stage, serving more as a formal audience than as active participants in the *tsam* – the *chakravarti* king, his wife and son, and Kashin, the king of Kashmir who welcomes the Buddha. The royal figures take their seats; occasionally, they rise to greet the arrival of the protectors of the dharma, including Lhamo, Mahakala and others. Lama meditators enter wearing hats and carrying ritual knives. Then enters Yama, the lord of death, swirling and dancing, who symbolically kills the enemy of the law. Turn by turn, each figure performs the mandalic dance and exits.

The *Mahabharata* has been the epic halo of the Hindu-Buddhist mind, so poetic, so melancholy, and so vibrant. It has journeyed to Japan in the Far East and Indonesia in the Southeast. The well-known *Kabuki* drama in Japan, *Narukami*, is derived from the legend of Rishyashringa from *Mahabharata*. The sage had never seen a woman and is seduced at first sight by a princess, the daughter of the king Lomapada. The sage appears in the mask dances in Tibet and Japan, while in China clay images of the sage were made. Traces of the legends from *Mahabharata* are scattered in Chinese Buddhist literature. The influence of *Mahabharata* is also seen in the moral stories prevalent in Thailand. Two classical Thai works deal with the stories in which the hero is the son of Pradyumna and the grandson of Krishna. The *Mahabharata* has turned into a prime cultural phenomenon as we see it rendered in the performing arts, and in forms like Wayang (Indonesian puppet play), it has reached a high level of sophistication.

DRAMA

The dramatic art, or *natya*, is described as audio-visual poetry or *drishya-kavya* by Bharata Muni in his *Natya-shastra*. Here, *sangeeta* is expressed through bodily action and the use of facial and eye expressions. Music was the very life of the art of drama. Tracing the history of drama, Bharata Muni says that it was originally performed on the slopes of the Himalayas before the assembly of gods. Later, it developed into classical Sanskrit drama with songs remaining its principle constituent. All the dramas began with prayers, a devotional song offered to the gods or the presiding deity, to ensure a successful performance, and ended with the Bharatavakya, an epilogue wishing welfare and happiness to the people in general. Its aim is not merely to entertain, but also to elevate the minds of the spectators and offer them lessons to be better citizens. The dramas were not to end in tragedy, but to culminate in the success of the hero or the heroine. The drama represented a total view of life not only of this world, but of all the three worlds.

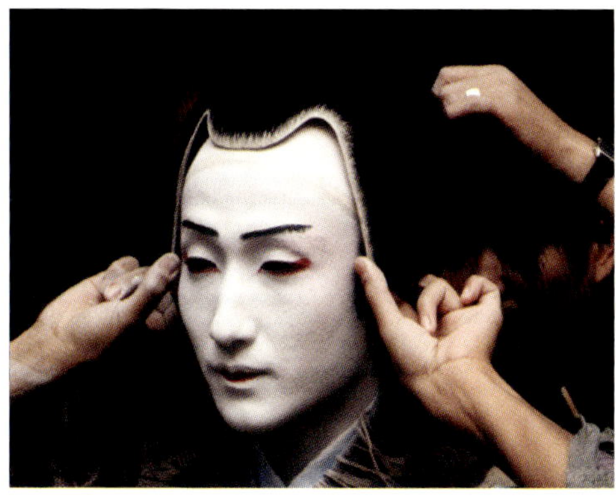

Facing page top: *Kabuki* actors on stage. *Kabuki* is the traditional form of Japanese theatre.
Facing page below: *Tsam* dancer. *Tsam* is a ritual dance performed in Tibet and Mongolia to exorcise the enemies of religion.
Left: A Japanese *Kabuki* Onnagata, a man playing the role of a woman, is helped with his wig.

Greek drama has always been closely associated with religion. A Greek tragedy or comedy was a religious service sanctioned by the state to one of its gods. Plays were performed at the festivals of Dionysus – at the festival of the winepress in January; in the villages in December; and in the city, in March. Parallel to this developed the Mystery and Miracle plays in the medieval period. These were first attached to the church, but later they were dissociated from the litturgy and formed true dramatic literature – the actors performed their plays wherever convenient, whether in the church or at an inn-yard.

Roman theatre for the most part was a continuation and development of the Greek prototypes, as they existed in the Alexandrian period. A Roman play was an act of worship to the gods. It was, therefore, presented at festivals that the state itself had set apart for the purpose of public worship. The plays were merely one item of the ritual observed. One's seat at the theatre was determined by one's position in the state, as theatre was a religious institution under the aegis of the government. The usual time for a play to begin was early in the morning. Around the 2nd century BC, a favourite act was parodying the rites of the Christian church, especially baptism. The candidate was brought to the stage accompanied by bishops, priests and deacons. A number of early saints had been converted then and there by the divine power of the rite they were parodying – they had confessed their faith from the stage, and attained martyrdom soon after.

The Chinese classics frequently mention music and dance. Services were held in the ancestral temples of princes and nobles. Dancing of a slow and dignified character formed a part of civil and religious ceremonies. According to one theory, Chinese drama had gradually evolved from dance forms. The

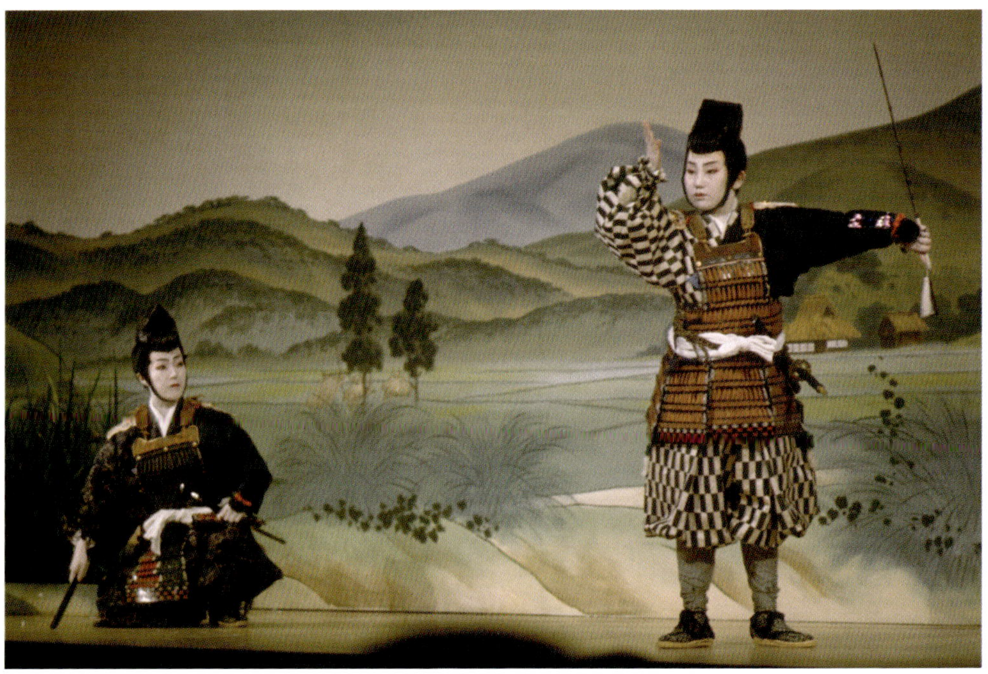

Top: A *Noh* mask belonging to the Momoyama period. *Noh* is a major form of classical Japanese musical drama. ***Below:*** Actors perform a *Noh* play in Kyoto, Japan. ***Facing page:*** *Noh* performer. *Noh* developed as a temple dance or lyric drama as early as the 14th century and involves singing and posturing.

earliest reference to drama goes back to the 8th century AD. An actor called 'the introducer of the play' recited the prologue. Later, by the 10th-11th centuries, it was customary to sing the greater portion of the play. Chinese drama saw its golden age under the rule of the Yuan Dynasty (1126-1367). Every rank of life was represented, from an emperor to a humble slave girl. Even gods and goddesses appear and speak.

The drama in Japan goes back to mythological times, when the Sun goddess Amaterasu-no-omikami was angry with her mischievous brother, the god of wind and thunder, and hid herself in a cave and refused to come forth. The gods, distressed by the eclipse, try to lure her by means of a play that was known as 'Play before the Classical Gate'. This play is looked upon as the root for the origin of classical Japanese drama. Later, *Noh* developed as temple dance or lyric drama and comprised singing and posturing. *Noh* appeared in its perfected form in the 14th-17th centuries.

Shintoistic dances were connected with nature worship. With the spread of Buddhism later, these incorporated Buddhist teachings and were performed by monks. During the ninth and tenth centuries, there were itinerant monks who used to attract people to watch the dances and religious performances that they enacted for teaching the principles of Buddhism.

The *Ramlila* is a drama that seeks to create awareness about the religious fervour and values of the Hindus. The presentation of the story of good triumphing over evil told through the story of Lord Rama, is an annual festival when most Indian cities wear a festive look with nooks and corners spruced up to stage the grand show that requires just makeshift structures. Women keep away from

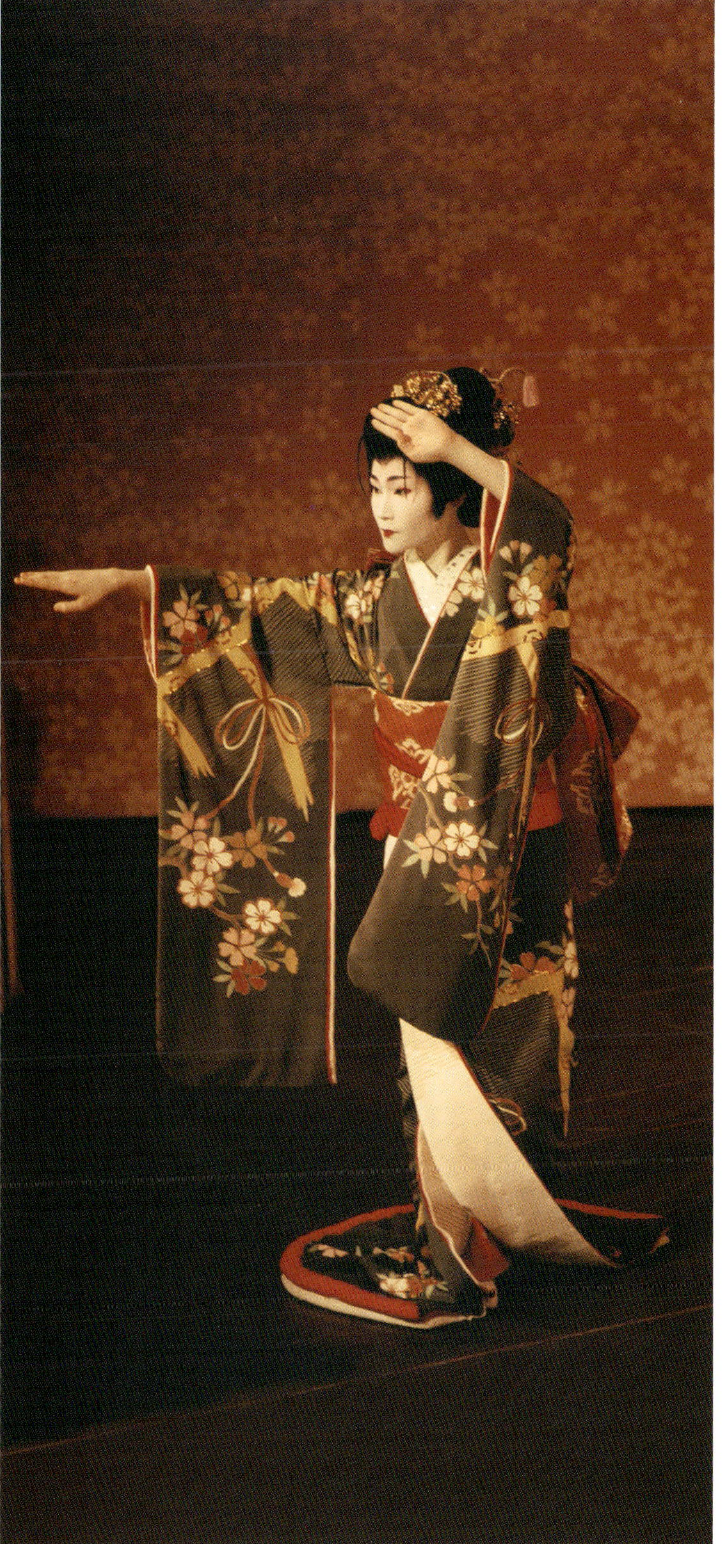

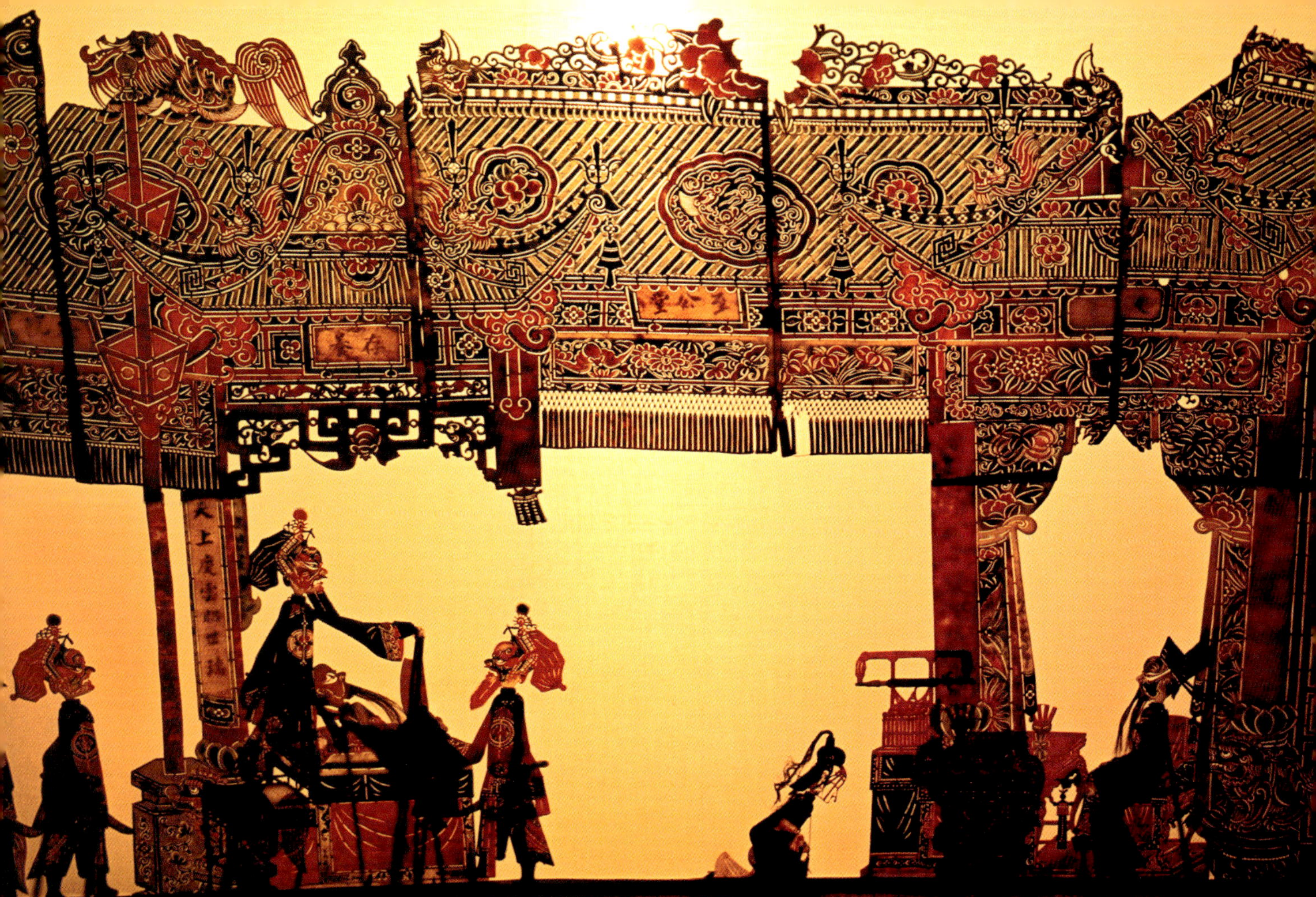

Above: *Wayang*, Indonesian shadow theatre, is an art form based on the chapters of *Mahabharata* and *Ramayana*. A group of *Wayang Kulit* puppets kept together (**facing page above**). Traditionally, *Wayang Kulit* performances, lasting all night, feature leather shadow puppets (**facing page below**).

participating, giving a chance to the male members of the troupes to act as Sita, Kaikeyee, Kaushalya, or any other female characters of the *Ramayana*. The voices of those acting as Hanuman or Ravana have to be deep to create a powerful effect. The drama concludes with the burning of the effigies of Ravana, Kumbhakarna and Meghanad on the 10th day, Dussehra, of the month of Ashvini. It is not possible to trace its beginning, but one theory proposes that Goswami Tulasi Dasa wrote the epic in AD 1554, when a saint arranged the first-ever *Ramlila* in Chitrakoot.

The *Ramayana* has played a creative role, manifesting itself in the narrative arts of recitation by storytellers, in the performing arts of classical ballad, theatre and shadow play, in the arts of stone engraving, wood carving and painting, and in creative writings whether prose or poetry. The *Ramayana* was rendered as a *Jataka* tale in Chinese in the third century AD. In the 6th century, the Sri Lankan poet-king Kumaradasa composed *Janaki-harana*, the earliest Sanskrit work in Sri Lanka. It has been eulogised in several Sinhalese works.

The word *Wayang* means 'shadow'. Shadows of puppets are projected on a canvas stretched out on a wooden frame. Through Wayang – an art form combining in itself the virtues of self-control, contemplation, charm and grace – the story of the *Mahabharata* becomes energetic and mysterious. It represents the combination of the beauty of body and colour. Texts for *Wayang* are based

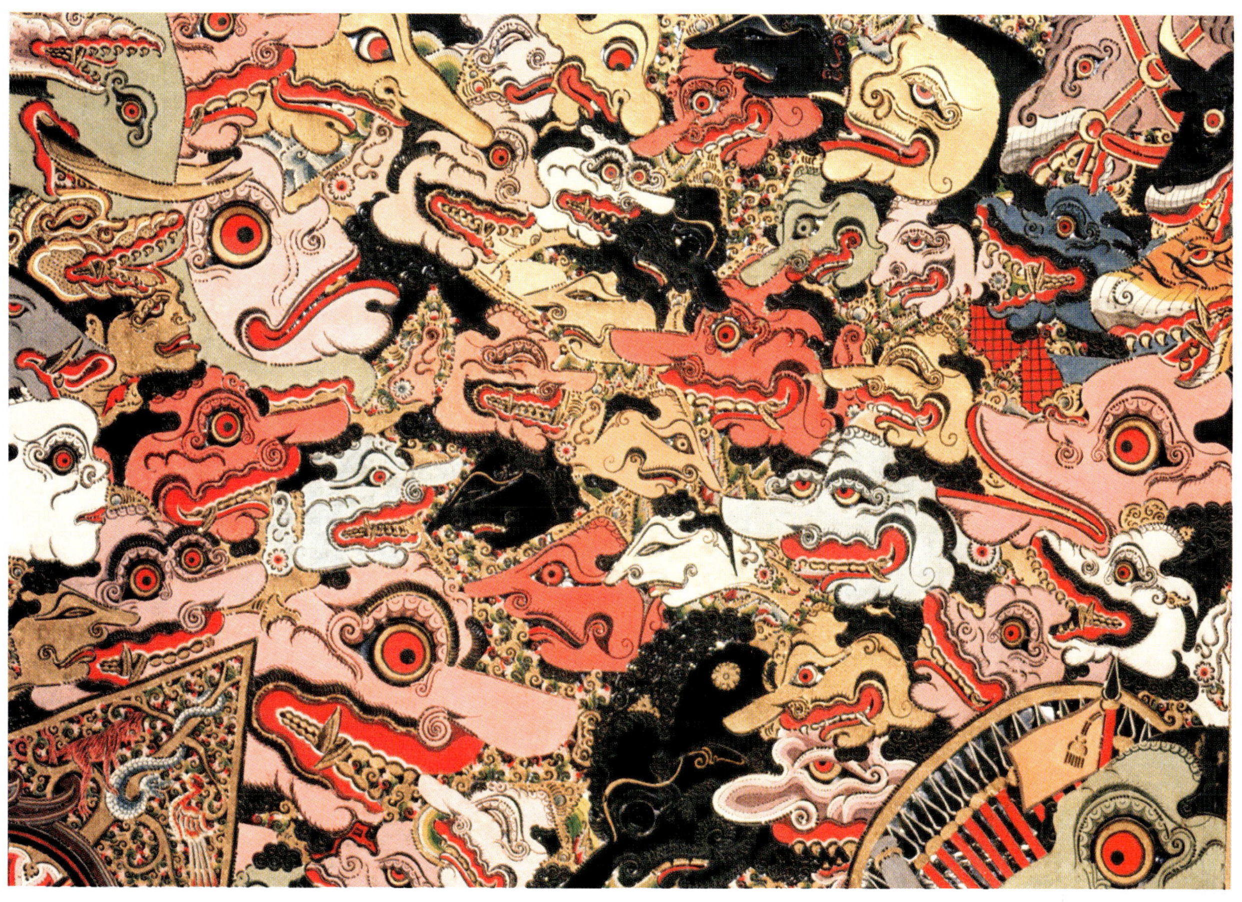

on and inspired by the *parvas* (chapters) of the Mahabharata or the Ramayana, but are modified to suit its distinct form. The dalang is the ritual performer and a skilled entertainer. He recites in varied voices giving indications of a change of character. *Wayang* is undoubtedly religious in origin – offerings are made to the spirits, incense is offered before a presentation begins, and plays are often presented at night when the spirits are thought to be away. The presentation is considered to be a meritorious act for the patron who hires the troop.

Khon, one of the Thai classical dances, is known from time immemorial. The stories for *Khon* performances are taken from the Thai version of *Ramayana* called Ramakien. They are composed for the classical dance that exists in many versions. Performers of Khon are normally male, but at times women also participate. The dress of a *Khon* performer is designed according to the character. The dress for a demon creates a sense of ferocity and strength for the demons, while that of a human hero is full of majesty and grace, and that of a female character is imbued with beauty and gentleness. The earliest reference to shadow play is found in *Therigatha* ('Songs of the Nuns'), where a young nun, Subha, spurned the love of a young man too engrossed with worldly realities.

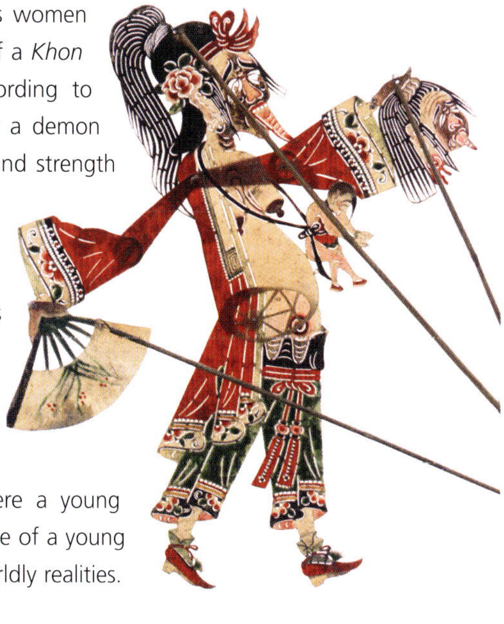

A young Sikh girl carrying a sarangi for the *kirtan*.

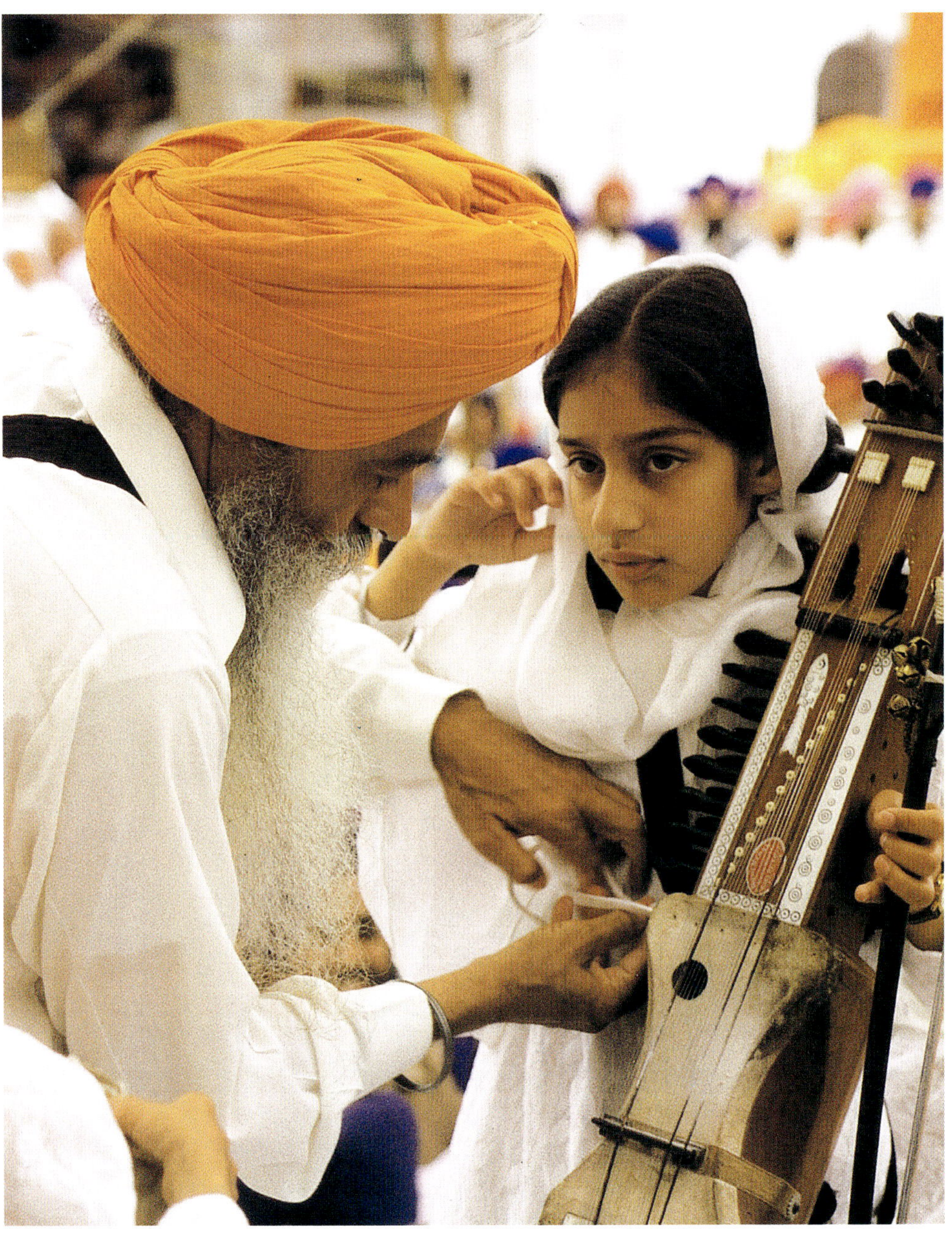

Devotional songs like *kirtan*s effectively convey their message. A *kirtan* creates agreeable and pleasurable emotions in the minds of the listeners. Such experience is most desirable for a state of *samadhi*. The singer forgets himself and is carried along by the song's ecstatic quality.

Bhajans are devotional songs of praise and prayer, or love songs in praise of Krishna, Rama, or other divine beings. *Bhajans* may also convey advice, *pravachan*, given by the storyteller, or tell a moral story explaining the characters of those who have influenced the past and present generations. The tradition is supposed

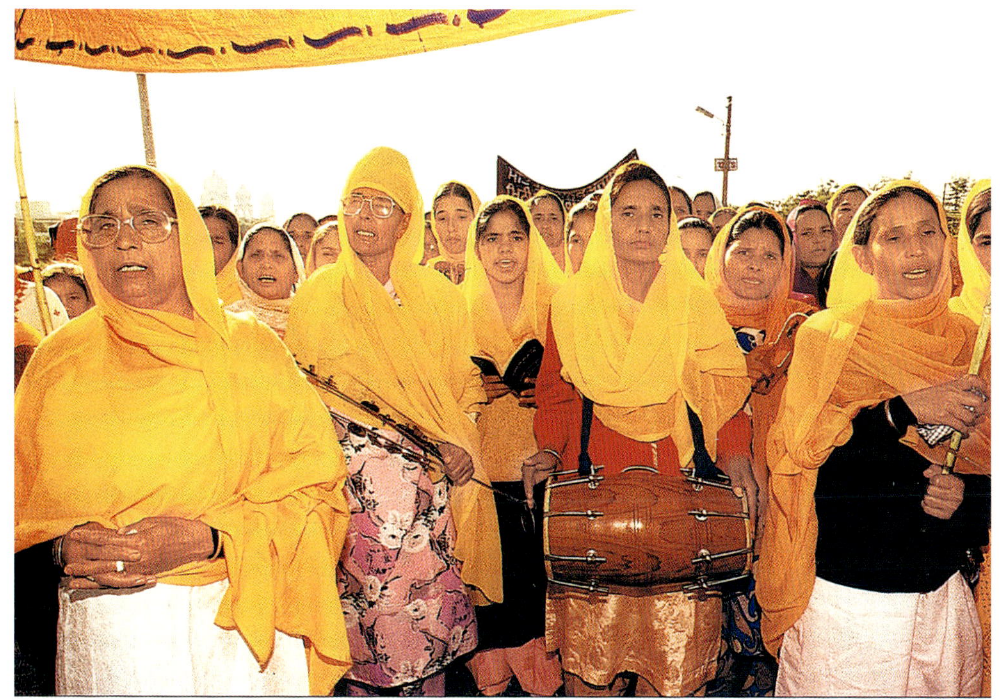

Devotional songs of prayer and love in praise of Krishna, Rama and other divine beings.
Following pages 70-71: Buddha statues, Schwedagon Pagoda, Yangon, Myanmar.

to have come down from Narada, the first storyteller of divine origin.

The power of the sound of chanting is a creative means for spiritual gain. Sacred chanting brings forth creative and spiritual resources on a common platform. Hindus and Buddhists, Zoroastrians and Judaeo-Christians, Sufis and Shamans, possess a rich heritage of chants. The human voice is specially trained for chanting. Sacred chanting combines the depth of voice with artistry and spirituality, revealing one's profound inner belief.

Vedic prayers or *mantra*s are often accompanied with sacrificial rites. Prayers are offered and rites are performed to uphold order in the society. Chanting *sutras*, according to the Buddhists, is an artistic way to communicate certain ideas and attitudes. This is a powerful medium to reach the hearts of the people. The sound of the *sutras* has a positive bearing on one's mind, making it calm and serene. Chanting helps in meditation. Lay Buddhist organisations in Japan organise group-chanting sessions, while Tibetan monks chant to large gatherings. Indonesian chanting sometimes includes drumming and performing rituals for daily life, for instance while entering a new home or a boat, for celebrating an important event in one's life, or for an epidemic or even crop failure. Sikhs recite from Guru Grantha Sahib, chanting the sayings of Guru Nanak. Some artists have integrated Jewish traditional music and sacred chanting into contemporary music and theatre.

It is generally believed by the Hindus and the Buddhists that the best way to impress a deity is to sing its praises and offer prayers, by muttering his or her name continuously – that is, through the discipline of *japa*. This is thought to be the best way to concentrate and, thereby, reach the level of trance. The Chinese also believe that 'music hath the power of making the heavens descend on earth.'

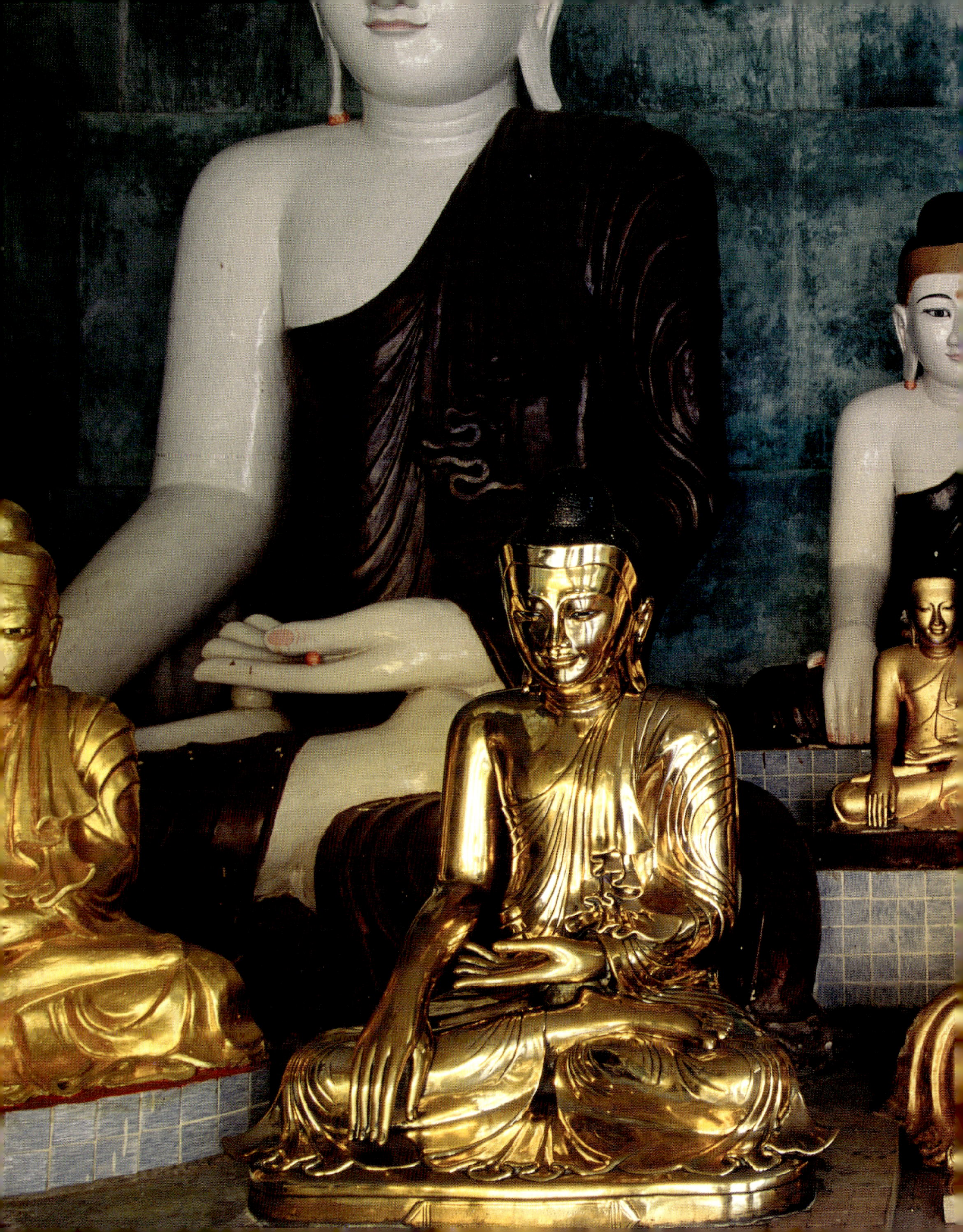

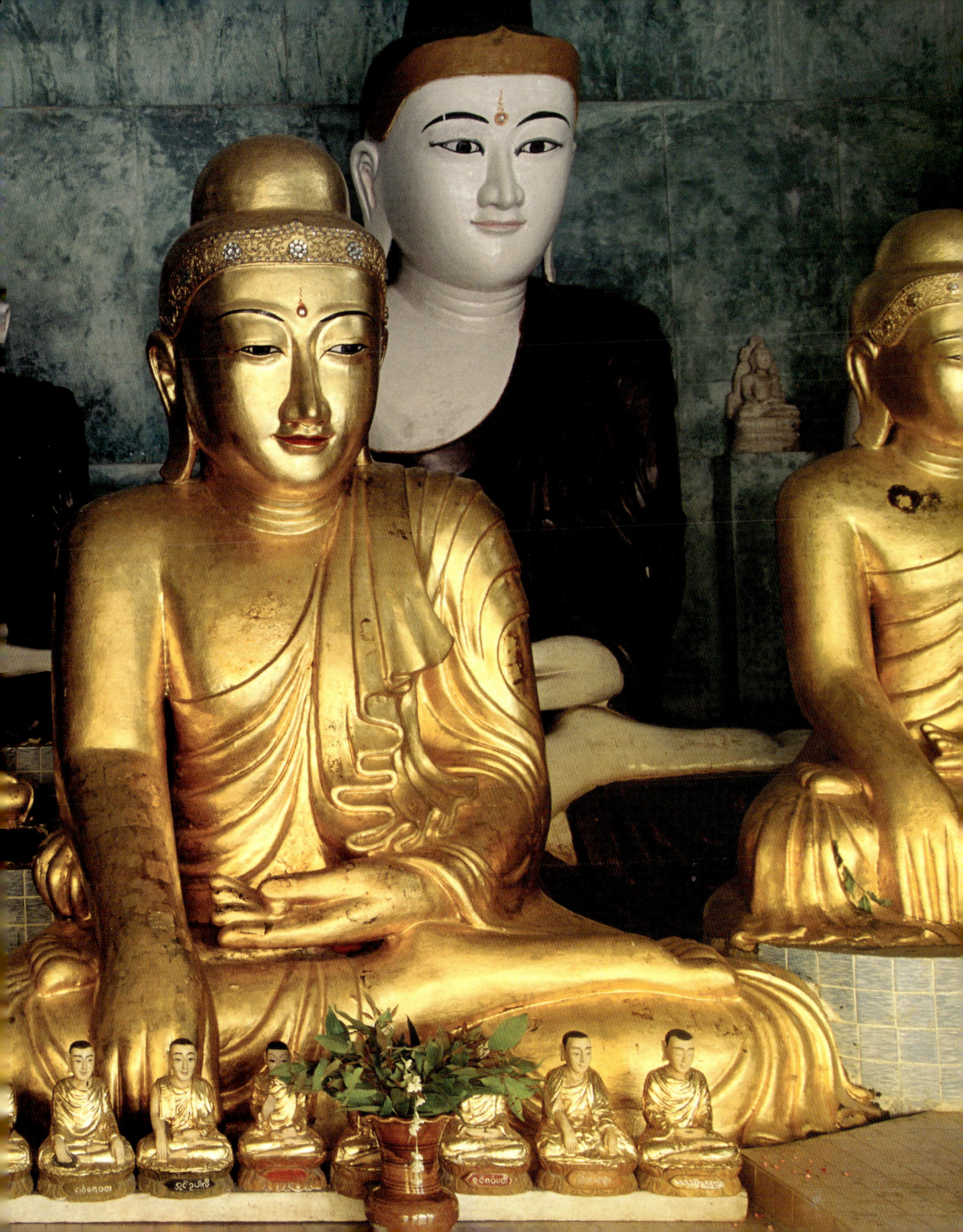

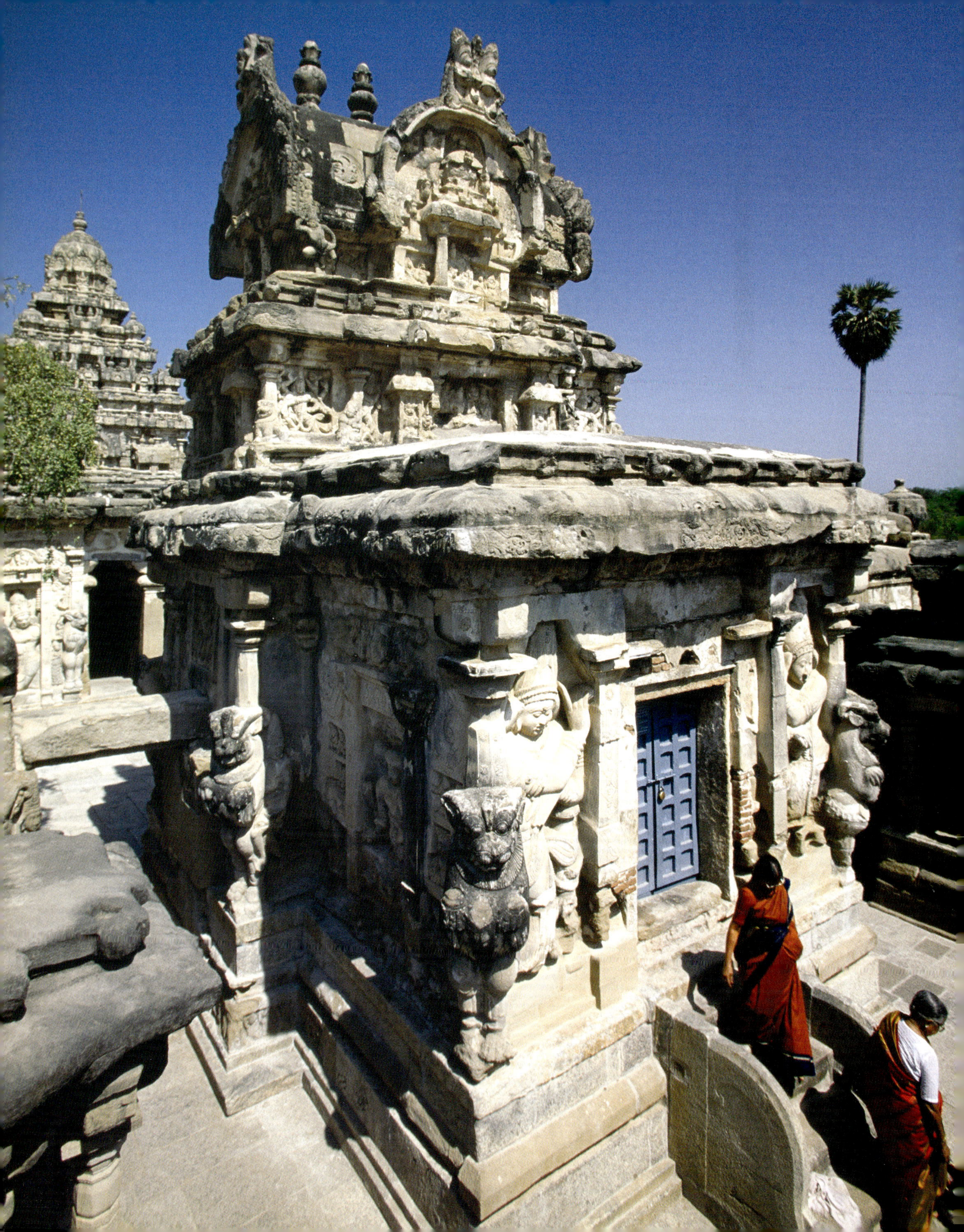

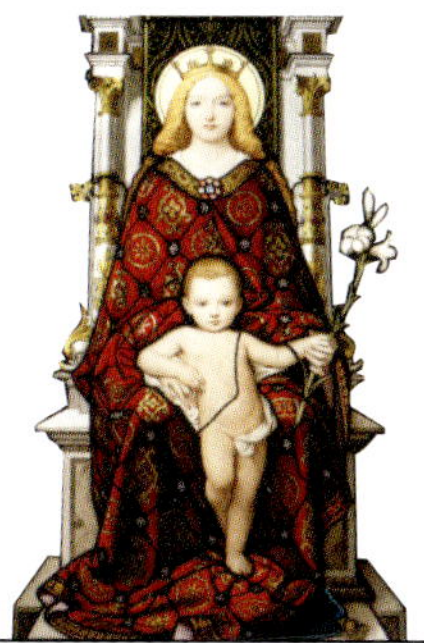

DECORATION AND ILLUSTRATION: DIVINITY IMMORTALISED

A temple is a place where one can contemplate; it relates to the paradigms of space and time. Intricate systems of thought are encoded in its architecture. The term *tempus* in Latin means 'time', and *templum* means 'space marked out', a 'sanctuary'. A temple is an earthly imitation of the celestial paradise of the divine on a reduced scale. It is a heavenly mansion composed of levels of pavilions, terraces, ponds and gardens.

In India divine places began to be built at the beginning of the Christian era, in the regions of Gandhara, Mathura and Amaravati. Due to a strong cultural intercourse with the west, Indian architects assimilated Iranian and Hellenistic ideas into their own creations. The Hindus built temples ranging from the simplest forms and designs to the incredibly complex ones. The simple ones constitute a porch, a main room, an inner sanctuary containing the principal image, and the superstructure – the surmounting tower. There are traces of the earliest freestanding building at Bairat near Jaipur, dating from the 3rd century BC. The next landmark in temple architecture is found at Jandial, in the city of Taxila, featuring an inner sanctuary, a meeting hall and a courtyard. The Sun temple at Martand in Kashmir is the most famous 8th-century-AD temple. No temple survives from the pre-Gupta period.

A number of temples in western India follow almost the same pattern. Their pillars are usually ornate with heavy bell-shaped capitals, which form the top of a column, surmounted by animal motifs, while mythological scenes and figures are carved at the entrances. They are smaller in scale. The finest examples of Gupta temples are at Deogarh near Jhansi, where iron dowels are used to hold the masonry together while the sanctum is surrounded by a covered verandah.

A small, dark room forms the heart – the focal point – of a temple, enshrining the main idol of worship, and opening into a hall meant for the devotees to gather in. The main hall of the temple has a porch. The central sanctum is topped by the superstructure. In the east-

Above: 'Madonna and Child' painted on a stained glass window, at the Vatican.
Facing page: Kailasanatha Temple sanctuary, Kanchipuram. This temple was built around 7th century AD and received patronage from the Pallava and Chalukyan kings.

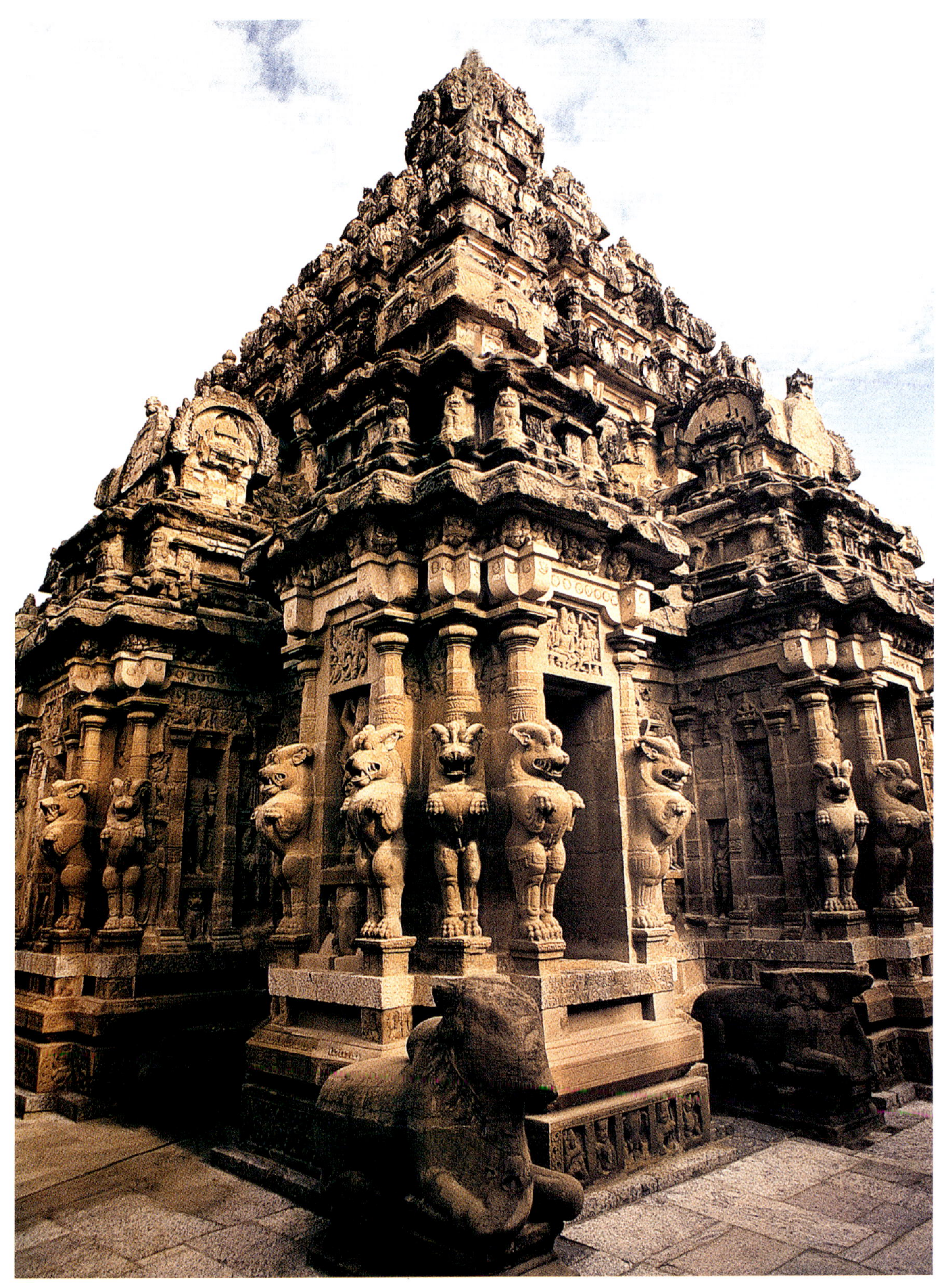

facing temples, the first rays of the rising sun consecrate the main image because the sun is the symbol of stability of the state and the cosmos.

In the Middle Ages, new temple styles were created with better techniques of stone architecture. Books were written on strict canons of design both in architecture and sculpture. Temples were ornately decorated with heavy cornices, strong pillars and towers. In north India towers with rounded tops and curvilinear outlines were erected, while in the south they were given the shape of a rectangular, truncated pyramid.

The soaring multistoried gates of the south Indian temples symbolise Sumeru, the central mountain of the universe that carries the realms of the celestials on its summits. Vast, tube-like horizontal roofs called *vimana*s crown them. The Sun Temple at Konark is the divine chariot of the lord of the world.

Temple building was given much patronage by the Pallava and Chalukyan kings in the 6th-8th centuries. The Ganges valley played a paramount role in the sphere of arts during the Gupta and post-Gupta periods. It was during this time that stupas were built at Nalanda, Rajagriha, Sarnath and Mathura; a number of temples were built in the central regions; caves were dug at Udayagiri and Bagh; in Maharashtra, caves were carved at Ajanta, Ellora and Elephanta; and temples were built on a large scale in Andhra Pradesh. Kailashanath Temple at Ellora is the best example of the Rashtrakuta style. The Pallava style of art developed in the south. Around the 6th century, several temples were erected in the region of Aihole, in what is now known as Mysore. They continued with the Gupta style but incorporated some new elements. They reflect two different styles: Nagara and Dravidian. The monolithic temples and Shore Temple at Mamallapuram and the temples of Kanchipuram in the south provided prototypes for the Dravidian art that developed in the following centuries.

In Dravidian architecture, the emphasis shifted from the tower above the chief shrine to the entrance gateway of the surrounding wall. These walls were strong and high, and protected the temples. From the 12th century onwards, temples were fortified by three concentric walls with gates on the four sides. The gates were surrounded by watchtowers that

Facing page: Kailashanatha temple, Kanchipuram.
Below: The earliest structural temple in stone, built in Tamil Nadu by Rajasimha. It marks the evolution of the Dravida architecture.

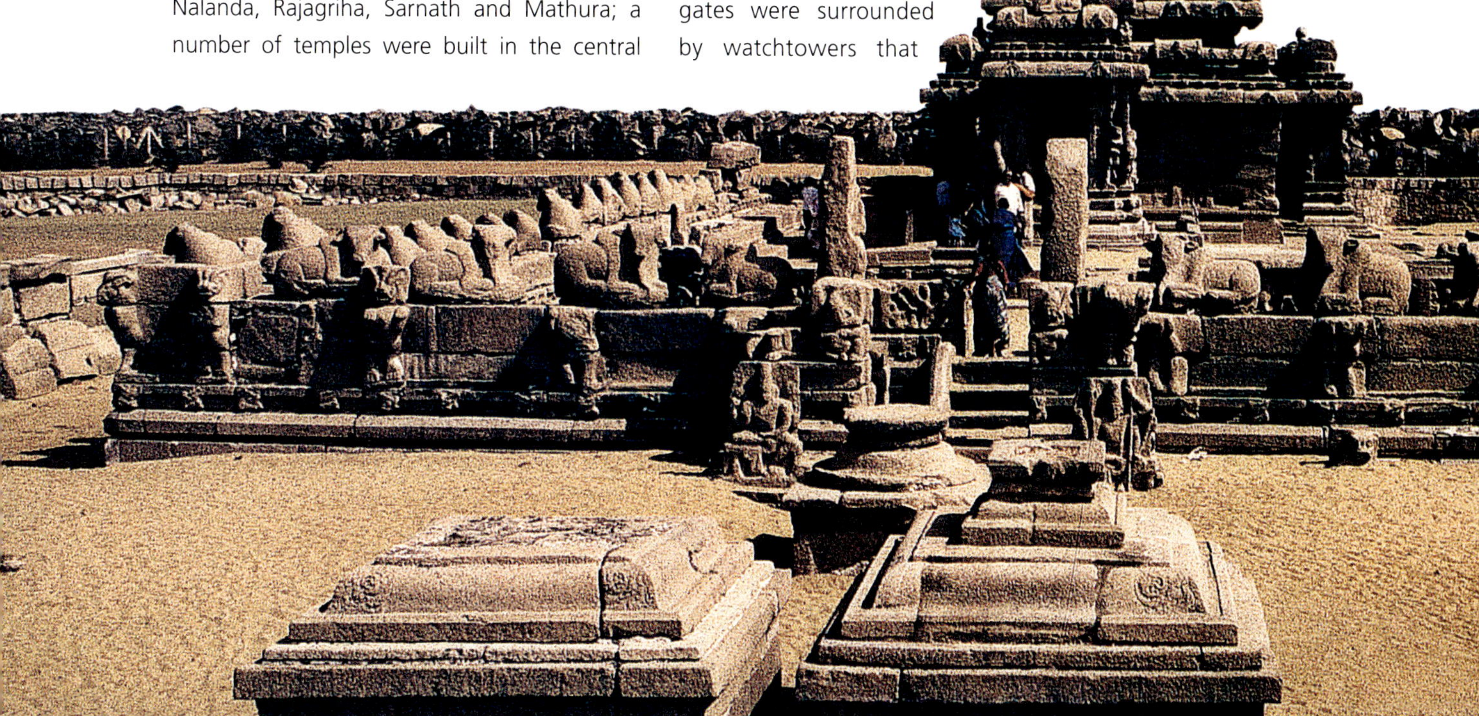

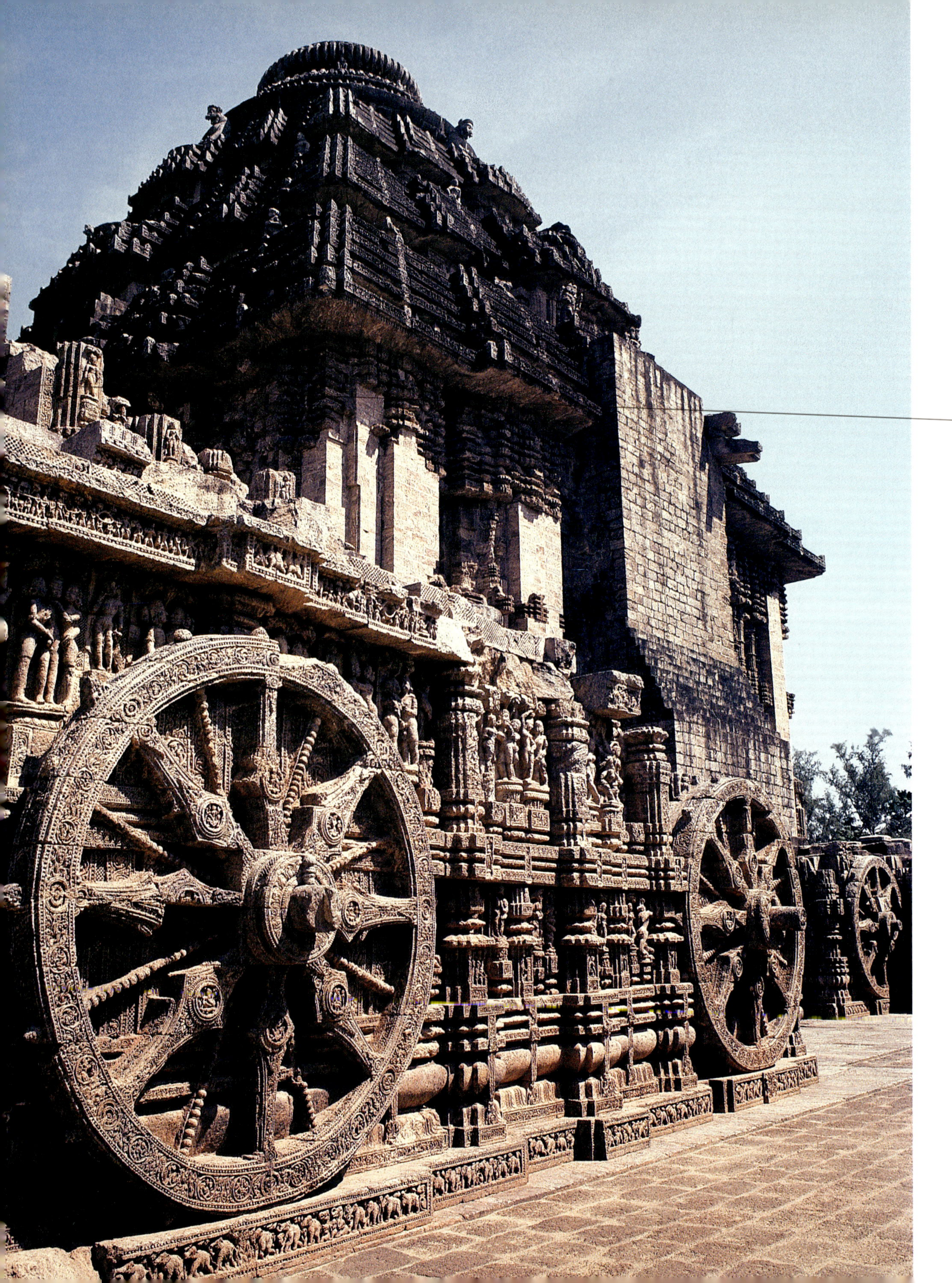

developed into soaring towers, generally much taller than the *shikharas* over the central shrines. They were elaborately ornamented.

By the 8th century new features developed in the Deccan. The Chalukyan temples were known by their wide, overhanging eaves. Later, Chalukyan and Hoysala temples became polygonal or stellate, raised on tall, solid platforms. The school that flourished under the Vijayanagara Empire and reached its apogee in the 16th century shows both Pandyan and Hoysala features. Florid carving was developed with greater exuberance. Delicate carvings adorned the pillared halls.

Medieval north Indian architecture is best illustrated by three schools – those of Orissa, Bundelkhand, and Gujarat and south Rajasthan. Besides, Kashmir developed its own style. The major temples of the Orissa school lie in and around the towns of Bhubaneswar and Puri, Linggaraj being the finest, bearing an inward curve in its superstructure called *shikhara*, with a rounded top crowned by a flat stone disc (*amalaka*) and a finial (*kalasha*).

The temple of Vishnu Jagannatha at Puri and the Sun Temple at Konark are the best known and the most important among the temples of Orissa. There are two halls built separately from the main shrine erected on an imposing platform along with the assembly hall. Twelve wheels, 10 feet each in diameter, decorate each side of the outer wall of the platform of the Sun Temple. The whole structure symbolises the chariot of the Sun god. The Shaivite temple of Kandariya Mahadeva, built in about AD 1000, is the finest among the beautiful temples at Khajuraho built by the Chandela kings of Bundelkhand. Sculptures are carved both inside and outside of the temple. The wonderful friezes of statuary contain figures of graceful vitality and look warm and attractive.

Stupas are symbolic structures integral to Buddhism. They symbolise the presence of the lord. From massive monuments to tiny votive offerings, they have many levels of meaning. At the deepest level they are symbols of Dharmakaya, attributed to three main functions: as reliquaries they contain ashes of the Awakened Ones; as memorials they mark important events of the life of the Buddha; and as votive stupas they are symbols of meritorious acts. These divine structures began to appear during the life of the historical divine. The first stupas were built by the two traders, Trapusha and Bhallika. They requested the lord for a relic to worship him. The Buddha acceded and cut off a tuft of his hair and nails, with which he asked them to construct topes. They constructed stupas at Keshasthalin for the hair and at Valuksha for the nails.

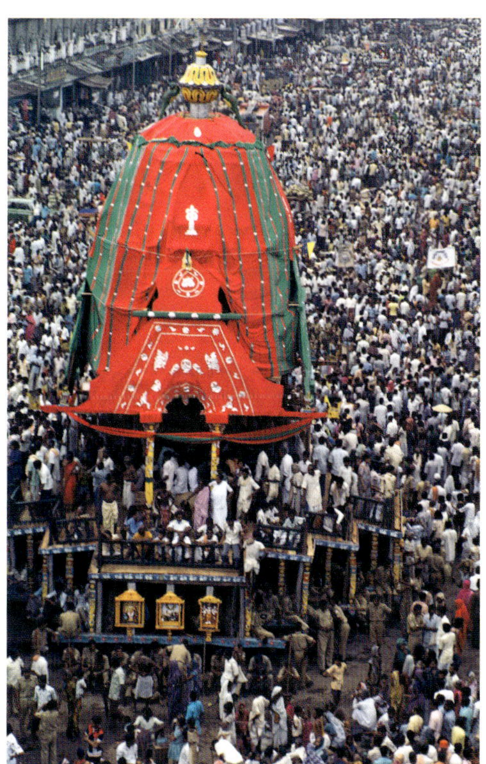

Facing page: The Sun Temple in Konark, Orissa, 13th century AD.
Below: The famous rath yatra festival of Jugannath at Puri (Orissa). Puri is a major pilgrim centre, attracting people from across the globe.

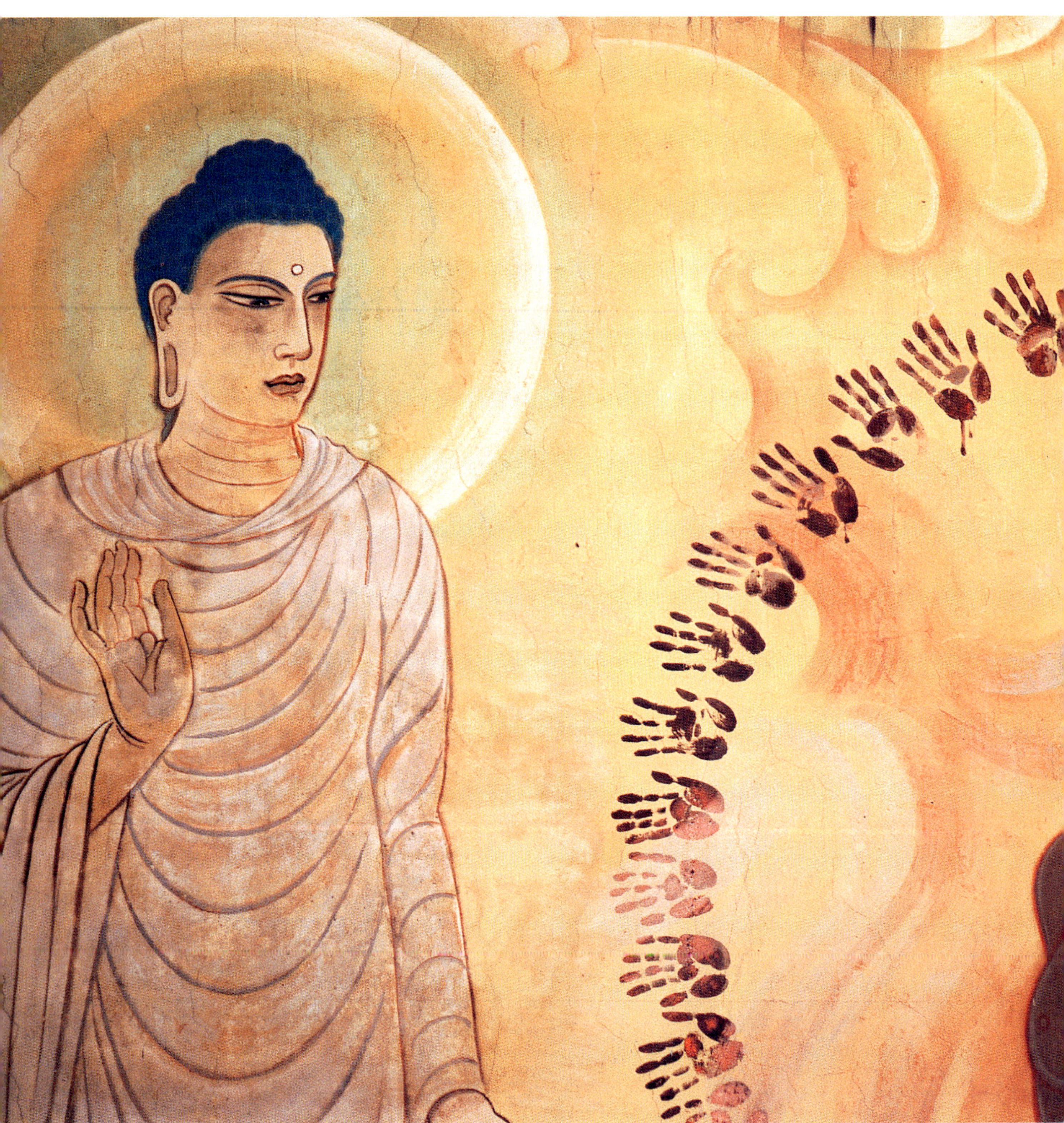

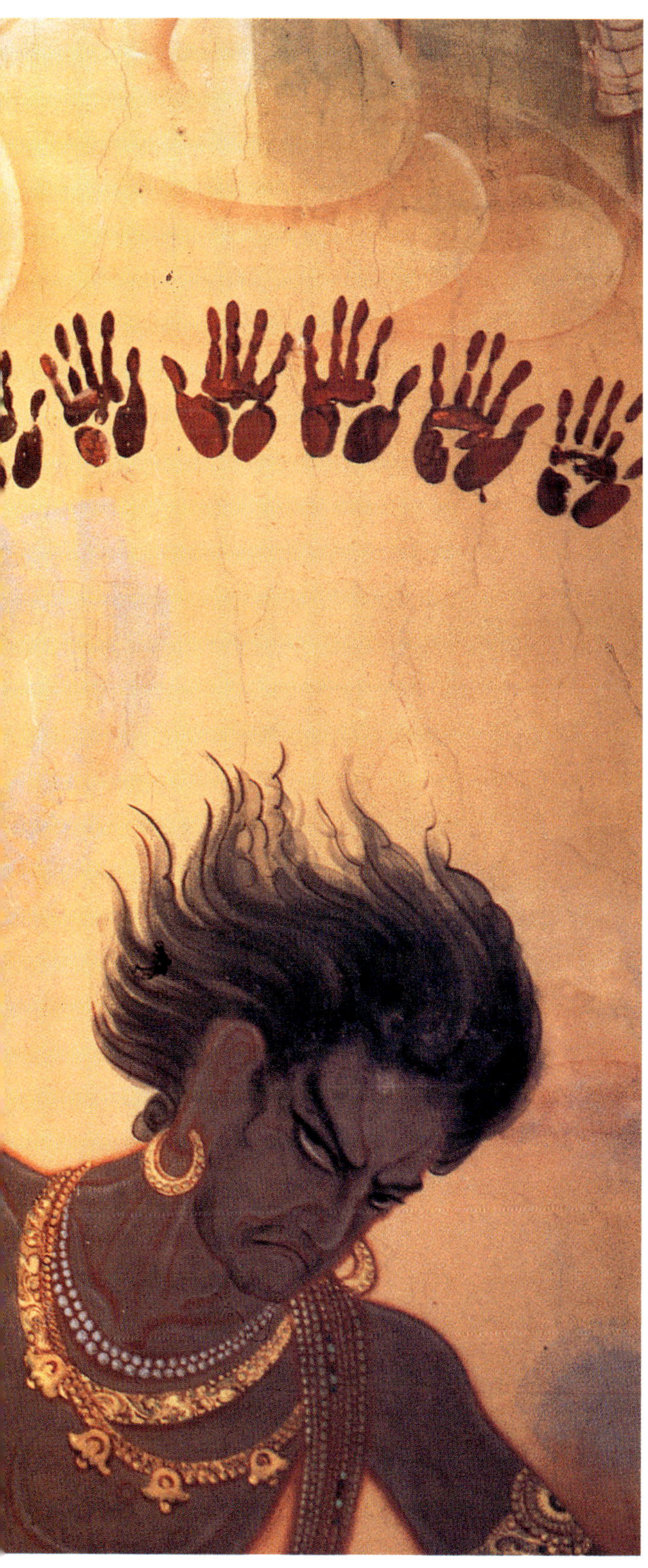

Left: A painting depicting Angulimal, the bloodthirsty bandit who was later redeemed by the gentle and persuasive ways of Buddha.

Caves with a temple's silence, darkness and solitude, were the earliest dwellings of man where he also first tried his hand at visual art on walls. The Buddhists were the first to carve out natural rock shelters in India. Indians too began to cut rocks, by the 3rd century BC. In order to cut and carve, first an outline was marked and then cutting was begun downwards from the ceiling with sharp and heavy instruments. Solid blocks were left for pillars and other constituents. These caves served as temporary retreats during the rainy season for travelling monks. It was not a final retreat because after enlightenment they used to re-enter the world of the common people and show them the path of the Buddha.

Inside the caves, although it was dim and dark, sculptors carved a divine world out of lithic masses, while the painter's brush touched the walls to paint murals to create a refreshing atmosphere of heavenly bliss. Buddhas and Bodhisattvas, nagas and garudas, hell and heaven, flying goddesses and guardians were painted in full glory and noble grace as symbols of purity and dignity. Travelling monks brought their dharma to the caves. Mystery and charm intermingled there.

Monasteries serve as centres of both religion and wisdom. The environment around them inspires a divine feeling. A soothing murmuring sound created by prayers chanted by the devotees adds to their transcendental beauty. Normally, an outer wall separates the sacred from the common. The main gate welcomes outsiders, but the guardians standing on the sides keep a watch to protect the dharma. Within the halls are installed smiling and compassionate figures of Buddhas, Bodhisattvas and goddesses, inculcating hopes and aspirations, and assuring peace and protection. The paintings or sculptures created inside are intended to

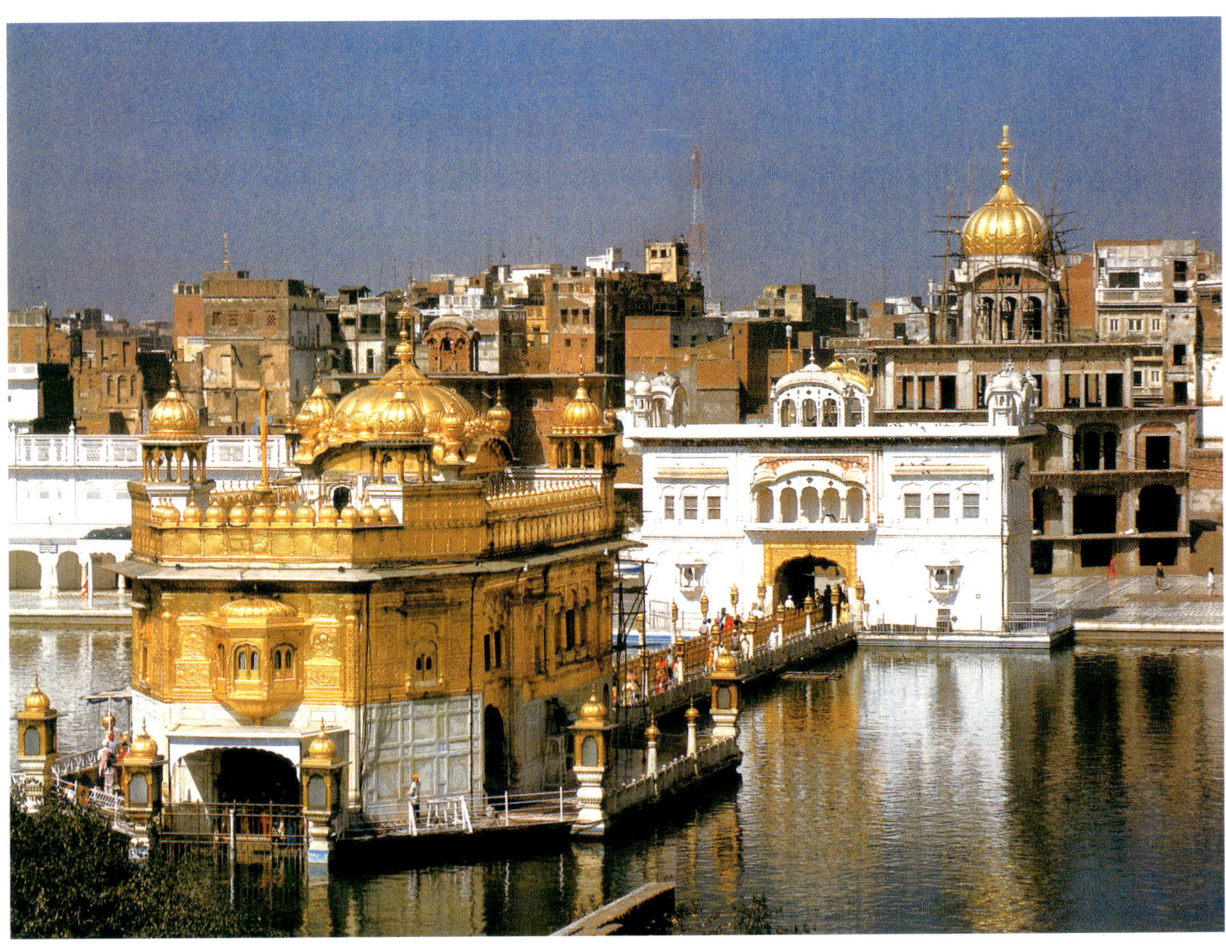

Above: Harimandir (foreground), the Darshani Deodi and the causeway to the Golden Temple, with the dome of the Akal Takht (far back). It is the primary seat of Sikh religion and the central point of political assembly.

attract devotees. Pictorial representations of the *Jatakas* are often used to embellish monastic interiors.

A gurdwara is a place of worship for the Sikhs. It is a gateway to reach the Guru, a place where devotees gather to listen to the teachings of the divine teacher and the hymns chanted by the gurus. Guru Gobind Singh introduced the term 'gurdwara'. It enshrines the divine scripture, the Guru Granth Sahib. Free distribution of food without any discrimination is one of the major functions of a gurdwara.

The chief place of pilgrimage of the Sikhs is Harimandir Sahib, also known as the Golden Temple, at Amritsar in Punjab. It preserves their historical and spiritual traditions. The place is also honoured as the divine court, Darbar Sahib, which is a source of inspiration and embodies purity of the body and the mind. The glistening structure of the temple stands in a pond called Amritsar, the 'pool of nectar.' It receives devotees coming from all four directions through its entrances on the four sides.

In their architecture, gurdwaras owe much to the Mughal style as the artisans of the day were trained that way in Punjab. However, in the course of time, they developed certain prominent characteristics, such as repeated use of *chhatris* and ornamental parapets, corners, angles and other permanent projections. Over the doorways, florid ornamentation is sometimes found. Artists have provided decorative embellishments through various disciplines in some of the temples, especially in the Golden Temple, the Akal Takht and the Baba Atal at Amritsar, and at the shrine at Taran Taran and Baoli Sahib. Another artistic endeavour was the inlay work – studding of precious and coloured stones into marble slabs. The slabs often have florid or simple borders and sometimes flowery designs, into which stones are inlaid at appropriate places. Metal workers emboss pictures and other designs on copper or other metals.

Beautiful designs are made on the walls. Verses from the Granth Sahib have also been engraved. Cut glasses, coloured as well as mirrored, and sometimes precious stones, are also set in. This is called *tukri* work. Frescoes are to be found in some of the shrines and they generally depict episodes from the lives of the gurus. Vines, plants, flowers, birds and animals are also represented. The largest number of such frescoes is on the first floor of Baba Atal. In a staircase in the Golden Temple is a fine painting of Guru Gobind Singh on a riding horse and accompanied by some of his followers.

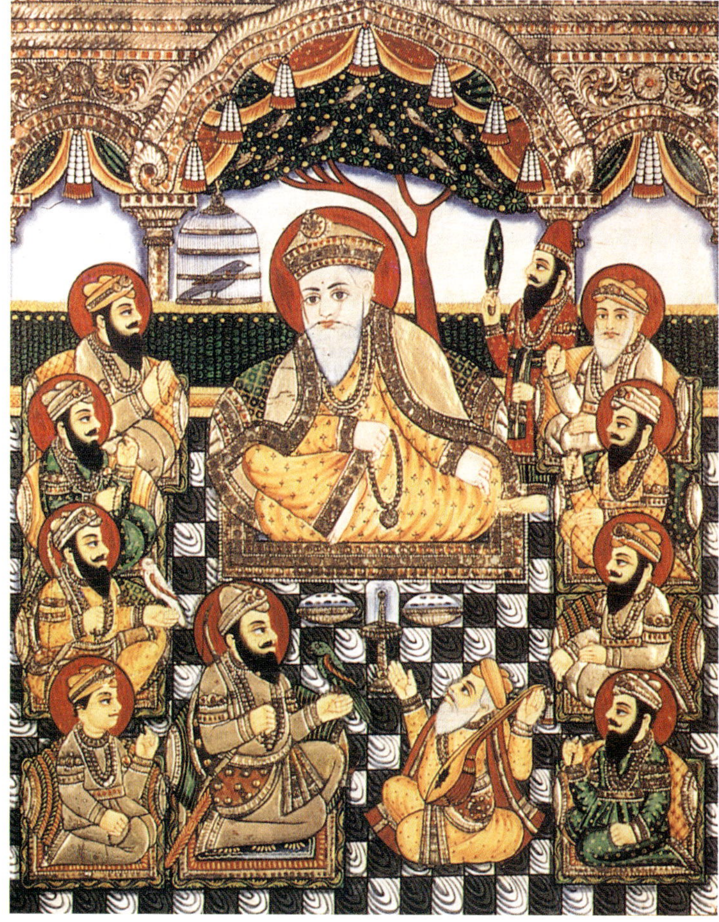

Above: A Tanjore style painting of the 19th century depicting the ten gurus with Bala and Madana.
Below: A panel in gold depicting Guru Gobind Singh with his disciples.

A gurdwara can be spotted from a distance by the yellow triangular flag hoisted from a pole in the compound. The flag is called Nishan Sahib. The top is always a dome, especially on older historical shrines. It is mostly white, and sometimes gilded, as in the Golden Temple, Taran Taran and Sis Ganj. Apart from the big central dome, there are often four other smaller cupolas, one on each corner. Several turrets decorate the parapet. The big domes are always ribbed or fluted and usually have an inverted lotus symbol at the top. At the bottom of the dome, one may come across floral or other artistic designs. Starting with a wide base, the domes reach the maximum circumference when they are less than halfway up. On the pinnacle is a *kalash*, a short, straight, cylindrical construction often with some concentric circles and a very small canopy at the absolute top with pendants hanging from the outer rim.

The Jains are atheists; they do not worship the transcendental God, but have constructed magnificent temples dedicated to the two sects,

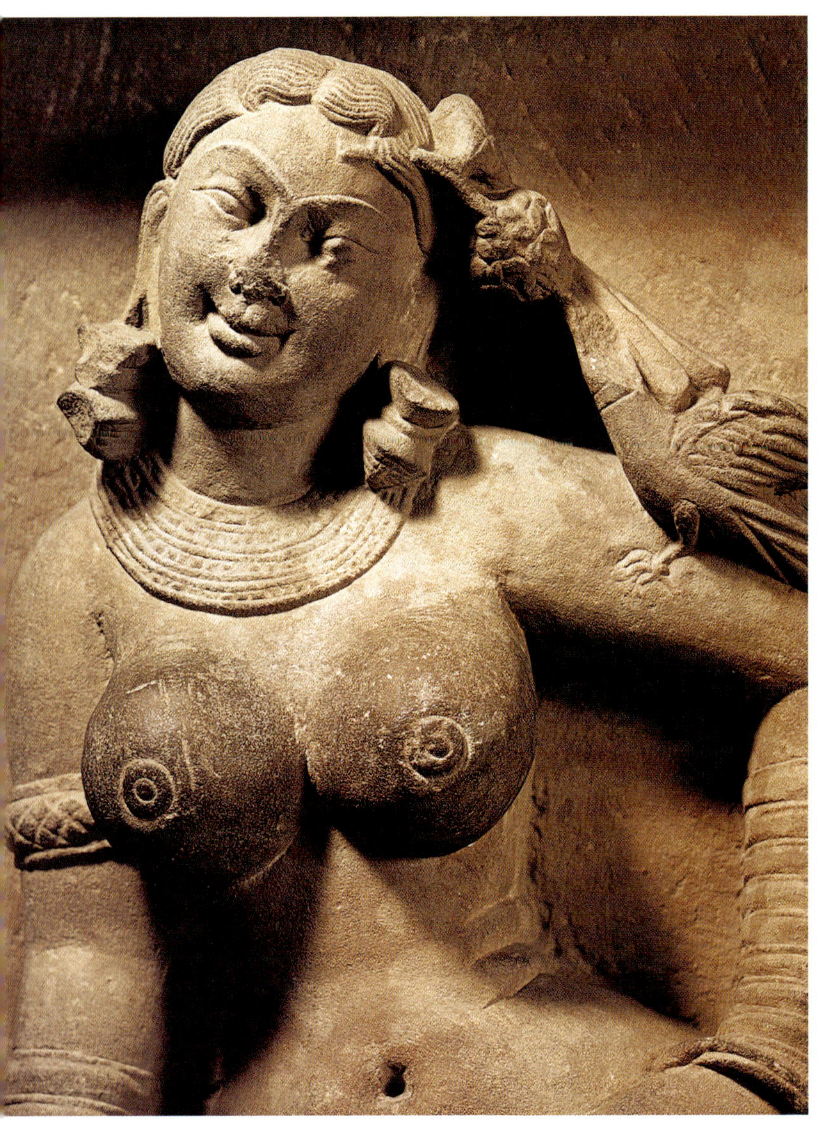

Image of Yakshi talking to a parrot. The image of a full-bodied woman, signifying both fertility and charm, is a recurring leitmotif in Indian art.

Shvetambara and Digambara, and have evolved a complex set of rituals. They adore the Tirthankaras, or Jinas, who had attained Nirvana, the highest liberation achieved by purifying the soul through meditation and asceticism, trying to put an end to all misery. Thus, the Jain temples house images of Tirthankaras. Temples are open to all members of the community. They own precious jewellery, silver chariots and other expensive objects used for worship and rituals.

The inner chamber is secluded from the outer hall by a surrounding wall that enshrines the cult image. A small ritual image is placed in the outer hall, in front of the inner chamber. Tables are placed there to keep offerings like rice grains and fruits. A circumambulatory path runs around the inner chamber. Large temples can have two worship halls and shrines, one for daily worship by men and another for women. In many Shvetambara temples, musical instruments are kept for use in rituals. One corner is reserved for preparation of sandalwood paste used in daily rituals. Apart from the main cult image, each Jain temple has several smaller shrines of other deities in the surrounding chambers. The pillars, walls and ceilings often feature paintings of gods, goddesses and places of pilgrimage. In a corner there is usually a small shrine of Kshetrapala, a guardian deity who is also very popular in village cults. The cult images undergo the ceremony of installation through a series of rituals. Large diagrams of Arhats, Siddhas, Acharyas, Upadhyayas and Sadhus are depicted on the floor.

The earliest works of Jain art are the cave monasteries at Udayagiri and Khandagiri in Orissa. An inscription of King Kharavela, a follower of Jainism, dating to 150 BC has been discovered at Udayagiri. The reliefs engraved in the caves resemble the carvings at Bharhut and Sanchi, representing warriors, charioteers, men and women, animals and vegetation, and other characteristic motifs. A hoard of Jain antiquities found at the Kankali mound, Mathura, date from 150 BC to the end of the first millennium. Jains adored the Tirthankaras through their symbolic representations like stupas, *chaitya*-trees and *dharmachakras*. In addition, there were symbols such as *srivatsa*, *swastika*, lotus bud, a pair of fish and a full vase, which later crystallised in the set of eight auspicious marks of both the sects.

Monuments of Digambara faith from the medieval period are mainly in central India. The most noteworthy examples are the Jain temples at Khajuraho; the shrines of Deogarh in Uttar Pradesh, and Chanderi Gyeraspur and Gwalior in Madhya Pradesh; and the exquisite pillar of glory at Chittorgarh in Rajasthan. Also, in southern India the Jains created important monuments of art. In the Chalukya period several shrines were constructed at Aihole and Pattadakal, of which the Meguti hill temple at Aihole is the most remarkable for its plan as well as for the sculpture of Mahavira's yakshi, Siddhaika, riding a lion. At Sittanavasal, there are remains of Jain paintings of the 9th century. In the 10th century, the famous 21-metre high colossus of Gommata was installed at Sravanabelagola in Karnataka. Characteristic creepers entwine the body of the majestic ascetic. On the opposite hill there are remains of monasteries, cult images and reliefs with scenes from the life of monks. All South Indian monuments belong to the Digambara sect. In a later period, under the Hoysala rulers, many Jain shrines such as Lakkundi were built in local style in Karnataka.

The temples of Shvetambara faith are mainly in western India. The marble shrines at Mount Abu and Kumbharia in north Gujarat are magnificent monuments of fine and intricate workmanship. At Mount Abu the 16 Mahavidyadevis, the goddesses of magic, appear in full iconographic detail, and so also the yakshas, yakshis and the guardian of directions. Of the same period and mode, but somewhat lesser known examples, are the Mahavira temple and the Taranga Hill temple in north Gujarat.

The early Jinas were depicted seated in *padmasana* – with open palms, placed one over the other, resting on the lap, and eyes closed in concentration. They are shown meditating with heads shaven or with hair arranged as curled locks. Each Tirthankara had a pair of his attendant yakshas or yakshis. Most of the basic features of the standard Jina image through the centuries remain the same. In the Gupta period the Jain cult image was evolved three-dimensionally. The figures became more sophisticated and lightweight in modelling. In

Bottom left: A quadruple structure of the four Tirthankaras polished in red sandstone in Mathura, Uttar Pradesh.
Centre: Yaksha of Pitalkhora, Uttar Pradesh. The raised right hand identifies the carver as a goldsmith.
Bottom right: Chauri-bearer in polished sandstone. The bearer of the fly-whisk (Chauri) gives an impression of grace, embodying the classical gait of the swan.

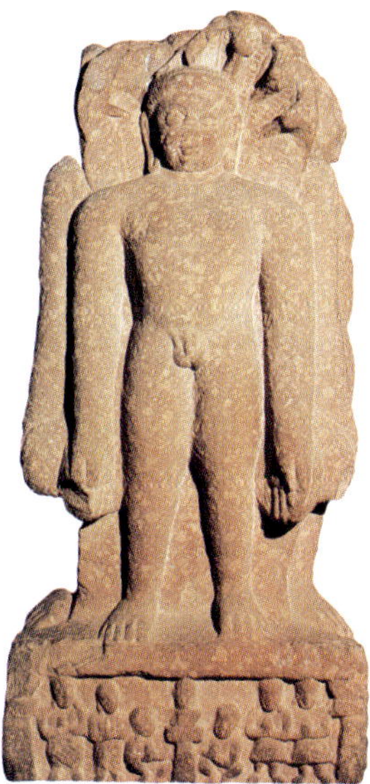

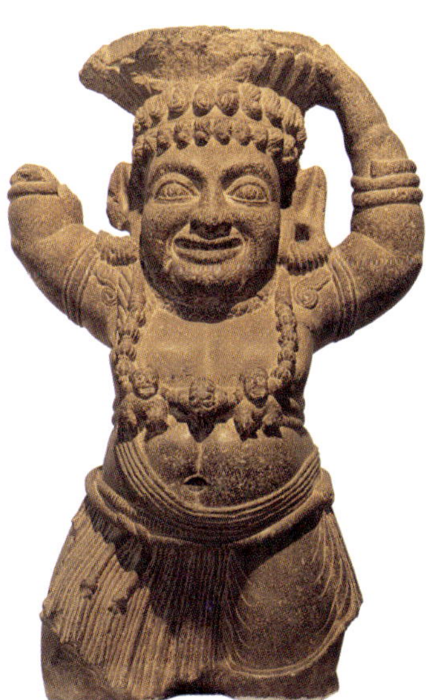

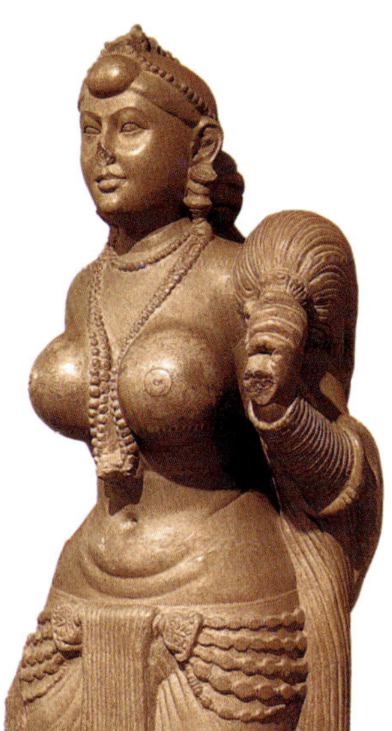

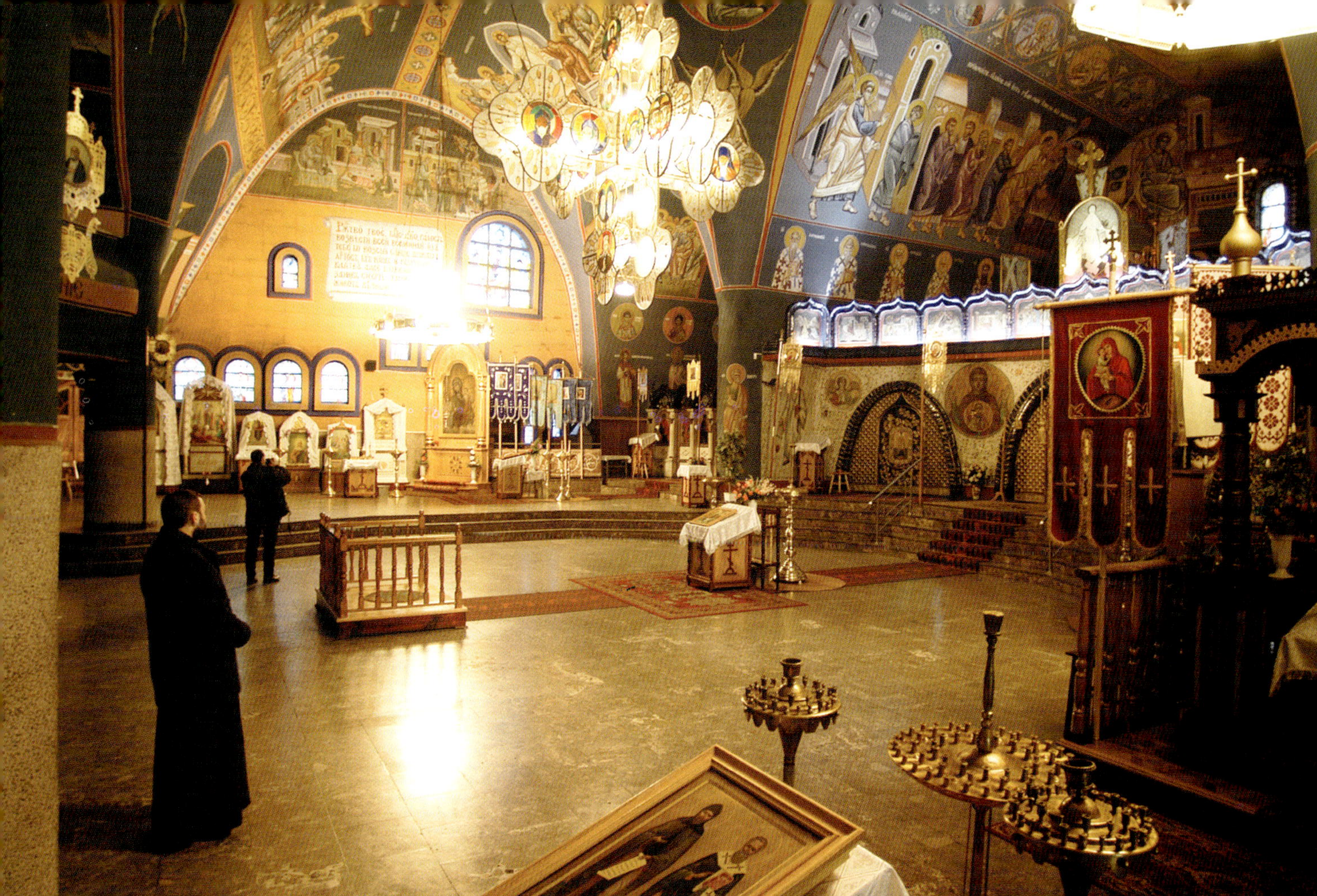

Elaborate decorated interior of an Orthodox church.

the post-Gupta period the Jain pantheon, as depicted in art, was enlarged. The symbol of cognition became a regular feature. A triple umbrella over the head and the figures of nine planets started to appear on the pedestal. Hundreds of images of this period have come to light from Deogarh, Chanderi and other places in central India. Belonging to the early post-Gupta period are the remarkable examples of the Jain temples at Badami and Ellora.

In early Christian architecture, great importance was given to luminosity, to the inlaying of precious metals, to mosaics glowing with gold and colour, and to stucco work in basilican and central plan churches. Architecture and image formed a single whole, and gradually iconographic repertory and technique of execution were refined and enriched. When monasticism was consolidated as a temporal power and as a guide to society, the Cluniacs cultivated magnificence in architecture, in decoration of churches, in church hangings, and in liturgy and the ceremonies associated with it. In the rich decoration of churches, Christians particularly favoured, apart from symbolic representations, those images capable of arousing the fear of sin, divine wrath, and hell or the expectation of the Last Judgement, represented in their churches with the image of Christ as judge.

Pilgrimages, which were encouraged by the Cluniacs, contributed to the renovation and enlargement of churches. Episcopal churches are located in the cities and open to the masses of the faithful. There, grandeur of space, opulence of decoration and richness, and variety of images are justified by the need to arouse popular devotion through material ornamentation. In the abbey churches that serve only monks, any grandeur, sumptuousness and opulence would be not only superfluous, but deserving censure.

The architecture of Gothic cathedrals in France and in the rest of Europe was influenced by the philosophical idea based on numbers, and also by the revival and elaboration of the Platonic concept of light as the image of divine power and love. The revival of this idea was responsible for the dominance of void over solid in the walls of Gothic cathedrals, and also for the predilection for storied windows – more allegorical than narrative – that were themselves, in a sense, created by light.

An Italian Thomist philosopher wrote on the didactic function of sacred images, asserting that they have a place not only in churches but also in private homes where they could be particularly useful for the instruction of children. Such images must not be adorned with gold and silver. Later, a bishop from Florence wrote that it is necessary to place

Left: Mosaic of Christ from the Basilica of Santa Prassede in Rome.
Below: A painting of the Madonna and child with saints from the San Branaba altarpiece by Sandro Boticelli.

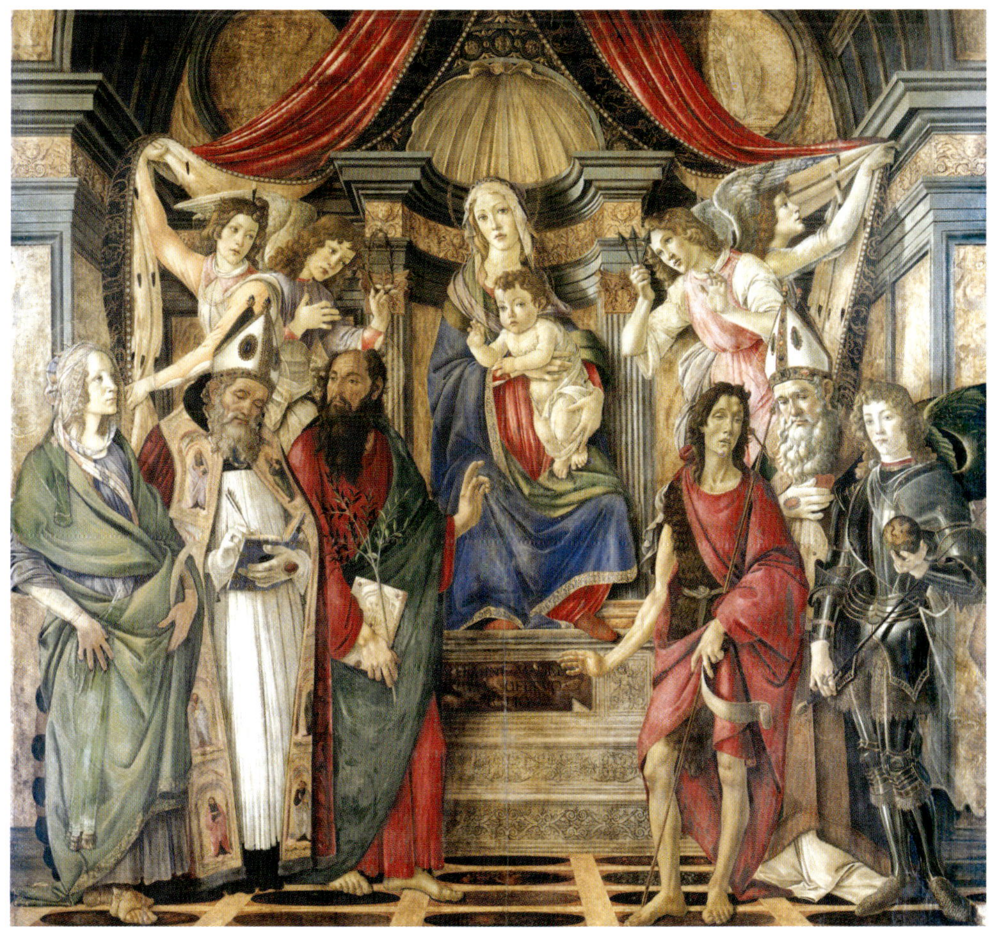

Evening prayers at the grand mosque in Mecca.

images of saints in the churches not in order to offer them worship, but to impress their virtue more effectively upon the minds of men. So, works depicting the desired characteristics intended for the laity were narrative, vivid in colour, and imbued with a lively feeling for nature. In works expressly intended for religion there was greater austerity of attenuated colour, and the introduction of symbols rather than narrative as an object of meditation.

In Catholic churches, sentimental significance prevails over aesthetic quality. Some of the more recent devotional subjects – the heart of Jesus, the Heart of Mary, and the Madonna of Lourdes – have inspired iconographic formulas, among the most popular in standardised productions.

In the last quarter of the 19th century, various symbolist artists turned to Christianity as a source of inspiration. Their art is filled with mystical-religious feeling. The church began to use serious artists for mural work. During the first half of the 20th century, more and more artists turned to Christian art, just as the church turned increasingly to contemporary artists. One effect of this revival, especially in the period after World War II, was the creation of a host of Catholic and Protestant churches in all parts of the world, designed by outstanding architects. The figural arts – murals, stained glass and sculpture – also played a role in the revival.

Protestant architecture differs from that of the Catholic world because the emphasis is placed on the Word of God, rather than on His presence. Thus, the idea of a single room is dominant in such buildings – and the figural arts, by definition, are more appropriate to Catholic than to Protestant worship.

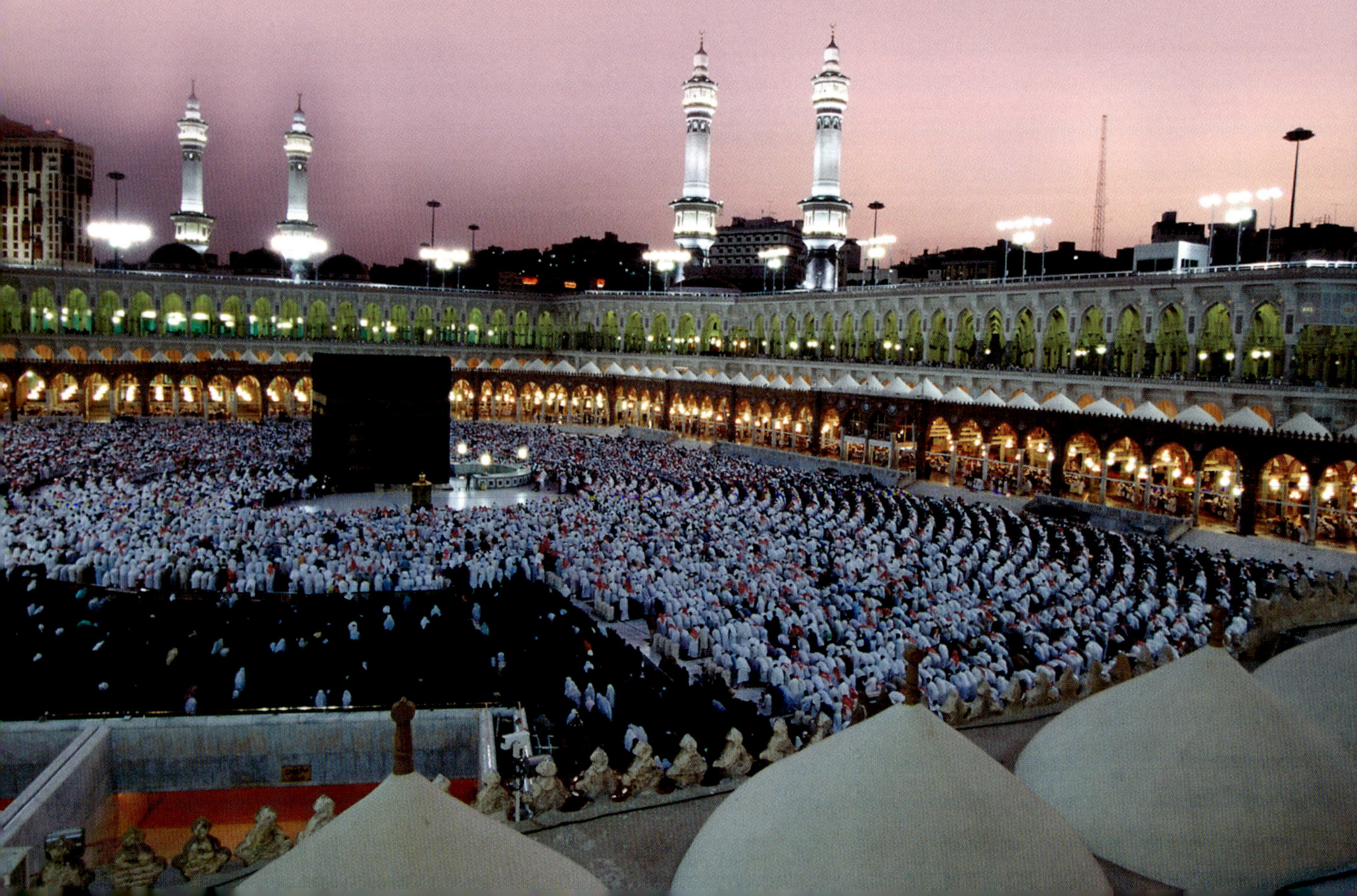

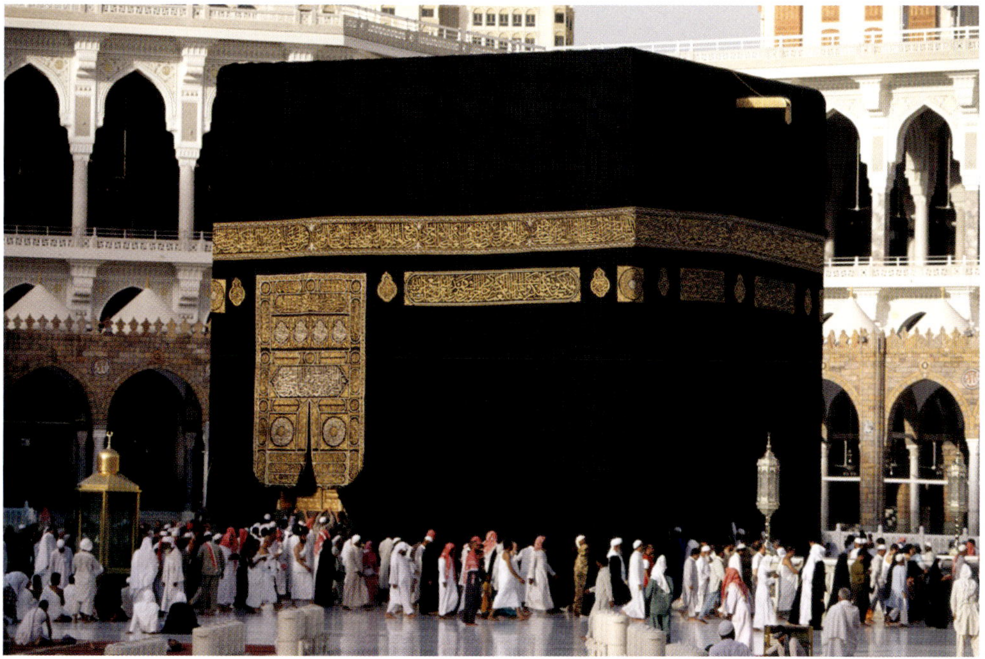

The Kaaba in Mecca is the holiest place in Islam and shelters the black stone treasured by Muslims.

The Kaaba in Mecca and the Dome of the Rock in Jerusalem are two monuments that stand out in Islamic architecture due to their extraordinary importance in the Muslim world. Originally, Kaaba was a modest structure sheltering the black stone that had been treasured by the Arabs in pre-Islamic times; over time, it came to be surrounded by numerous structures, as it gained ascendancy as an important centre of worship. The Dome of the Rock was erected in AD 691 over a holy rock that was regarded by the Jews as the foundation stone and axis of the world, and by the Muslims as the spot of the Prophet's mystic ascent to heaven. The building is octagonal, with a double inner colonnade supporting a wooden dome mounted on an elevated drum.

Mosques are constructed as assembly halls for the faithful. They serve primarily for recitation of prayers in groups. Friday sermon called *khutbah* is delivered in the larger or main mosques in every city. Moreover, they are used for religious instructions and memorial services, and also as hostels for travelling scholars and as places of asylum for the prosecuted. In earlier days, if a mosque was endowed as a memorial to a deceased person, his tomb was built on the premises.

The plan of a mosque was based on the so-called *musalla*, a simple walled precinct used for prayers in pre-Islamic times. Its *qibla*, 'orientation,' was changed and directed towards Mecca by Muhammad. It is a feature that became canonically binding in all Islamic places of worship. In many cases Christian basilicas were transformed into mosques, simply through change of orientation.

The ground plan of the early mosques showed the basic characteristics of the more solidly built and widely constructed courtyard mosques. The flat roof was constructed with beams and supported by planks on the ground or horseshoe arches that, in turn, were supported by columns, placed in regular rows either parallel or perpendicular to the *qibla* wall. The courtyard, which had a fountain for

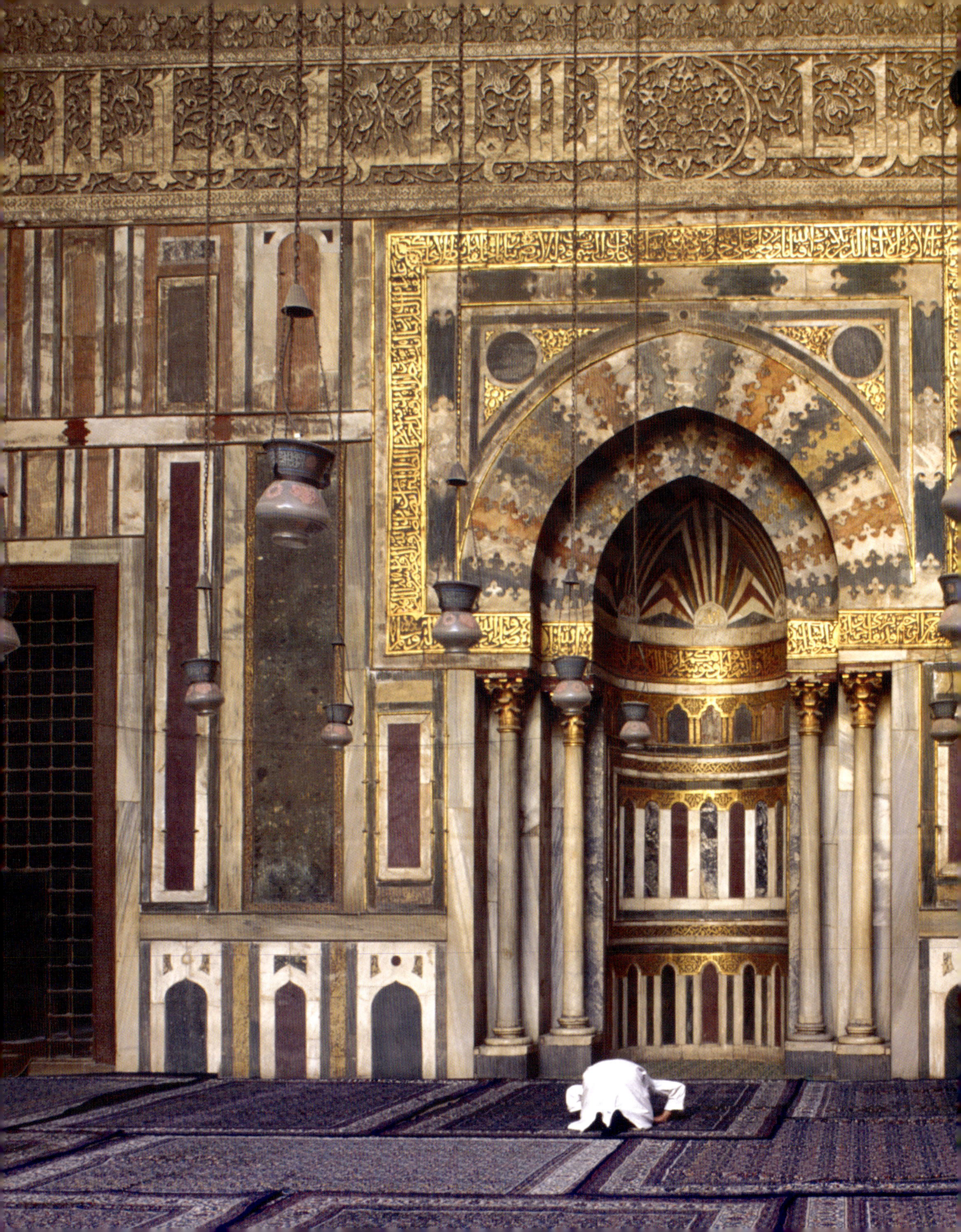

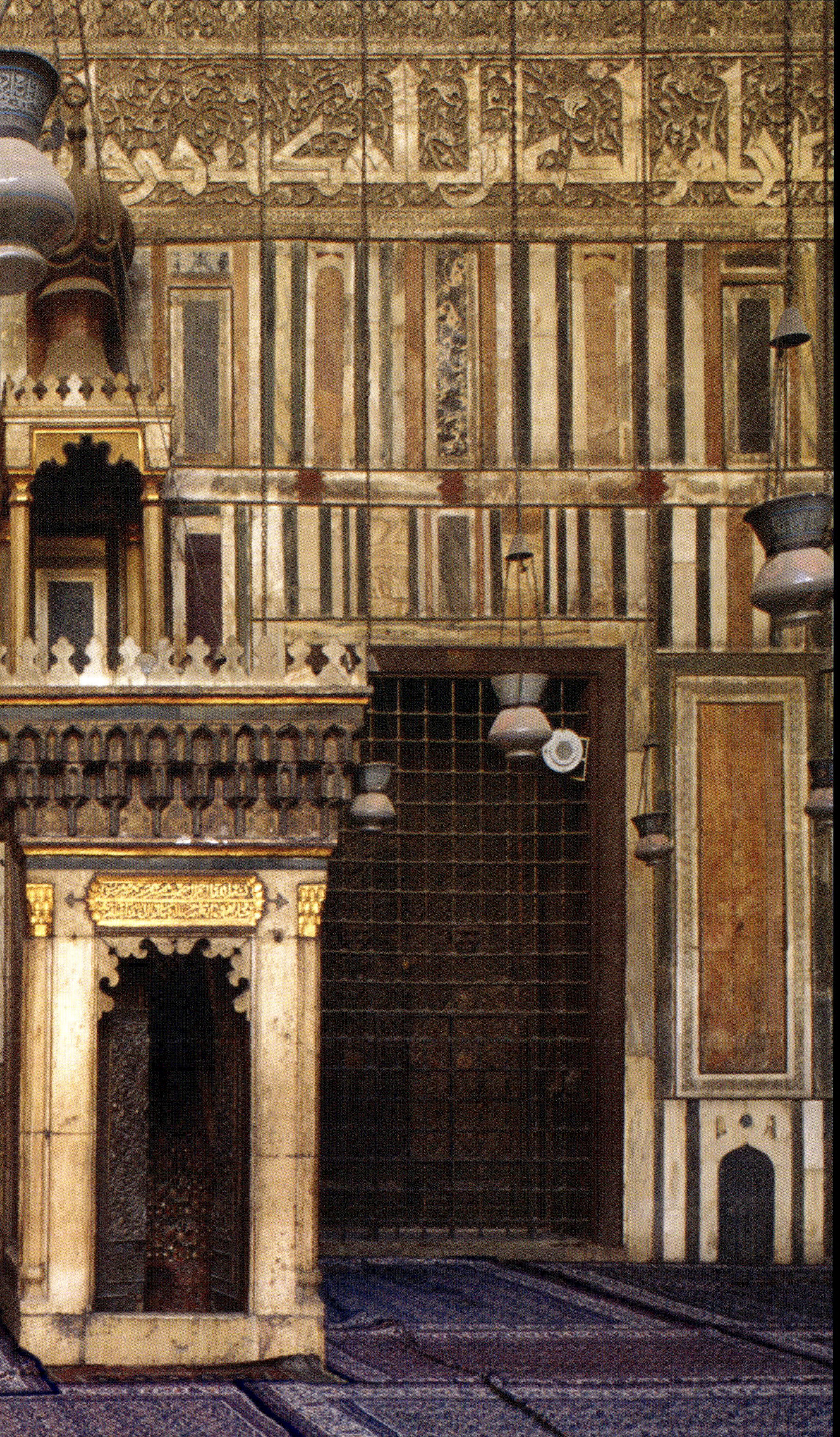

Il Mihrab (prayer room), Madrasa di Hasan. The first *mihrab* was built in the memorial mosque in Medina in honour of Muhammad, in 644 AD.

Bottom right: An example of embedded decorative tile work with ornamented calligraphic script at Mir-i-Arab Madrasa's twin dome in Bukhara, USSR. ***Extreme left and centre:*** Iranian Islamic tile work at Jami Masjid. ***Facing page:*** Exquisite ornate inscriptions combined with tapestry-like patterns in cobalt blue tiles adorn the entrance of Esfahan's Imam mosque in Iran.

ablution in the centre, was usually surrounded by an arcade and sometimes by several rows of arcades.

The *qibla* wall of the early prayer hall was provided with a niche called *mihrab*. The first *mihrab* was built in the memorial mosque built in Medina in honour of Muhammad, in AD 644. The significance of the niche was emphasised by decorative effects and by its position as the centrepoint of the wall.

An indispensable feature of the mosque is the minaret, the tower from where the call to prayer is made. The earliest minarets were generally placed at the front of the courtyard on the axis of the *mihrab*, in a corner of the courtyard, or entirely outside the mosque. They can be accessed by means of a staircase or a ramp.

Monastic establishments were also found in the Islamic world. The oldest and most important were the *ribat*s – fortress-like structures housing soldiers who propagated their faith through holy war and also provided protection against enemy attacks. The *ribat*s served as military encampments at strategic points and as guardposts against invasion. They had powerful walls, cells for living quarters, special areas for storing weapons and provisions, a watchtower, and a prayer room.

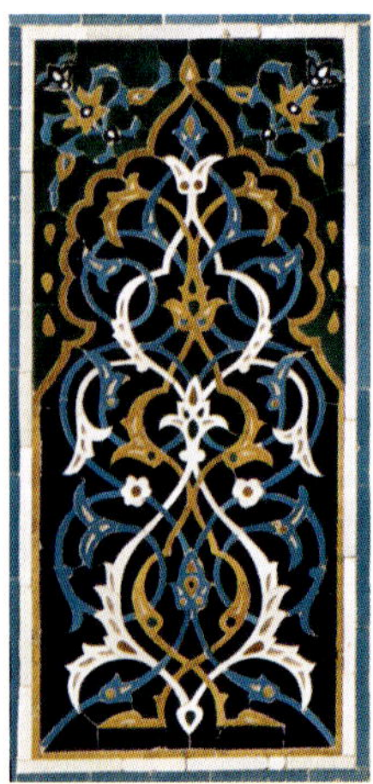

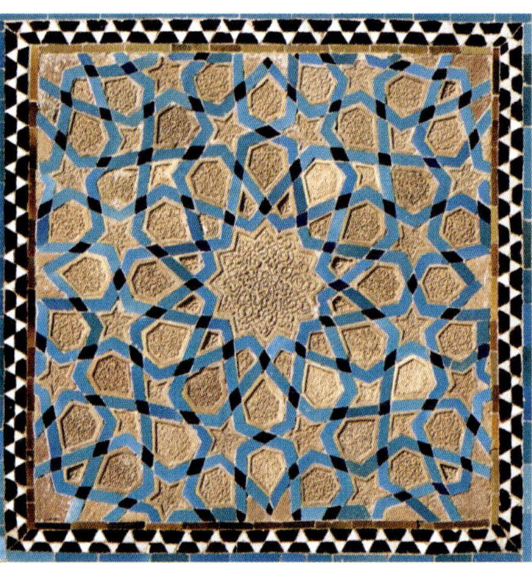

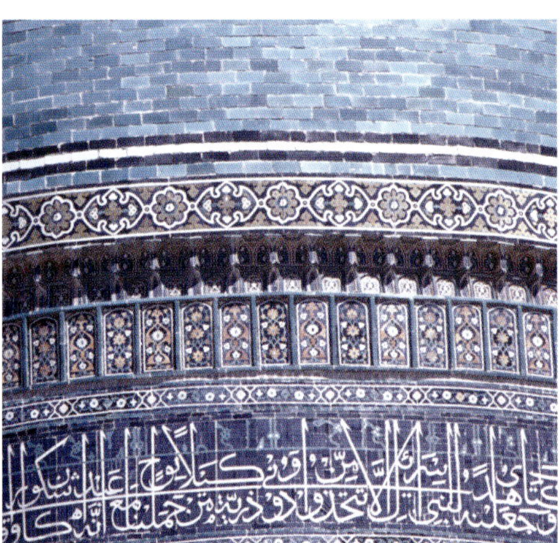

The Islamic art style evolved principally from the artistic resources of older cultures that Islam simulated to new efflorescence. An important aspect of architectural decoration in Islamic art was the use of the honeycomb pattern. *Muqarna* work was used in domes and all types of vaulting, including portals and prayer niches, as well as friezes carved in very high relief. The art was not limited to stone and wood, but was executed in brick as well. Graceful arabesques, colourful floral forms, imitation medallions, cartouches and friezes of exquisite ornate inscriptions were combined into tapestry-like patterns of glowing colour with a predominance of cobalt blue.

The use of ceramic mosaic in architectural decorations reached an unprecedented level of perfection during the 14th-15th centuries. The Turks employed huge quantities of faience tiles in decorating the mosques of Istanbul and, eventually, of the Ottoman Empire. In Egypt, walls were covered with wood panelling. A taste for the rich effect of ornamental and figural designs executed in lacquer painting was probably derived from Persia.

A new and important element that exerted a powerful influence on decorative

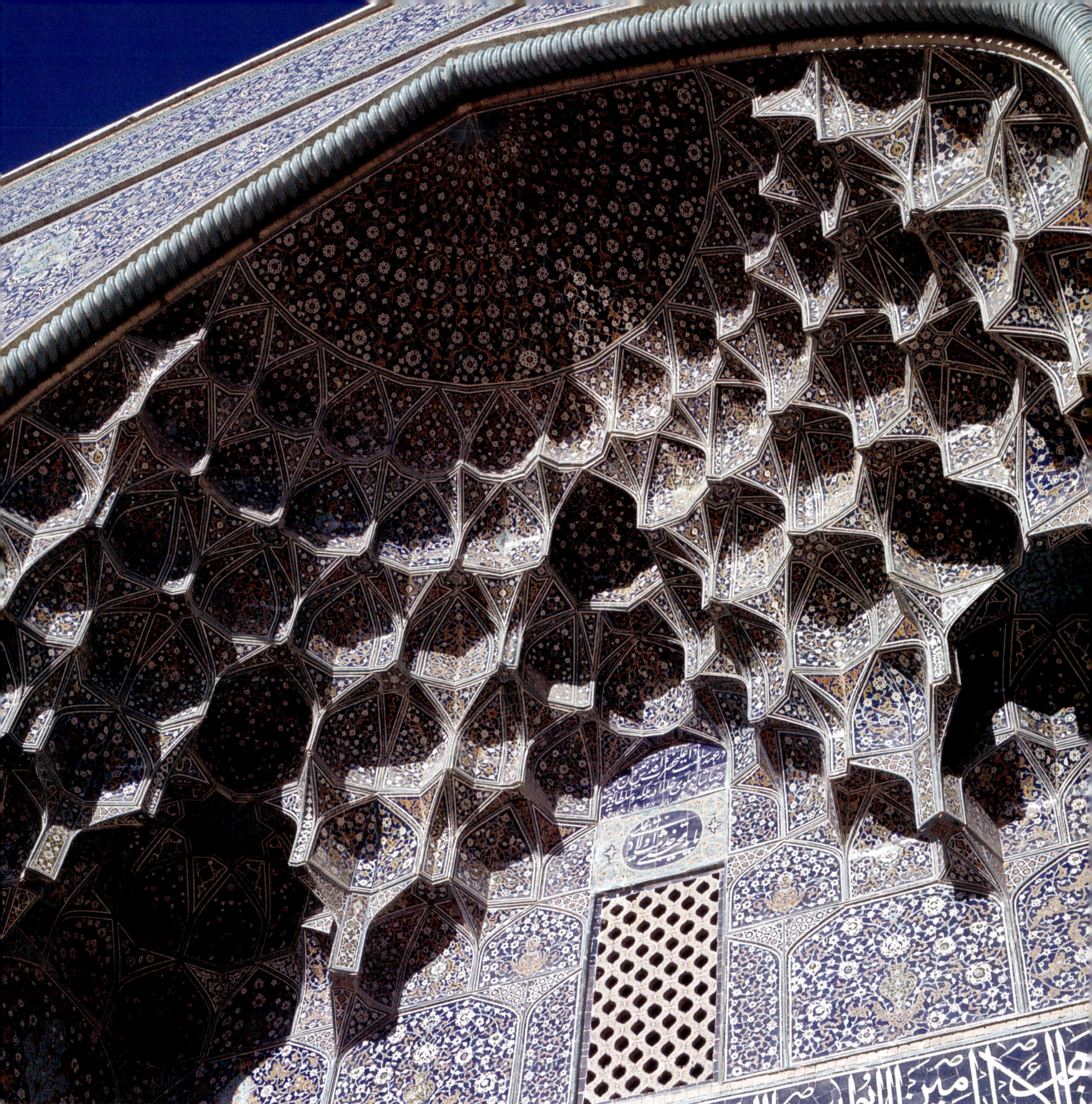

forms was the Arabic script. It lent itself easily to the formation of evolving variations. The angular and massive characters of the Kufic script as well as the round and readily changeable forms of Naskhi writing were used in elaboration of monumental epigraphy. The text used in the decorative scheme of religious buildings was for the most part taken from the Quran. The execution of calligraphic flourishes called for considerable feats of artistry and in

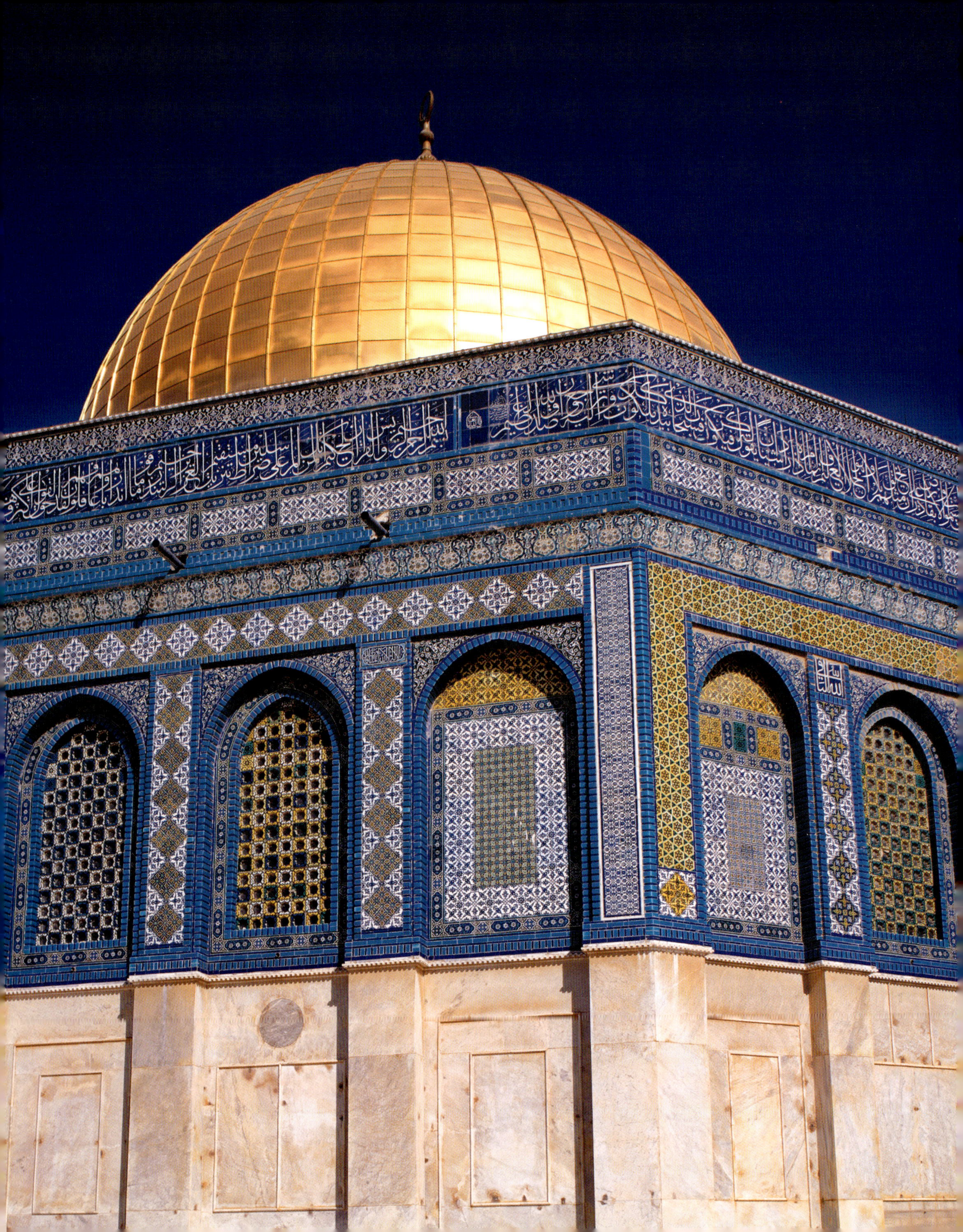

this domain, Islamic artisans were unsurpassed. At the height of their art, large surfaces were covered with inscriptions written out in geometricised Kufic script.

Jewish art has acquired great richness and variety due to the dispersion of Jews in other nations, but on the other hand, the origin of a Hebrew nation is closely bound with a religious covenant. Both biblical and rabbinical laws governed their representational art. Jewish art in the Middle Ages was influenced by Islamic aniconism on one hand, and by the artistic freedom of Christian Europe on the other.

The earliest reference to a Jewish temple, the temple of Solomon, is found in the Bible. The greatest monuments of Herodian architecture were the temple and the palace of Herod in Jerusalem, of which just scant remains are left. Their measurements, layout and components were dictated by tradition. They served as sacred buildings as well as fortresses. From the 2nd century AD, a series of monumental stone synagogues were built. They were erected with the façade looking towards Jerusalem; the wall facing the 'holy city' was made particularly ornate, with a triple entrance imitating Syrian temple façades.

According to the plan, the synagogues were basilican, with a central nave surrounded by three aisles. Columns placed on high pedestals supported the roof. The main hall of the synagogue had a gallery; the richest part of architectural ornamentation was reserved for this feature of the building. The doorjambs, lintels and especially the great frieze of the gallery were decorated in high relief. Mosaic pavements have been preserved in various synagogues. In succeeding periods, various experiments were made leading to the general adoption of the basilican plan, with a nave and two aisles, culminating in an apse directed towards Jerusalem. While earlier the Ark of the Law was apparently movable, the new plan had the advantages of proper direction and of concentration of the focal point of synagogue worship.

In the 6th-7th centuries, a significant change was visible in the mosaic pavements of synagogues. The figural subjects tend to disappear, and the images are restricted to representations of the Ark of the Law, of a seven-branched candlestick, and of lions or other beasts and birds. Spanish, and in general eastern Jews followed the tradition in which the focal point of the synagogue was the Ark of the Law firmly set up in the wall facing Jerusalem. They favoured the type with several ows of columns perpendicular to the wall opposite the entrance.

Jewish architecture in medieval Europe was limited almost exclusively to synagogue

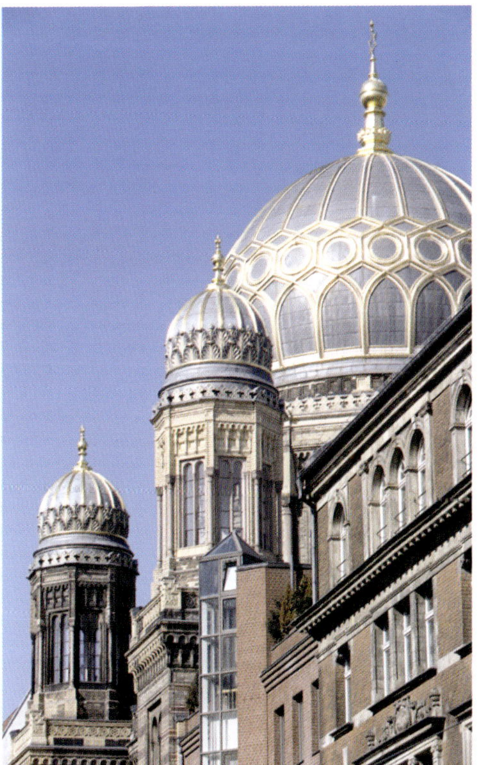

Facing page: The exterior of the Dome of the Rock adorned with tile work in Jerusalem. It was built by Abd al-Malik between AD 687 and 692, inspired by the Church of the Sepulchre as well as the Church of the Ascension at Mount of Olives.
Left: The Neue Synagogue in Berlin. Synagogues in Germany served as sacred buildings as well as fortresses.

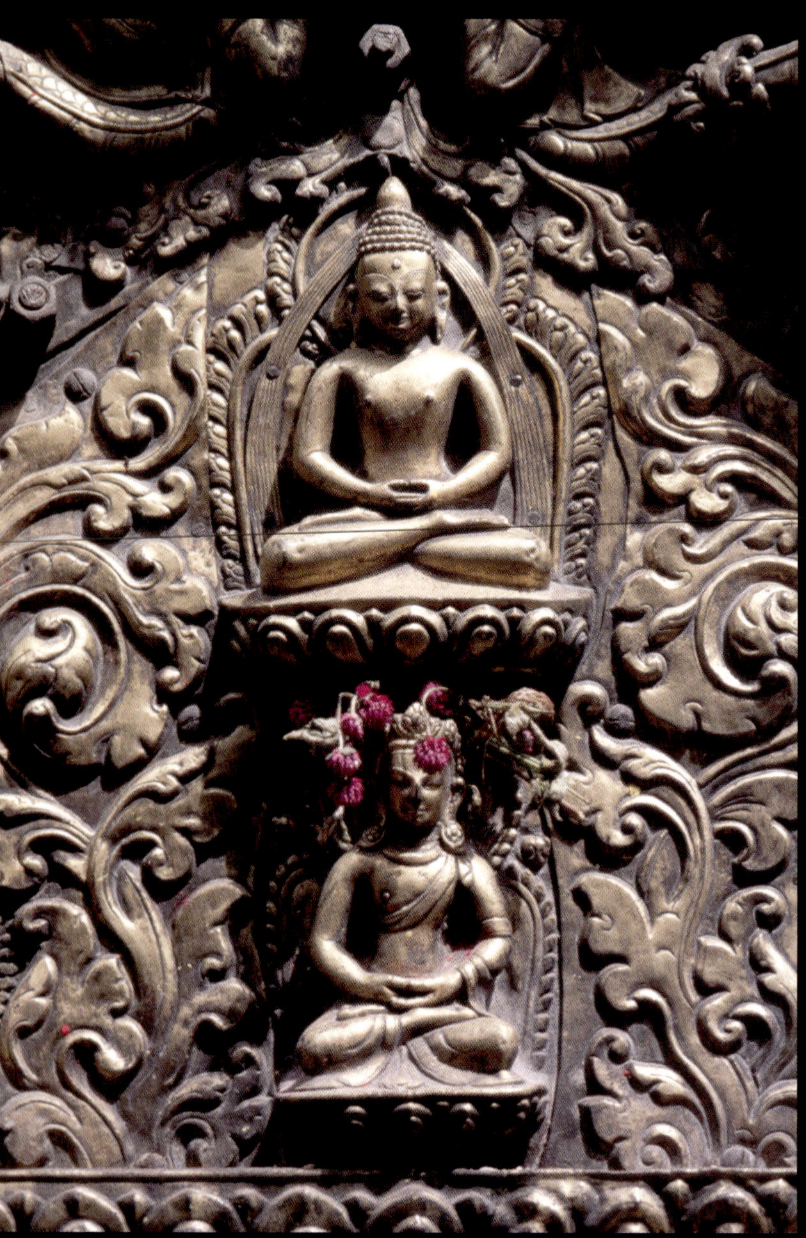

building. French and German Jews preferred the tradition of a movable arc. The focal point was a raised platform placed in the middle of the hall, around which the worshippers were grouped. The women's section was placed either on the same level as the main prayer room, or in two-storied synagogues, a level below.

Medieval synagogues were in general of two types: those in which central columns supported the vaults, usually two, dividing the synagogue into two aisles; and those in which the vaults were not supported centrally. Until the 19th century, Jewish art was created primarily to serve the synagogue and the Jewish community, and was limited mainly to illustrated manuscripts and ceremonial objects. While always employing the prevailing art styles of their countries of residence, Jewish artists adapted these to conform to the specific religious purpose of their works.

WORKS OF ART IN METAL

Works of art in metal began to appear in the early centuries of the Christian era, bearing Hellenistic features. Some looked so un-Indian, that they may have been imported from or produced by foreign craftsmen. A number of bronze and copper figures have survived from the Gupta period. The most impressive among them is the Buddha from Sultan Ganj, measuring seven-and-a-half feet in height. A feeling of life, a sense of movement, a slight tilt in the body, delicate fingers, and the impressively delicate face give a transcendental look to the image.

Great works in metal produced under the patronage of the Pala kings were even exported to the countries in south-east Asia, and to Nepal and Tibet. They served as prototypes for indigenous divine works of art. They are delicate in design and ornamental in detail. Gilding and the use of semi-precious stones lend them an impression of great brilliance and smoothness.

In South India the Cholas created the greatest metal works – the finest among them are very large and heavy, yet graceful and simple. They follow the proportion fixed by the canons laid down in iconographical textbooks,

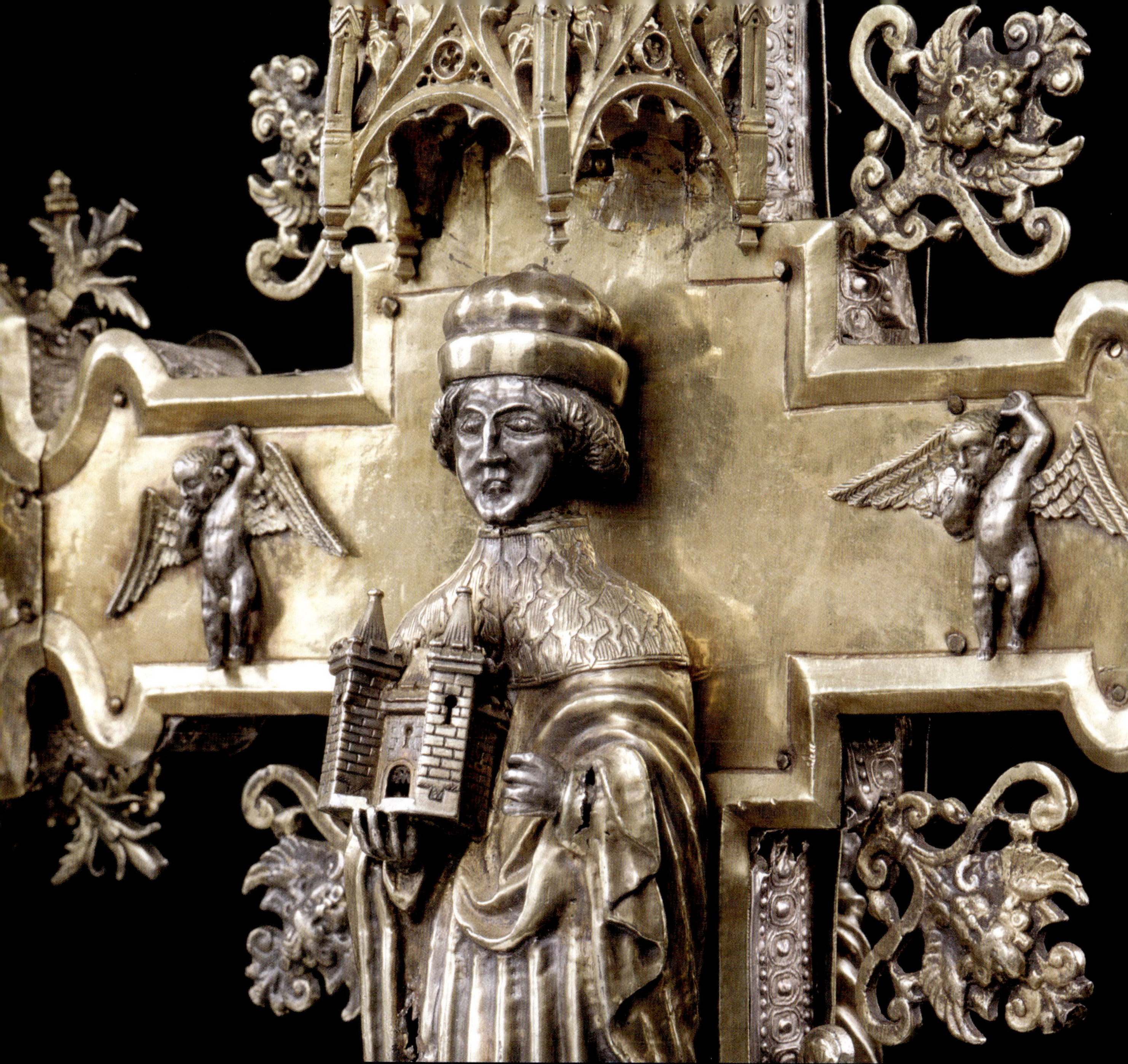

and though the attributes of the deities are determined by convention, they still convey individuality. Apart from gods and goddesses, figures were created representing saints of devotional theism and portraits of kings and queens. The greatest and the most triumphant achievement of Tamil bronze casting is undoubtedly the dancing Shiva, or Nataraj.

DIVINE FORMS

The earliest divine images produced in India were the female figurines discovered from the remains of the Indus Valley civilisation, later worshipped as the mother of the universe, the goddess Earth, or the female power. The goddess of power assumed various forms such as Kali, Durga and Chandi. Sarasvati is the

Above: Detail showing bishop St. John holding a cathedral on a ceremonial cross from San Daniele Friuli.

Facing page: Brass sculpture of Buddha (top) on the shrine of Amitabha, in Kathmandu.

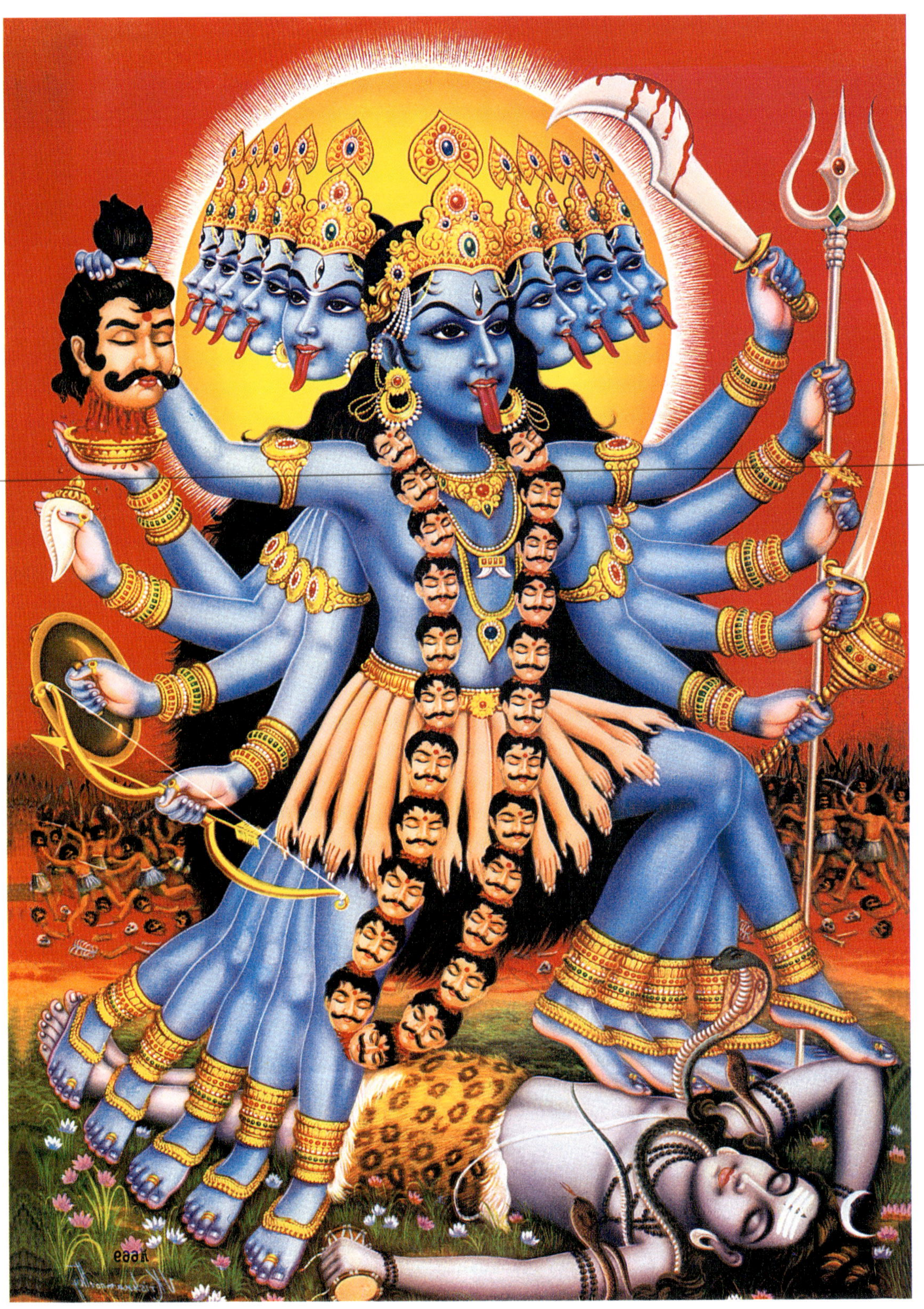

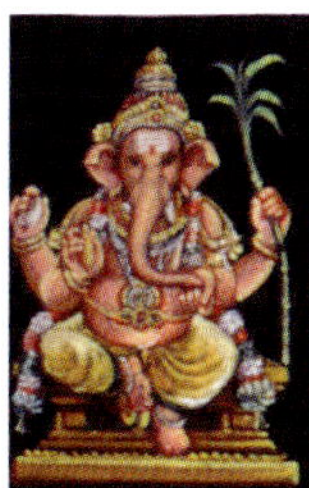
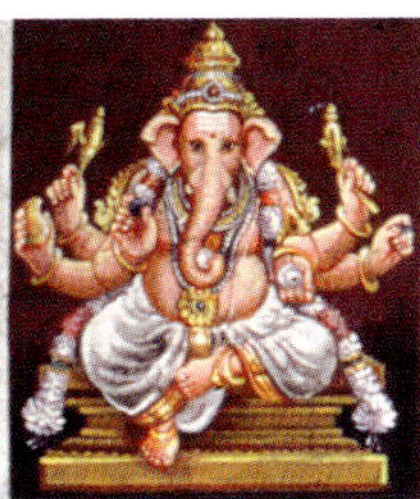
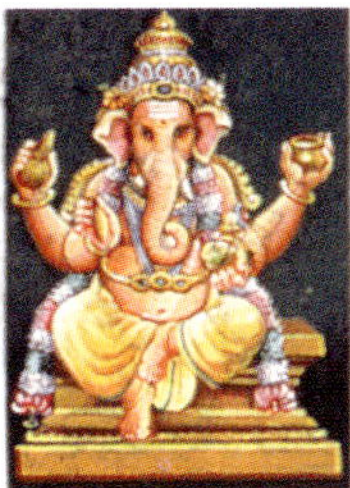
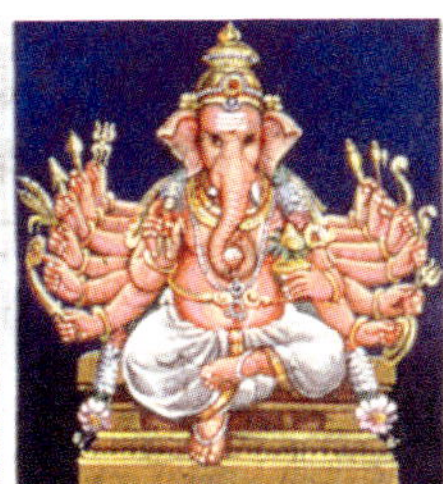
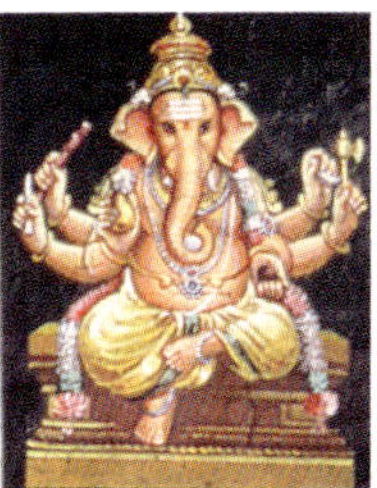

Left: Different forms of the elephant-headed Lord Ganesh, the god of wisdom.
Facing page: Kali – the goddess of power and destroyer of evil in the Hindu mythology, is the female counterpart of Great Time – Kala.
Below: Hanuman, the monkey god, known for his courage, strength and selfless devotion to Lord Rama.

goddess of wisdom, the flowing eloquence, the transcendent word, who wears pure white clothes and sits on a white lotus. Her serene aspect is reflected in the modelling of her graceful, narrow eyes and placid lips. The rivers flowing perennially and carrying water to satisfy the daily needs of the living world, are venerated as mothers – thus, the Ganges is called 'Ma Ganga' and a dip into her waters adds to the merits of a person.

Brahma, Vishnu and Shiva constitute the Hindu Trinity – Brahma being the creator; Vishnu, the sustainer; and Shiva, the destroyer. The three forces are constantly in action, creating the world anew every moment. Kali, the dark one portrayed as absolutely black, is the female counterpart of Great Time, Kala. Kali and Mahakala connote time and eternity in the highest cosmogonic principles. Time brings forth everything and presently destroys it, obliterating, swallowing and annihilating the beings that originate from it and then are carried on its flow for the brief periods of their lives. Durga is the fierce-looking goddess, one who is difficult to go against – that is, she is the unassailable. She is the fairest in the three spheres of the universe, *tripura sundari*. She is the divine incarnation of the supreme power of womanhood and feminine charm incarnate, both in its spellbinding and devastating aspects. She is also known as Mahishasura-mardini; she crushes the demon buffalo to rescue the universe from its tyranny.

Shiva is the personification of death and time, a creator, a destroyer, the divine lover, and the lord of dance. His wife Parvati is the goddess of love and beauty; his son, the elephant-headed Ganesha, is the god of wisdom. The Shiva *linga* is the eternal embrace of the cosmic male and female that procreated the universe and all the forms of life processes in the world. The union is symbolised by the *linga* and the *yoni*.

In Jain temples, the main image along with several smaller ritual images of bronze are installed. The earliest bronze objects date from the 1st century BC from Bihar. From the Gupta period, there are bronzes from Chausar in Bihar, and from western India the superb bronzes of the so-called Akota hoard. Jain bronzes of Chola style from Sittanavasal are remarkable for their refinement of modelling. From the medieval period, there are hundreds of Jina images. Other bronze objects include *yantras*, replicas of samavasarana (the divine preaching hall for Tirthankaras), figures of goddesses, models of the mythical mount Meru, and plaques depicting auspicious symbols. Most of these objects are worshipped in temples at Surat, Patan and Ahmedabad in Gujarat; Jaisalmer and Jaipur in Rajasthan; and many other shrines in Madhya Pradesh and Karnataka.

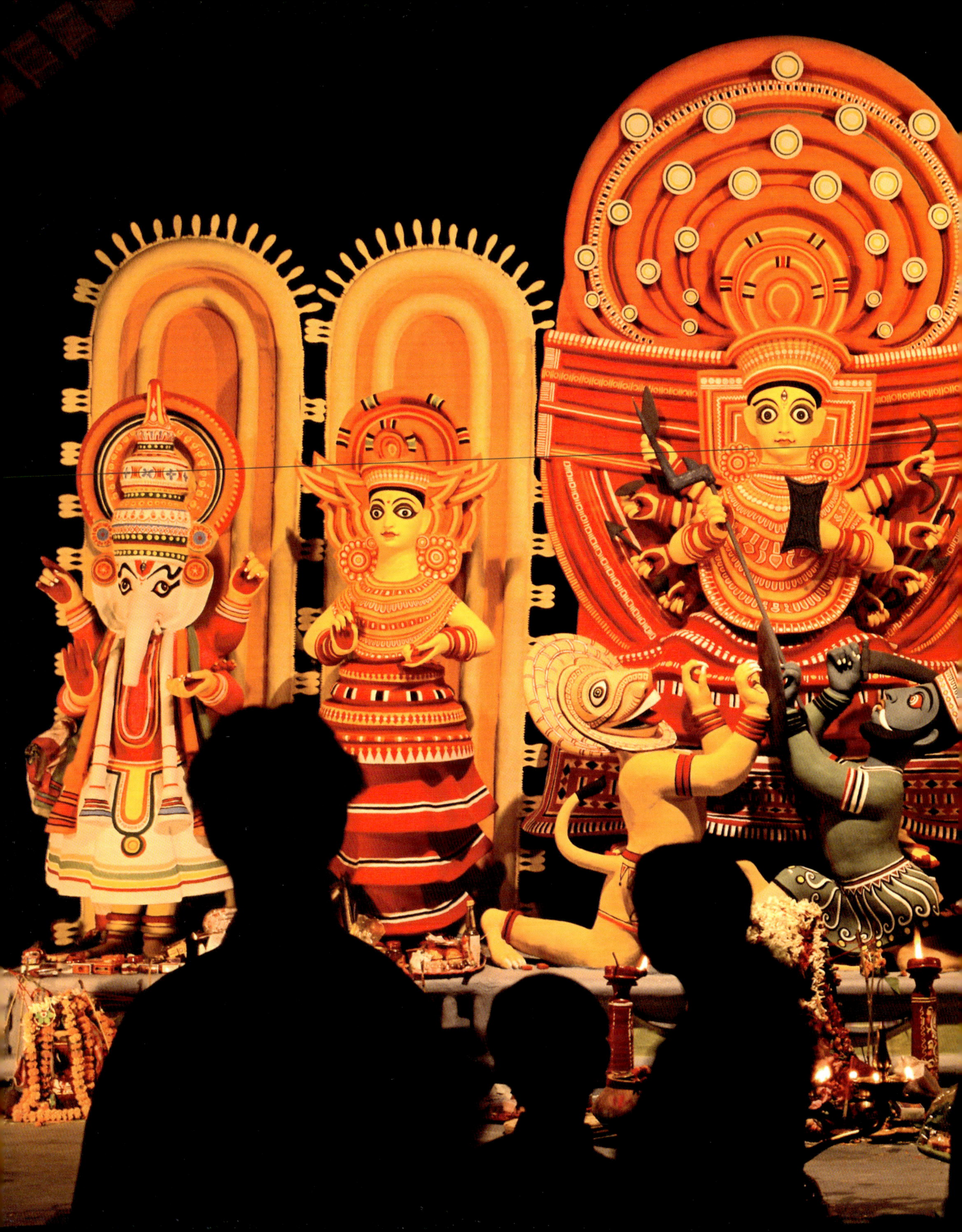

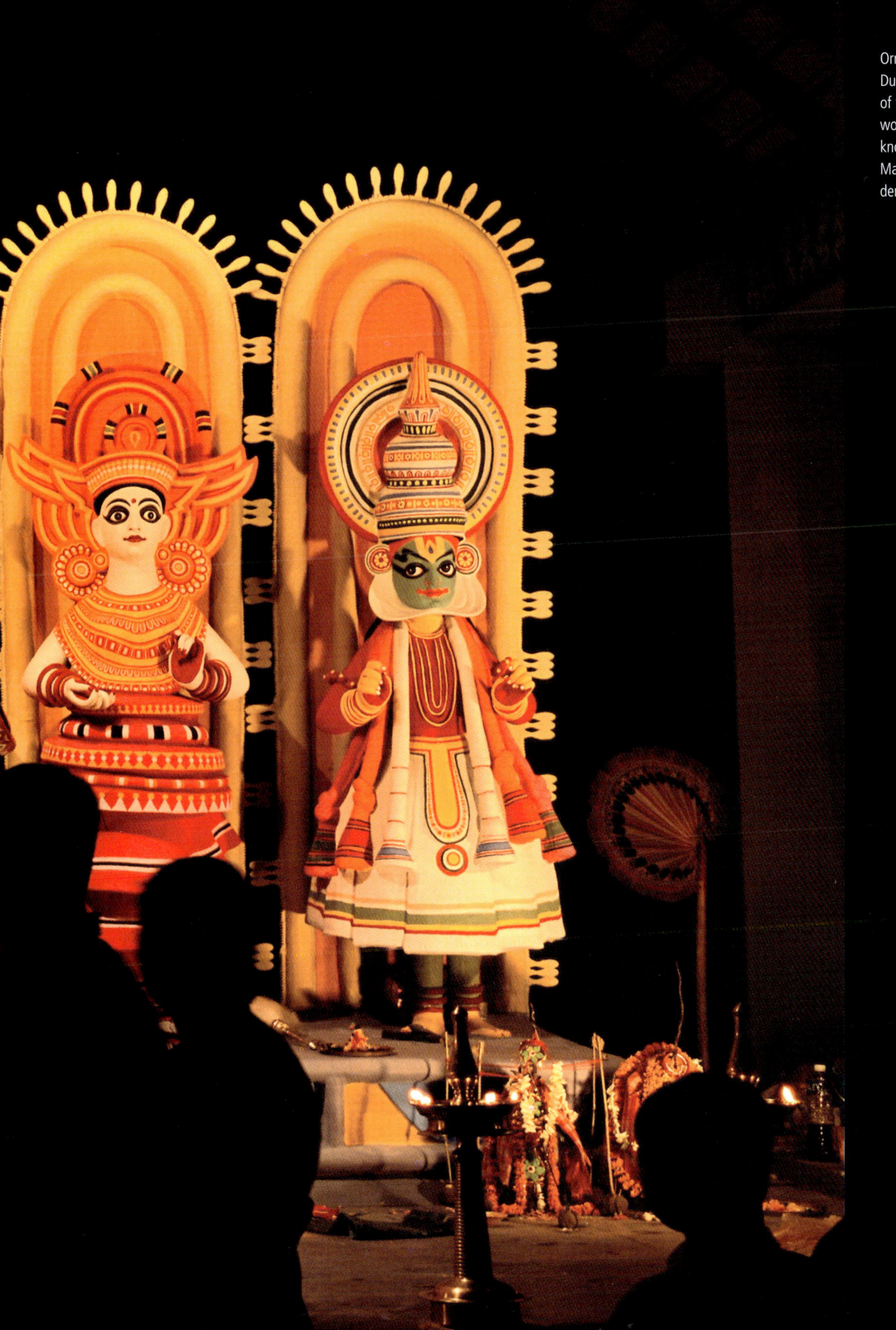

Ornamented idols of Durga, the divine incarnation of the supreme power of womanhood. She is also known as Mahishasura-Mardini (conqueror of the demon Mahishasur)

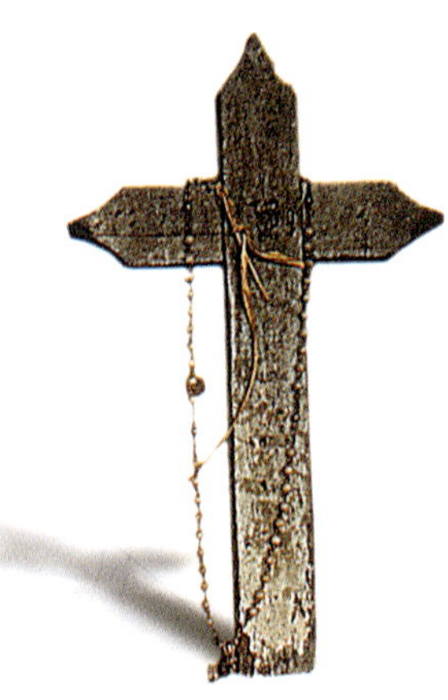

Above: An ornamental metallic cross, with a hanging rosary. ***Facing page:*** Pathos in Christian iconography was introduced in the 14-15th century. The image of the suffering Christ upon the cross symbolises salvation.

CHRISTIAN ICONOGRAPHY

Christianity has also created a vast iconographic system. This was linked not only to sacred history, but also to the need for representing new subjects related to its doctrine as well as to the demand for new forms for existing religious and political concepts. Further, it also met the pressure of popular and devotional demands.

With the advent of Christ, however, a new factor was introduced which was compatible with anthropomorphism. God had come down; he became a man in service of mankind. The Son of God was equal to the Father, and was his living image. The bearded, long-haired, youthful Christ proudly bears a cross and holds an open book. He supports the same youthful style when he stands on the globe of the earth among the archangels. In Romanesque and Gothic representations, Christ is almost always bearded. The Gothic period made Christ an ideal type portraying him as the supreme doctor. The Romanesque period often depicted him as the solemn judge.

It is believed that the earliest image of Christ showed him with beautiful eyes, joined eyebrows, a long nose, and a youthful appearance. A 3rd century sculpture found on a fragmentary sarcophagus shows Jesus with the face of an old man who wears a pallium that leaves his shoulder and breast uncovered. The image of Christ the king is represented neither with regal vestments nor with crown. Representations of Christ show him either enthroned or standing among the apostles and other saints – who could be described as his courtiers, or occasionally among the archangels, who take their place as the guardians of the divine flank of the sovereign. The standing Christ in the mosaic of the Confession in St. Peter's at the Vatican is one of the fine examples. The seated Christ holds a closed book and has an old man's face. The enthroned Christ is the teacher par excellence.

Pathos was introduced in art around the 14th-15th centuries. Tragic images of a suffering Christ with a crown of thorns were painted, followed up by painting the dead Christ. In the early Christian period, attention was focused more on the cross as a symbol of salvation than on the actual suffering of the crucified Christ. The childhood of the saviour was represented through scenes narrating events in the life of Christ. Another subject that has been frequently treated is that of the Virgin. She always appeared with the child Christ in her arms. The Byzantine world created distinct types of images of the Virgin.

The supernatural aspect of Christianity is underlined by the many representations of usually youthful angels. Raphael is shown in a pilgrim's dress with a fish or a medicine flask; Michael is connected with the cult of the underworld and of lightning. He is a warrior angel who slays the dragon and hurls the rebel angels into hell. Christian art gives a major place to saints who are represented either singly or in cycles narrating their lives and miracles.

Symbolic representations of the church were also of great importance. The form and structure of holy edifices were assigned the significance of symbolic representations of the community of the faithful. Representation of the Greek youth in the guise of divinities gave rise to figures that are admired for structural beauty, purity and human perfection. They represent a bond between men and gods. Gods were represented in Greek religion as idealised human beings.

PANEL ART

The outer walls of a temple welcome the devotees, uplifting one's consciousness, and inspiring respect for moral and social value

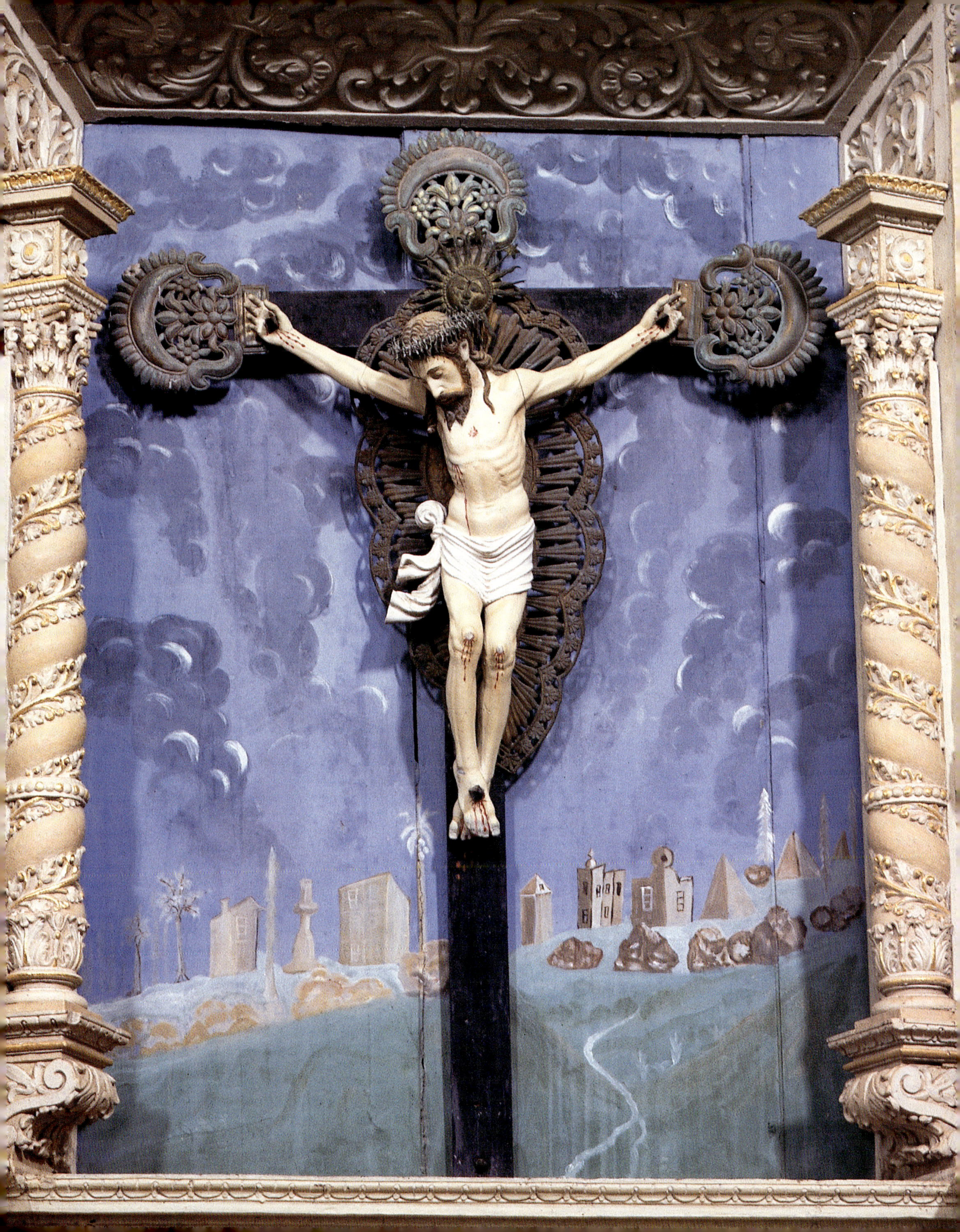

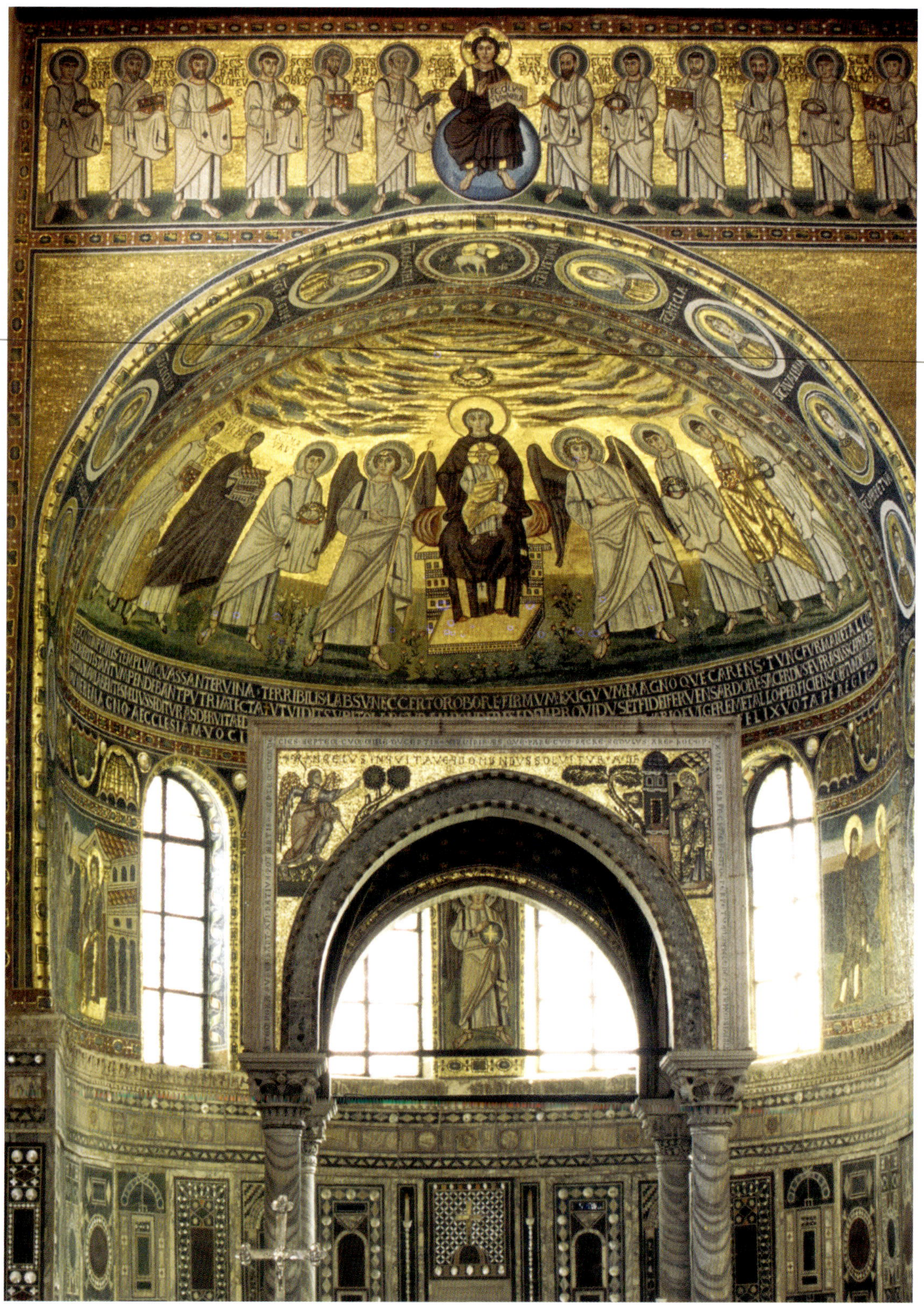

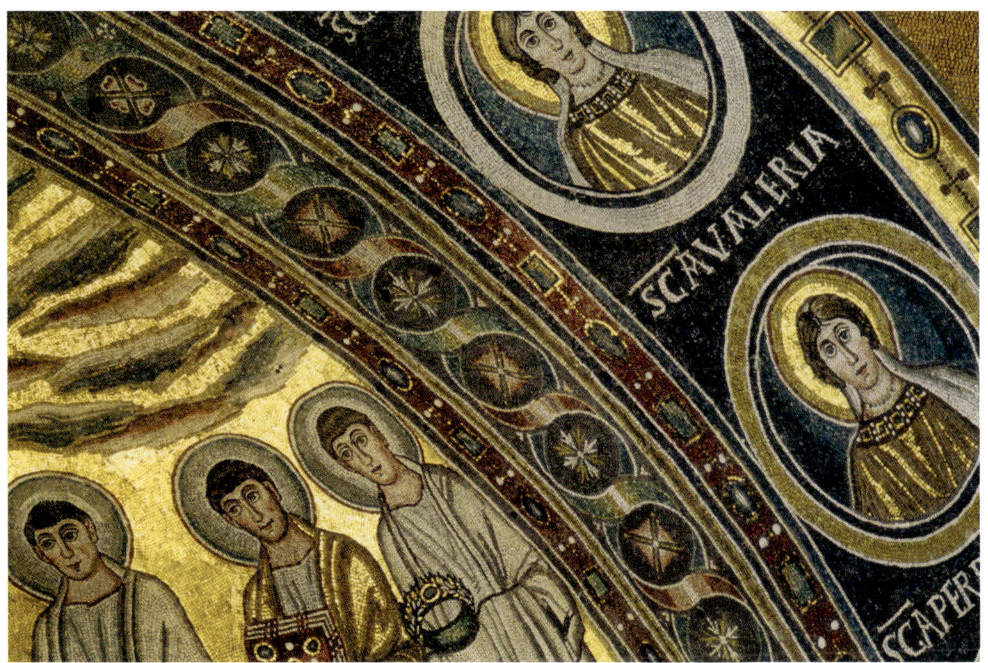

Facing page and left: Detail of the Apse mosaics in Basilica Euphrasiana in Porec, Croatia. They are a good example of panel art in Christianity.
Below: Panel painting of St. Francis with scenes from his life.

systems. They may record historical events and great achievements of the rulers, or celebrate the past lives of the Buddha. The earliest panels found in India, carved on the gates and railings of the stupas at Sanchi and Bharhut, depict events from the biographical legends of the Buddha. In most Buddhist temples, the walls bear scenes from Buddhist stories like *Jataka*s and *Avadana*s.

In Christianity it was sacrilegious to make a concrete image of any religious story or sacred figure, given that the Ten Commandments explicitly forbade the production of graven images of any kind. Nonetheless, Pope Gregory had decreed that religious images could be made in order to enlighten the illiterate. Thus began the depiction of sacred narratives. One of the most publicly accessible depictions was the large-scale fresco cycles that had been painted on the walls, domes and ceilings of churches and chapels for centuries. The practice continued during the Renaissance with new visual strategies. The story of Francis and the miracles he was believed to have performed after his death are depicted in the chronologically consecutive circles going from top to bottom.

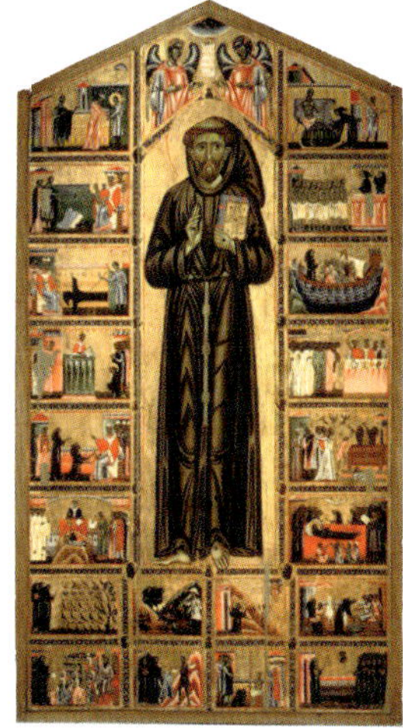

MOSAIC

Mosaic is one of the most specialised and most involved in terms of use of material. Special skills are required by the nature of its technique, based upon the use of small, hard components set side by side on large surfaces. After a preliminary planning, the procedure entails execution by groups of skilled workmen. Mosaic was the heritage and creation of a limited cultural area like the Greco-Roman world and the Christian and Byzantine civilisations. The technique of mosaic allows a freedom of design and, thus, sometimes rivals painting in effect. Its solidity and durability makes mosaic particularly suitable for monuments.

The oldest information pertaining to mosaic artisans dates to the 4th century BC. In ancient times, mosaics were made of pebbles and, later, of hard stones, marble shells, vitreous paste, terra cotta, mother of pearl, and enamels attached to the solid surface with cement or putty. A wall surface that was to be covered with mosaic received a triple coat of plaster. The artists made a rough outline of the proposed design either on the wall itself or on the first and second rendering of coat, and then paints were applied in full with red usually substituting for gold.

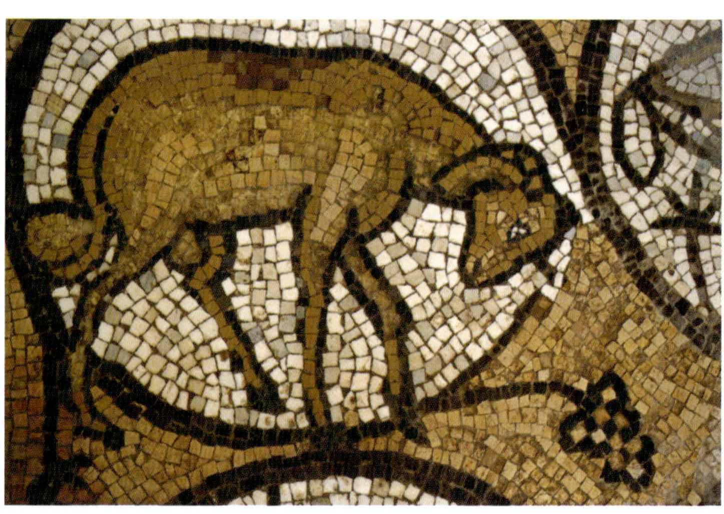

Lamb Medallion from Byzantine floor mosaic on northern aisle of Petra Church. Mosaics originally belonged to the Greco-Roman world and the Christian and Byzantine civilisations.

The first Christian mosaic floor dates from the first half of the 4th century. Given the religious continuity that has prevailed in Rome to the present, a relatively large number of mosaics have survived there. The mosaics on the Triumphal arch and in the nave of St Maria Maggiore are among the finest from the 5th century. The mosaics of the Triumphal arch depict scenes from the infancy of Christ. The mosaics on the dome represent a star-filled sky. Among the most important examples of mosaic art of all times are the mosaics of St Vitale dating from around AD 548.

STAINED GLASS

The translucent quality of stained glass gives a unique decorative effect. Glass panes of different colours are joined by a network of narrow lead strips and inserted into a metal framework. The decorative function of the mosaic style was replaced by stained glass in the medieval religious structures that became widespread in the 12th century. The earliest fragments of poured flat glass were discovered in Egypt from the second millennium BC. Examples of blown glass have been found in Rome and in various cities of the Roman Empire.

Glass was employed in early Christian architecture with other kinds of translucent screens made of natural material. Glass was mounted on wooden framework and on pierced screens of stone, stucco, or bronze. Clear references are found in literature of glass windows in medieval religious buildings. These windows must have been composed of pieces of glass that were coloured throughout, rather than painted, and it is likely that they bore no depictions.

Following the technique developed in the Islamic east, the vitreous fragments were 'let into' a stucco trellis – thereby giving rise to the creation of original compositions with fine architectonic and plant motifs – by alternating stucco and glass. This technique enjoyed success in Egypt during the 12th 13th centuries, and was continued in Islamic art. Probably it was introduced in the Byzantine empire, from where it spread to Europe.

The mentioned techniques have little in common with figural stained glass. Stories and

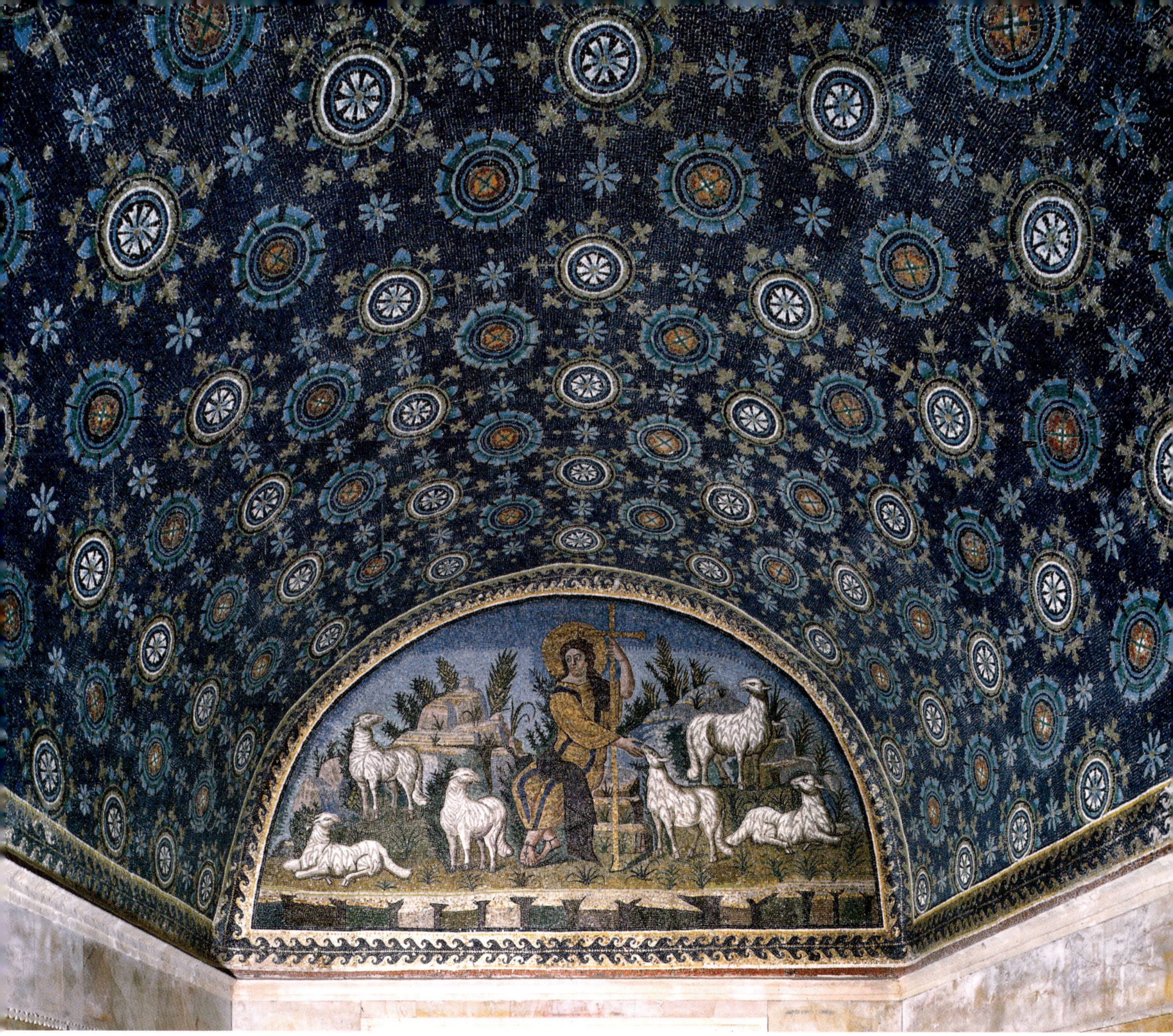

Mosaics at the mausoleum of Galla Placidia in Ravenna.

poems talk about glowing windows containing representations of stories. Stained glass developed into one of the richest aspects of medieval pictorial art. Beginning with the late 11th and early 12th centuries, the innumerable surviving examples of stained glass make possible the first-hand knowledge of its characteristics and direct observation of every technical detail of execution, mounting, and so on.

The model was the same size as the pane that was to be executed, and was drawn with a lead or tin point on a wooden panel smeared with chalk. The wooden panel was successively replaced by cloth, parchment, or paper. By the 15th century an Italian innovation, the use of cardboard, became prevalent. On top of the prepared models pieces of glass of different colours were arranged. Mineral salts and oxides of iron, copper, cobalt, manganese etc.

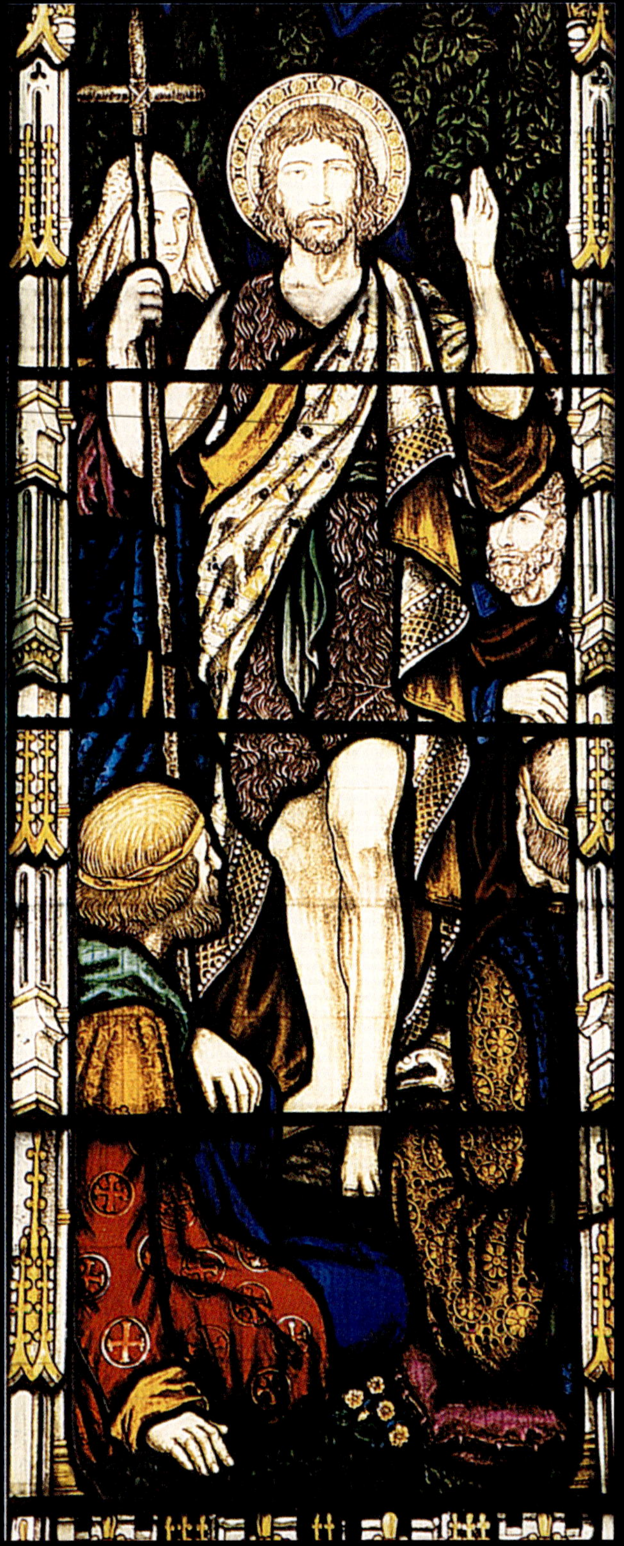

were added in the vitreous paste during fusion to sand and other component elements of the glass, to obtain various gradations. In some cases, pieces of coloured glass were composed of two layers – of the clear glass and a thinner layer of coloured glass, which was fused to the first by a process known as flashing. This was a normal practice in the case of red glass. Double panes were also used in combinations of yellow and red, white and blue, and green and red. In other cases, the red glass was placed between two layers of clear glass. The use of flashed panes made possible the practice of scrapping away the thin red film until the surface was exposed. The German masters used the 'Venetian glass' which consisted of thin multicoloured rods of glass incorporated in the body of clear glass during fusion.

After cutting the glass, it was mounted in a provisional frame in such a way that the glass master could check the overall effect of the composition and proceed to the painting. The procedure was carried out with a dark-coloured tint called 'grisaille' made of a powder of crushed glass, metallic salts and other pulverised minerals dissolved in wine or some other liquid. Resins and gums were later added to render the mixture more adherent to glass. This process is of primary significance in the creation of stained glass that is in the truest sense of the word both painting with glass and painting on glass.

The use of 'grisaille' is highly important in the production of stained glass because it partially modifies the tonality of glass as colours absorb light in varying degrees required by the painter. 'Grisaille' was also employed near the lead separating two panes of different tonality. It was used to outline the details of drawings, the lineaments of faces, the folds of drapery, and so on.

CALLIGRAPHY

Calligraphy is 'lines and curves of a written word.' It is spontaneous and is born out of a creative mind, an artistic hand, by brush or a pen dancing on paper to the rhythm of ink. It represents the civilisational development from speech to the written word. Calligraphy is the sacred beauty that decorates monastic interiors in China, Korea and Japan, and mosques all over West Asia. Calligraphy is auspicious beauty. Ornamental styles of calligraphy evolved for writing and illuminating religious books and sacred scriptures.

The earliest reference of veneration to calligraphy can be traced back to 2000 BC, when an Egyptian wise man said to his son: 'I shall make thee love writing more than thine own mother, I shall make beauty enter before thy face.' Calligraphy in East Asian traditions contains a continuous and complex flow. The personality of an artist is apparent through calligraphy – a line in Chinese calligraphy is executed with a single stroke of the brush. The 'slender gold' style of Emperor Hui-tsung suggests he was a handsome person, tall and slim, and meticulous. Some calligraphers withdrew to the mountains to practice in quiet. It is said about a Chinese master that he went to the mountains for 10 years to practice, and ultimately when he left, all the trees and rocks were stained with ink.

'Calli' in calligraphy means 'beautiful'; 'graphy' is to engrave, write, or design. Calligraphy became not only an art form, but also an object of worship in Egypt. In India, Ashokan inscriptions from the 3rd century BC are the earliest documents where a serif tops every letter and a vertical line ends in a curl. The North Indian scripts sought harmonious regularity in linear and angular elements. Aesthetic effects flowed from the inflexion of line. The South Indian scripts leaned towards rounded forms and curving lines.

About 3500 BC, the Egyptians created highly stylised hieroglyphics. In around 1000 BC, Phoenicians developed the writing systems and alphabets. Still later, Greeks developed their own form of writing, and in about 850 BC, Romans adapted writing in Latin, the lingua franca of the European churches in the Middle Ages. The monks began to scribe ancient texts in Gothic style. The art of calligraphy flourished during Europe's Renaissance when italic script was developed.

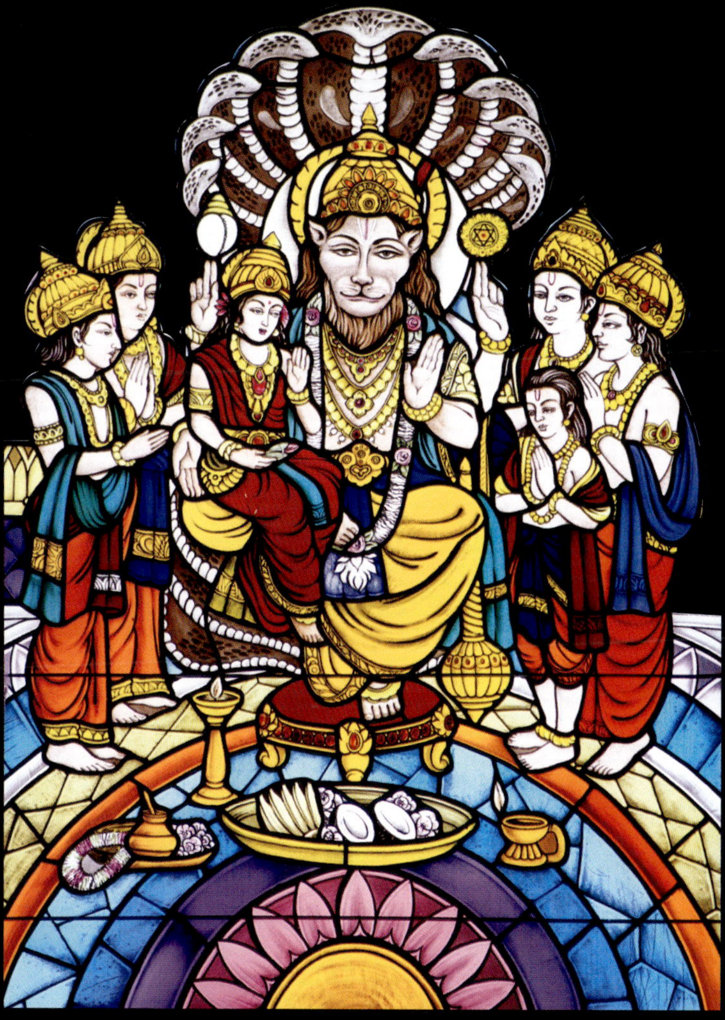

Above: Depiction from scenes of Hindu mythology on stained glass.
Facing page: A stained glass painting of Christ speaking to his disciples. These paintings are carried out with a dark coloured tint called 'grissaile.'

Hieroglyphics on a tomb in the Valley of the Kings on the west bank of the Nile at Luxor in Thebes. By 3500 BC the Egyptians had created highly stylised hieroglyphics.

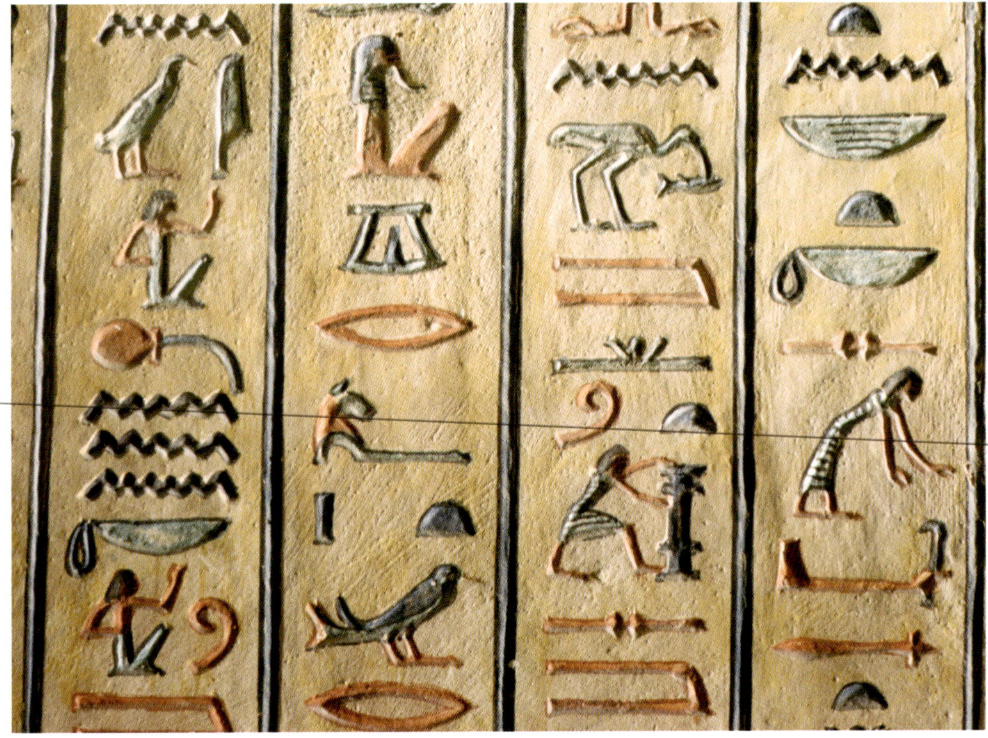

The advent of engraved copper plates and the invention of steel and fountain pens once threatened the art of calligraphy. In the mid-19th century, though, the British poets spearheaded a revival, reintroduced the flat-edged pen and elevated the art to its past form. Western calligraphy is rooted in the development of written symbols and letterforms, from the earliest scratchings and pictograms to the great classical inscriptions and the Medieval, Renaissance and Baroque manuscripts. Before the invention of the printing press, books were copied by scribes.

In the Islamic world, the art of calligraphy acquired enhanced artistic value since representational arts were prohibited. Iraq was the centre of the vast territories of the caliphate where art and letters flourished. The Arabs are famous for their calligraphy. They write in cursive hand from right to left. In Arabic calligraphy there are six major scripts: Farsi, Naskh, Kufi, Deewani, Re'qaa and Thuluth. They represent various traditions. The oldest Arabic calligraphy style was invented in Kufa, the medieval city of Iraq established in AD 641. Soon, the Arabic script was refined to an elegant and rather uniform script when Kufa emerged as an urban centre with vital cultural activities. Thus, the script became popular as 'kufi' or 'kufic'. It had a combination of square and angular lines on one hand and compact, bold circular forms on the other. As the Kufi script reached perfection in the second half of the 8th century, it became the only script used for copying the Quran for the next 300 years.

Serifs were added to simplify early Kufic on architectural monuments, and leaf-like vegetable ornaments appear as early as AD 866 at the end of vertical strokes. Of the use of calligraphy in buildings, the square style of Kufic developed during the 13th-14th centuries. It was the only calligraphic style used to carve entire buildings.

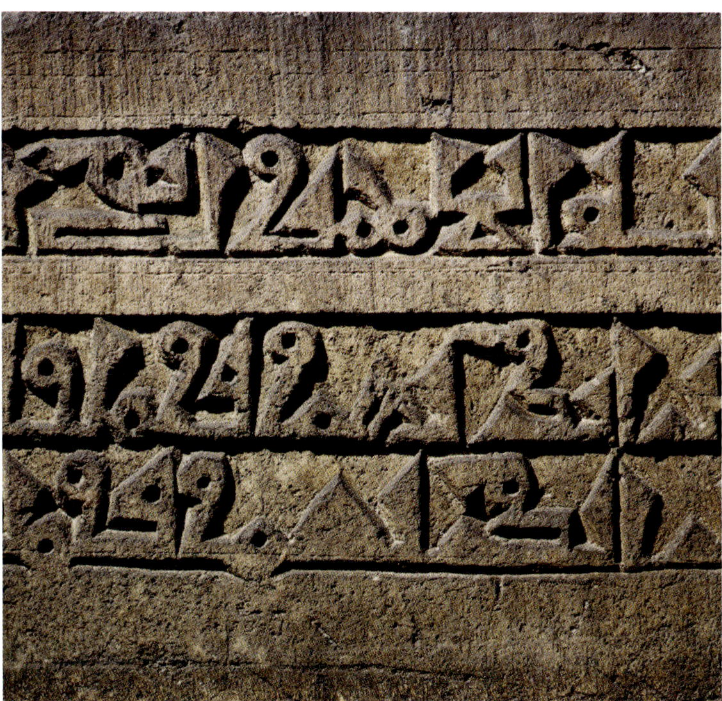

The cursive script dates back to the first decades of the Muslim era. The early examples lacked elegance and discipline. Naskhi was developed in the 10th century and refined into a fine art form in Turkey in the 16th century. It was then generally used to write the Quran. Thuluth is the more impressive and stately style often used for writing titles or epigrams. There are many styles used at different places and at different times. Some styles are more fluid and expressive, some have very short verticals, some are less round, and some have many ligatures. The Islamic world owns a rich heritage of creativity in writing styles.

Calligraphy became an art form in the Sino-Japanese world, too. They revered calligraphy and it became and it became an integral part of their lives. In China, calligraphic ideograms suggest a gentle feeling of purification. The Chinese master Kuo Hsi used to wash his hands and rinse the ink, put his desk in order, and burn incense on his right and left to calm his spirit and compose his thoughts.

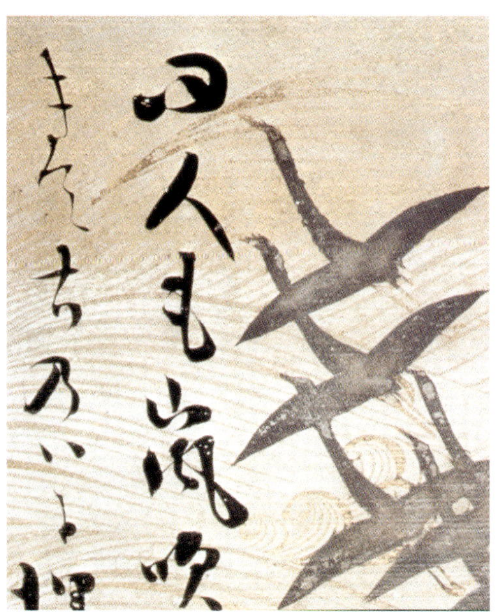

The Chinese calligraphy style called *'Shu fa'* is done with a brush that has a bamboo or a wooden handle and a tip made of different types of animal hair, making it soft and elastic. The artist holds the handle with different hand movements to dip the tip in ink. One has to undergo rigorous training in the various steps – from preparation of ink, making a brush, and choosing a paper, to holding the brush, stretching the paper, and finally creating a real art work worthy of veneration. Chinese calligraphy developed into different schools in the 3rd-4th centuries, when scripts in different styles came into being. Wang Xizhi (307-365), the sage of Chinese calligraphy, was the most prominent among the calligraphers. Among his works, the running-hand style is recognised as the best. Calligraphy touched new heights during the rule of the T'ang dynasty. Master calligraphers produced the highest level of

Above: Kufic inscriptions. Kufic is one of the six major Arabic calligraphic scripts.
Below: *Waka-Shikishi*, calligraphy painting by Koetsu and Sotatsu. Calligraphy flourished during Europe's Renaissance and later became an art form in the Sino-Japanese world.

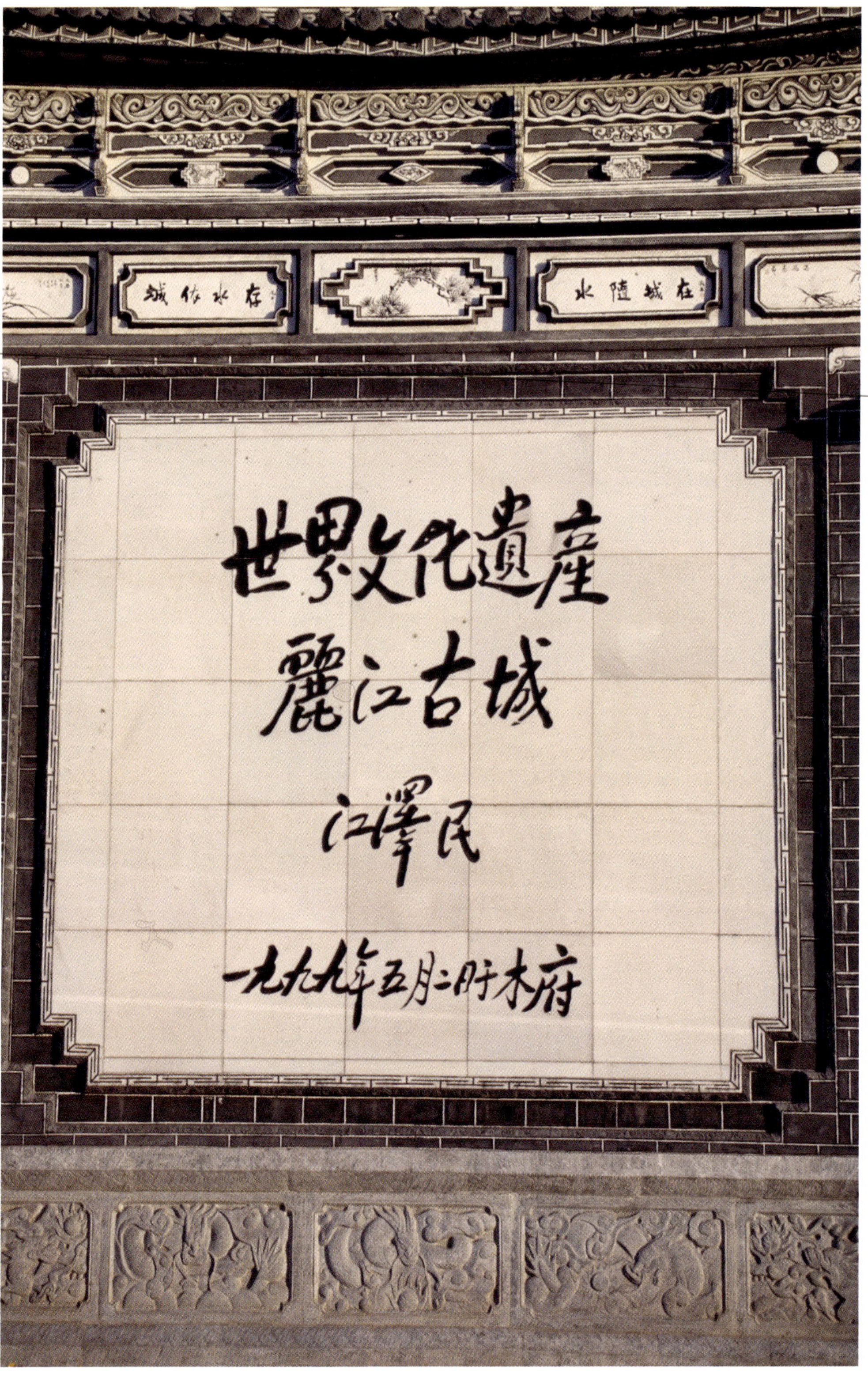

Chinese calligraphy on a ceramic wall in Lijiang, China.The word calligraphy literally means 'beautiful writing' and was used before the invention of the printing press. This subtle art, however, is being revived yet again.

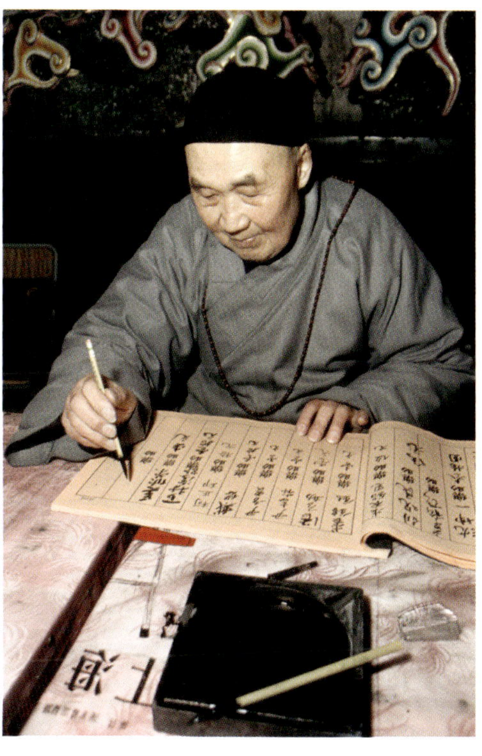

Left: A buddhist monk at the Jade Buddha temple, Shanghai, China, practises calligraphy.
Below: *'Shu-Fa'*, the Chinese calligraphic style, uses bamboo brushes with tips made out of fine animal hair, to provide elasticity.

works in all the styles. The regular script style in particular reached such a high point that even today, artists find it difficult to achieve that standard.

The brush is tipped with a fine point, made of deer's hair and covered with goat's hair. In Japan they are of two kinds: thick and slender. Thick brushes are normally used for the main body of the text, and the thin ones for inscriptions and signatures or for small-character calligraphy or fine cursive writing.

In Japan the art of calligraphy, called '*shodo*', is one of the three attributes of a cultured person, the other two being poetry and painting. With the introduction of Buddhism in Japan in the 6th century, *sutras* and their commentaries were written with brush and ink on paper in varied styles. The earliest handwritten text by Prince Shotoku Taishi is a commentary on the *Lotus Sutra*. It is written in the clerical cursive style. During the period from the 7th-9th centuries, the Chinese T'ang styles of calligraphy were adopted by the Japanese artists when the 'Bureau of *Sutra* Copying' was opened in Japan.

A variety of Chinese scripts are practised in Japan. The Tensho, or archaic script, is traditionally used for official seals. The Reisho, or clerical script, was once used for official documents. More common is the Kaisho or block-letter script. A faster movement of the brush and some consequent abbreviation of characters create the Gyosho, or the running-style script. This is normally used for informal writing. Sosho or grass writing is a pure cursive style that abbreviates and links parts of a character, resulting in fluid and curvilinear writing. The transmission of Devanagari, an Indian script, into the Sino-Japanese world gave way to its manifestation as Siddham, full of elegance and vitality. When a brush full of ink caresses the paper leaving empty spaces, it suggests the unsaid and the unwritten.

Zen calligraphy in Japan has seven characteristics. It is asymmetrically balanced. The strokes are as simple as possible, devoid of any complexities. It follows no rank and portrays sublime austerity. It is natural and has profound subtleties. Absence of hindrance in calligraphy means freedom from attachment.

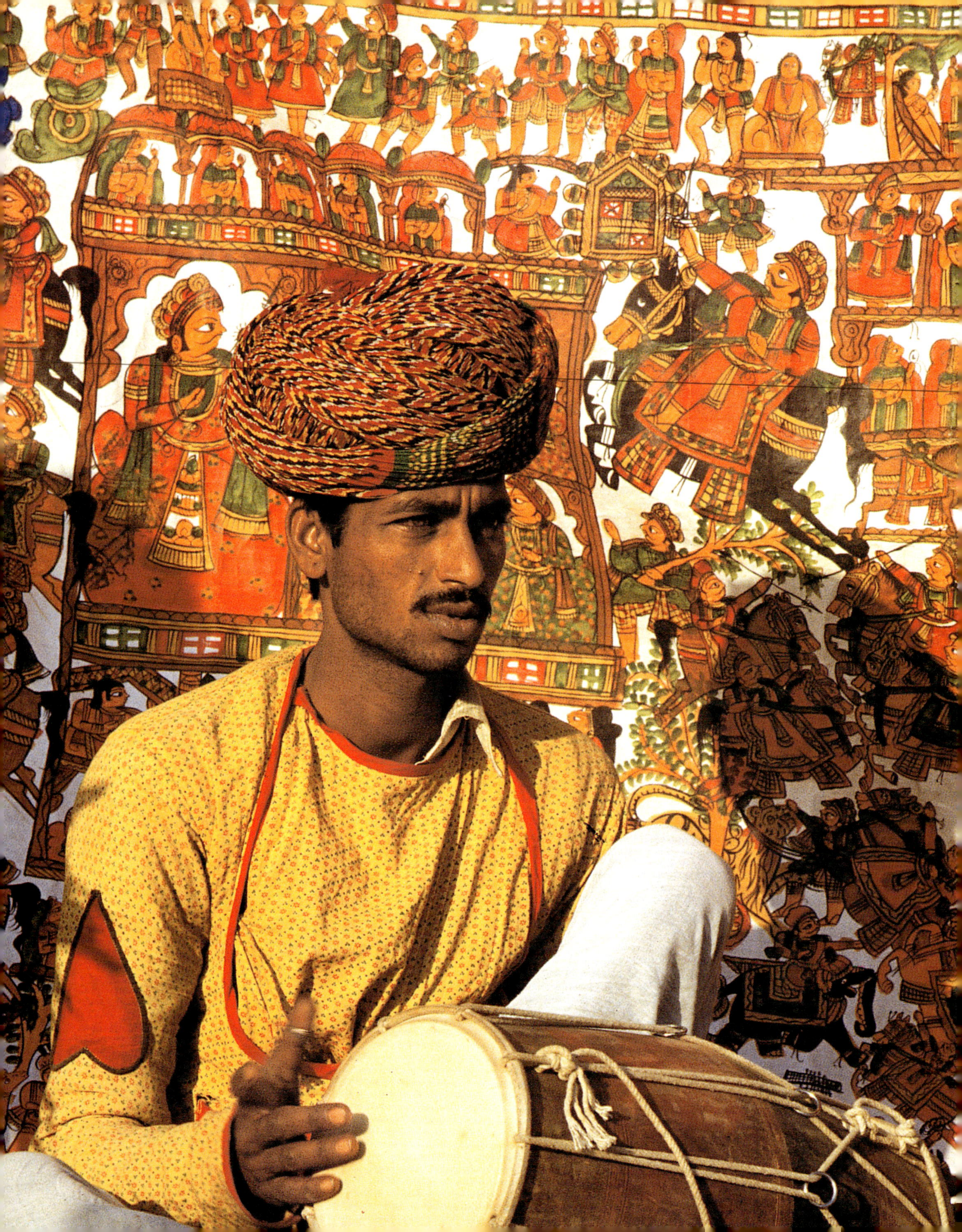

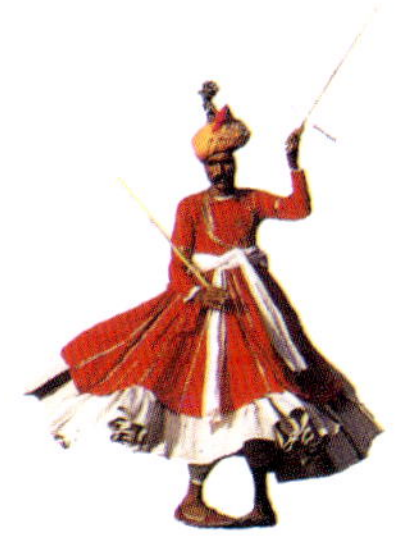

STROLLING MINSTRELS: SOCIO-CULTURAL REFORMERS

Strolling minstrels are highly skilled storytellers and actors who teach folk people through singing and dancing – making gestures and playing music, using oral and visual material like painted scrolls and shadow projections. They move from place to place, transmitting ideas, forms and various types of arts. They act as instructors to the society, and often instruments for socio-cultural changes. Their stories are often a satire upon the current socio-political state and can often mobilise public opinion. They have the power to please and enrapture the audience, narrating stories in a loud and overwhelming voice that stimulates the mind. They try to make their language as attractive as possible, but also easy to understand. Normally, it is a combination of poetry and prose. They create sketches or paint illustrations to accompany their presentations. When a minstrel performs, the whole atmosphere becomes so charming that the viewers sit spellbound. Their ultimate aim is to save society from the evil and the sinful. For the religious-minded, the performances are a medium through which they can be enlightened and be saved from the cycle of rebirth and death. They are a part of the village community in India, classified as Bhands, Nats, Gandharvas, Vairagis, and so on.

The art of strolling minstrels is termed as folk drama, traditional theatre, or folk dance. In India the epics, *Puranas* and other stories receive a different kind of treatment in the hands of minstrels, performing as professionals or non-professionals; nevertheless, they are dedicated academicians seeking a spiritual release. They keep art traditions active within a temple precinct or at the court of a king. They do not belong to any particular caste.

The traditional art can be traced in most parts of India from north to south and from east to west. Across boundaries, it travelled to various countries in the Southeast and to the Far East. The art developed in multiple forms, showing regional distinctiveness due to racial and linguistic factors existing in the society. The entertainers used to create their own copies with some modifications of various texts, folk

Facing page: Rajasthani folk performers sing and teach people with the help of '*Phad*' paintings in the background. '*Phad*' paintings reflect the age-old traditions of oral Indian literature.
Above: Rajasthani folk dancer in traditional costume at the Samode palace.

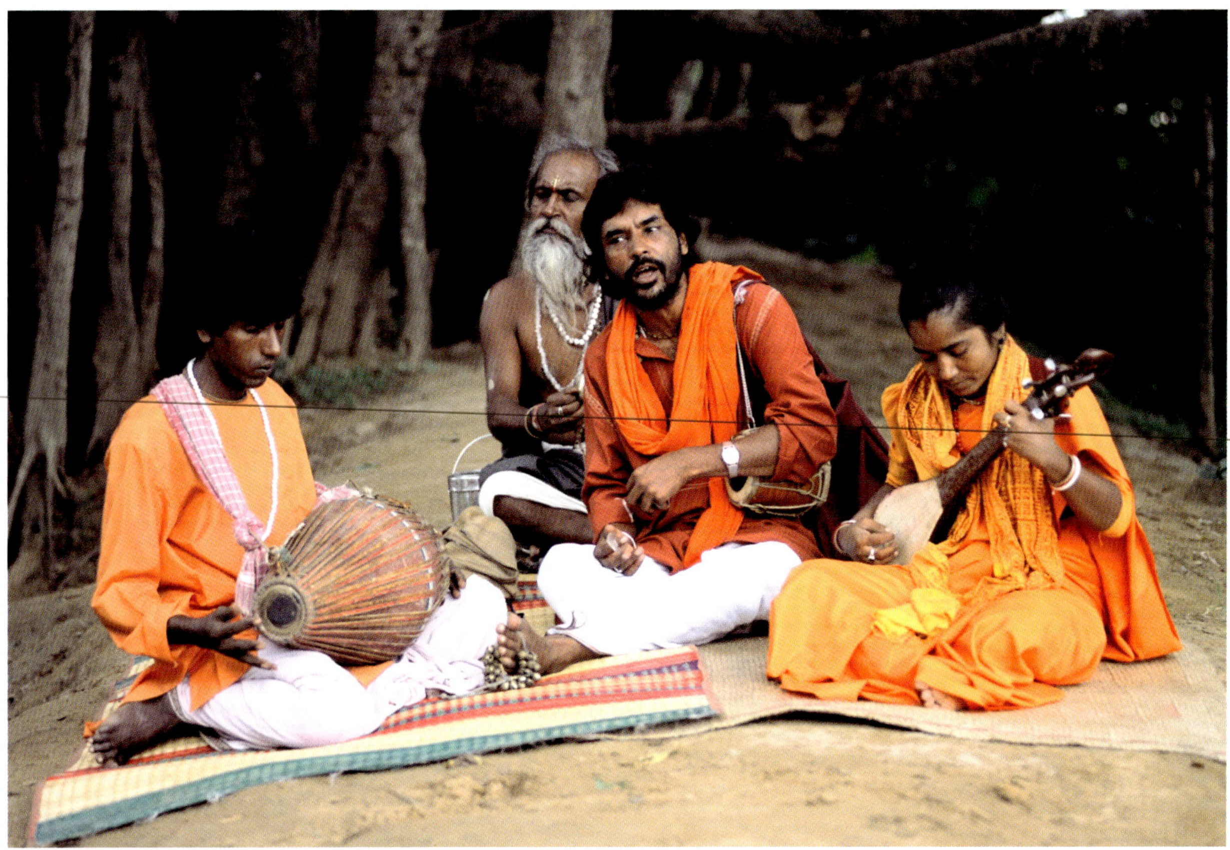

Above: A group of Bauls play music in Kenduli, India. Bauls are religious wandering minstrels known for their particular style of Bengali folk songs.

tales and legends. A large number of such versions are found written in a mixed style of prose and verse. Prose is highly conversational and verse is full of rhythm.

In ancient times, special endowments were made to temples in India to teach religious principles through the recitation of scriptures such as the epics, the *Puranas*, and other religious texts. Apart from discourses, storytellers made use of visual means to impart religious instructions. The earliest reference to such performances is found in ancient Indian literature, where the Shaubhikas were shadow players, the Mankhas are mentioned as mendicants showing pictures, and the Granthikas were narrators who, for example, discussed the fate of Kamsa from the beginning to the end. There were people who adopted this art for their living and could bring the stories alive in the viewer's mind. In a Sanskrit drama titled *Mudrarakshasa*, it is said that one of the characters, Nipunaka, disguised himself as a man who showed pictures of Yama and the punishments in hell, when he was to spy for Chanakya. Such people were known as Yamapattakas – carrying a canvas stretched out on a support of upright rods and showing the lord of the dead mounted on his dreadful buffalo. The Yama patas (*pata*, cloth painting) enjoyed popularity for more than a thousand years. People, including children, used to gather around to listen to their words. They used to chant verses expounding the features of the next world.

Until recently, the exhibition of such performances was popular in India, but is gradually giving way to other forms of religious folk entertainment such as puppet shows and shadow plays. In Bengal, the Patuas or Chitrakaras are still found as a class in rural areas. They used to paint pictures, go from house to house, exhibiting and singing. The narrators used to point to a specific spot on their paintings when narrating the events that they depicted. The pictures, termed as *pat*s, are classified according to their size and subjects. They can be square, rectangular, or in scroll form. However, with the decline of the profession of storytelling, the artists have taken up other occupations. A number of Patuas settled in Calcutta (now Kolkata) at the beginning of the 19th century.

The Chitrakathis were picture showmen in Maharashtra – like the Patuas of Bengal. They performed with wooden marionettes. A Chitrakathi in his collection had pictures of Rama, Sita, Ravana, Pandavas, Arjuna's sons, and other major characters of *Ramayana* and *Mahabharata*, along with pictures of famous kings like Harishchandra. Two performers sing and recite stories, using *tambura* and *damaru* for musical accompaniment. Performers used to squat on the ground. A wooden board of the size of a picture was propped against the knees and a piece of cloth rolled up in front of the board prevented pictures from slipping.

The Bhopas of Rajasthan have either scrolls or wooden boxes with folding doors called *kivad*. Colourful figures of gods and goddesses, men and animals are painted on the folding doors on a red background. The Bhopas fix the scrolls on two poles while performing. They sing and mime the story, while the women illuminate scenes with lamps. Scenes follow scenes without any dividing line in-between. Stories of heroes are popular with the Rajasthani audience.

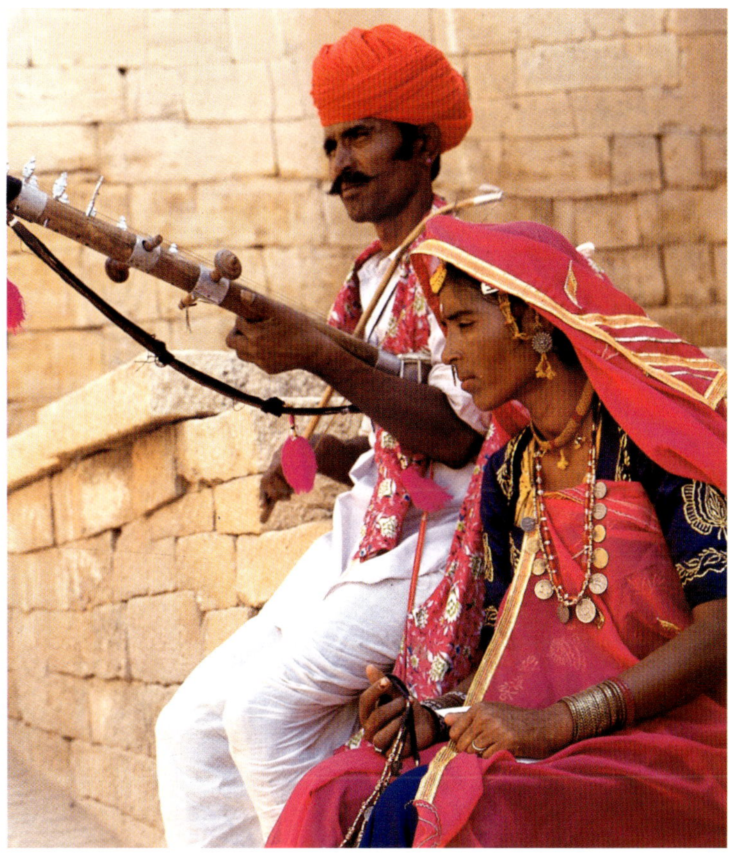

Above: The Bhopas of Rajasthan sing and mime stories of folk heroes, while the women illuminate the painted scenes on the scroll with lamps.

Teejan Bai, a devotee of Lord Krishna, is famous for performing Pandavani, a narrative folk form of the *Mahabharata*. She was a Bhilai girl from a village in Madhya Pradesh, and took up Pandavani not as a profession but as a passion. Since this profession was confined to men, her early audience largely comprised of plants and trees. Swimming against the tide, Teejan Bai began to sing the religious and mythological stories. She relates the familiar tales of the *Mahabharata* with gusto, through singing and enacting ballads of the Pandavas in the fiery Chhattisgarhi tradition. She has created her own style, one that has remained unchanged for three decades. She has saved a regional art style from the threat of extinction.

When Teejan Bai comes on stage, she infuses everything around her with the energy and charm of a little girl, in a style unique to her. Yet, she is unable to explain the source of this immense energy that ignites her body and helps her perform flawlessly. She always holds a *tambura* decorated with peacock feathers and bright flowers – regarded as representative of *bhakti* and *bhagawan*; it is her *shakti*, without which she cannot perform. It represents different things at different points of time during performances – sometimes it is the warrior's horse on the chariot and at other times, Arjuna's bow.

The sheer energy of her lyrical style adds to the charismatic performance. Her stories are interwoven with colloquial slang when she sings, dances and delivers dialogues at a high pitch. A harmonium, a *dholak*, a *banjo*, and a tabla accompany her performance. Teejan Bai skilfully weaves nuances of satire on contemporary societal habits through the stories of Arjuna, Karna, Krishna and several other characters of the *Mahabharata*, and also through important events in the epic – like the fight between Karna and Arjuna, the dialogues between Arjuna and Krishna, the episode where Draupadi was insulted, and the killing of Duhsshasana, Duryodhana and Kamsa. Teejan Bai has created a myriad of images, gestures and expressions personifying the inner being of the characters that she enacts. The dialogue delivery, with the requisite tonal ebb and flow, automatically transports the audience to the epic world of the *Mahabharata*, totally absorbed in the turbulent twists and turns of the tragic tale. Her passionate pursuit has created considerable stir in the world of aesthetics, with the audience left tapping their feet at the resonance of her *tambura*.

BUDDHIST TRADITION

The tradition of travelling monks, narrating the tenets of Buddhism through drama, goes back to the time of the Buddha, who himself had encouraged the use of storytelling to capture the attention of the audience and convince them of the precepts conveyed through a given tale. This approach would be certainly sanctioned by *upaya*, that is, 'skilful' means. Buddha's own *sutras* are full of interesting parables and tales. Buddha also sanctioned the use of local vernaculars so that people of various countries and regions would be able to understand his message in their own language.

The monks tell the stories from the *Jataka*s, *Avadana*s and *Nidana*s so that the more erudite Buddhist concepts are made easy and palatable. The tradition of telling unforgettable tales was transmitted to China and Japan through Central Asia, by monks who traversed vast deserts, mountains and oceans to carry the message of Shakyamuni to the oriental world. They composed vernacular pieces creating a new genre of folk song.

The monks derived themes from Buddhist literature and recreated them in their own way. Such books used by strolling minstrels were copied and adapted by performers in accordance with regional taste and the intellectual level of the audience. According to the colophon of a text, they were copied for pious reasons, usually by scribes and copyists who were students at the monastic schools.

The narratives were written in prosemetric style; the verse portion was chiefly heptasyllabic and written in semi-colloquial language, dealing with both secular and religious themes. They have an intimate relationship with pictures. A splendid example may be found in the 'Sutra of the Wise and Foolish', which consists of hundreds of long and short stories recorded by Buddhist monks from China who had heard them in 445 CE in the oasis city of Khotan in Central Asia.

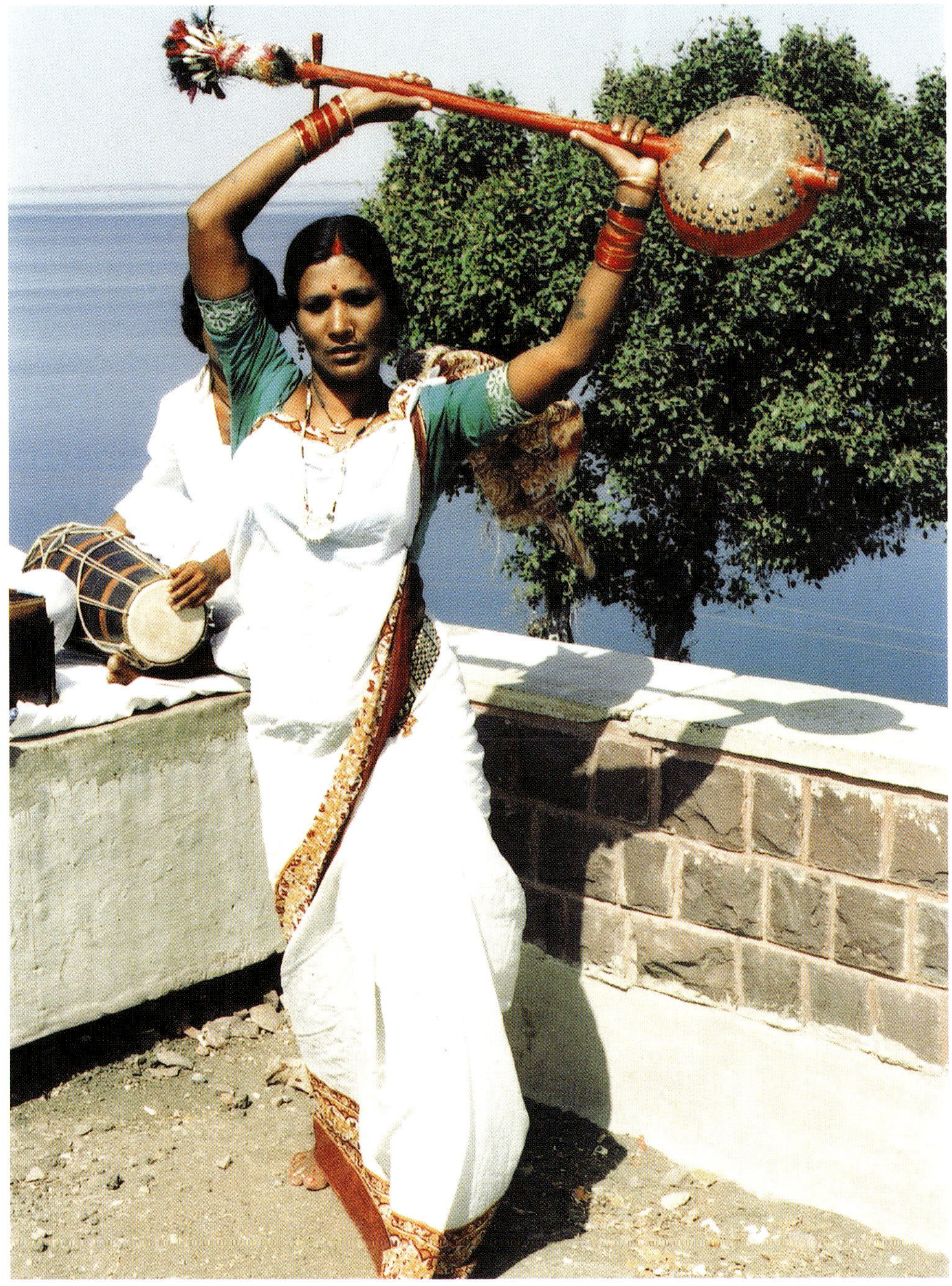

Teejan Bai, a devotee of Lord Krishna, is famous for performing Pandavani, a narrative folk performance that takes its stories from the *Mahabharat*.

Storytelling was established as a popular art form in the Christian world because one of the primary functions of Renaissance art was to communicate stories and ideas through visual means to contemporary beholders – in ways that were more enticing, vivid and memorable than was possible in a text, sermon, or speech. St. Ursula's tale became hugely popular throughout Europe and was as easily available as the Bible. It was illustrated in a series of large

A painting of Buddha and his disciples in the Tripitaka Koreana, collected writings of Mahayana Buddhism. It is a Buddhist treasure found at the Haeinsa temple, Korea.

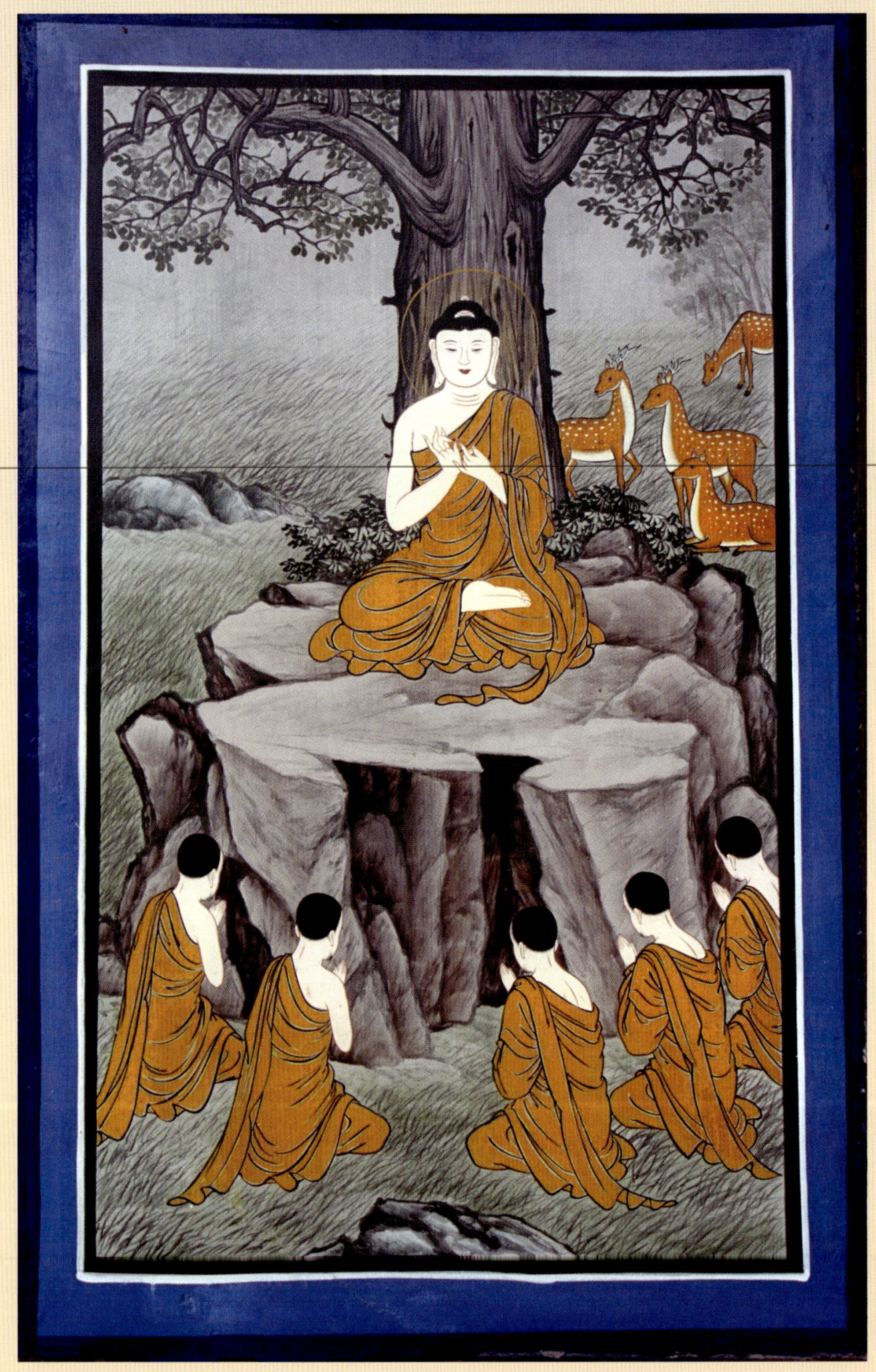

canvases, approximately three metres high and six metres long. The paintings, executed between 1490 and 1500, were hung all around the interior of the building that served as both the fraternity's meeting hall and its communal chapel. They depicted the life of Ursula, narrating episodes from her life. For instance she once asked her suitor to convert to Christianity and allow her to go on a pilgrimage with 11,000 other virgin women. Such episodes were often depicted on canvas emphasising the tale's ceremonial moments. Japan also had its storytellers and wandering minstrels, whose repertoire included stories and legends of gods, heroes, and personages famous in national history. One of the most popular of these stories was the history of *joruri*. The love story of this celebrated woman was so popular that it overshadowed all the rest and gave its name to the whole class of minstrel narrative, so that *joruri* came to be the generic name for this class of recitals. The *joruri* stories were originally unwritten, handed down from minstrel to minstrel. The first written text was created by the mistress of Oda Nobunaga, the ruler of Japan, in the late 16th century.

Japan developed the tradition of temple dance called *kagura*, which was performed at the cave of the Sun goddess and is still perpetuated in the *kagura* dances at shrines and temples. The Japanese assign the origin of the *Noh* lyric drama to the *kagura*. Over a thousand *Noh* dramas are known to have existed. Some of them are known as Kami-no or Shinji-no because they are related to the stories of gods or things divine, mythological pieces, or pieces related to the legends connected with some particular divine being or temple.

Buddhist monks in Japan practise mendicancy, asking for alms from door to door, chanting passages from the Buddhist sutras, and praying for the salvation of the people. Hokiichi Hanawa was a scholar who had lost his eyesight at the age of seven. He confined himself in the Tenjin shrine and compiled a book of classified quotations from classical books. He spent 39 years there and compiled 635 volumes.

Sightless musicians sang stories to the playing of the Satsuma-biwa, or lute. Even now, some of the best musicians in Japan are blind. A blind woman, called Goze, was a famous street singer.

The Korean minstrels chant Kosa-yombul, going from village to village in order to raise funds for building or repairing temples. Yombul, meaning 'invocation', is of two types, each having different texts and employing different instrumental accompaniments. Some of them are transliterations of Sanskrit texts, while some are Chinese translations from Sanskrit. They were chanted by professional shamanistic singers for exorcism, money raising and entertainment. The professional Buddhist chanters used to sing Hwach'ong, based on texts written in Korean and deriving its music from folk songs. The dance performed in conjunction with the chant is known as *chakpop*, 'making of the dharma.' In contemporary Korea, outdoor band music is one of the three components of performing genres in traditional Korean Buddhist rites.

The tradition was taken to Indonesia, where it became popular as *wayang beber*. A Chinese traveller who had visited Indonesia during the reign of the Ming dynasty, has described the performance of dramatic storytelling utilising a picture scroll – a series of individual scenes on cards. He felt the performance was very similar to the one that was common in China.

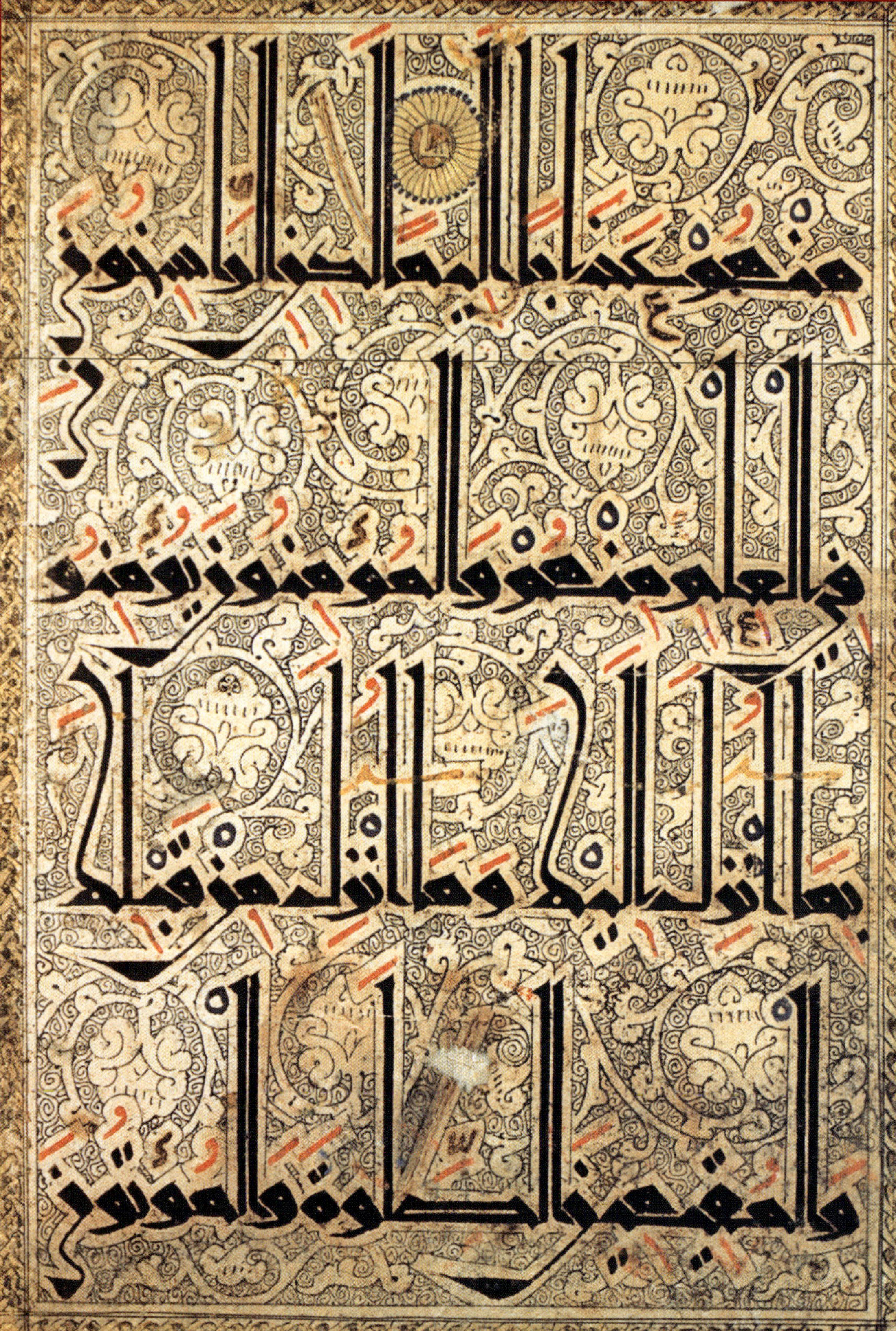

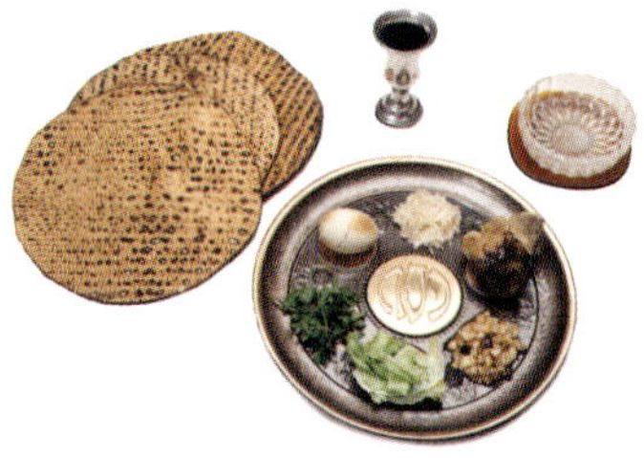

VOTIVE AND LITURGICAL OBJECTS: DIVINE METAPHORS

Votive offerings are voluntary offerings made to a supernatural being. Such offerings are made on many occasions, customary or special, public or private. Customary offerings at public feasts were common in ancient Greece. A worshipper who took part in a festival was expected to offer something.

The motive behind a votive offering may be thanksgiving, prayer, or propitiation, help or deliverance from peril, success in some undertaking or even to mark an important day in a person's life.

Worship springs from an inward feeling or a desire to earn the favour of supernatural powers or earn their sympathy, or to appease them or provoke their wrath. Some of the gifts are of direct use in the service of the divine. They may be temples and shrines and the articles used in them. Temples dedicated to special occasions are recorded in legends and also in history. Garments for the images, and some articles of intrinsic value such as ornaments or coins may be given as valuables. After coming back victorious, select objects are offered from the spoils of war – like a throne or statues from the temples of the conquered – to the deity who is believed to have helped in the victory. It can be a patron of his own city or tribe. There are instances when an artist dedicates his first or chief piece of work or a model of it. At a later stage, votive offerings became a means of self-glorification.

The term 'liturgy' is derived from the Greek '*leitourgia*' which refers to an act or work performed by or for the people. In the Greek city-states, it often had the technical and political sense of referring to the obligation placed upon wealthy citizens to undertake tasks relating to the common good, such as building a monument, outfitting a ship, and so on. Thus, liturgy is a system or set of rituals prescribed for public or corporate performance. In Roman Catholicism the importance of increasing lay participation in ritual activity is emphasised. Liturgical actions

Above: The *Kiddush* cups, *seder* plates, Sabbath lamps and spice boxes used for the Jewish *havdalah* ceremony. ***Facing page:*** Illuminated Quran leaf, early 11th century.

performed in public or in solitude are equally important. Sometimes, household ancestral cults end in public and corporate celebrations. Calendrical rituals are governed by solar or lunar cycles. Moreover, there are rituals marking turning points in the life of the community, such as preparation for war, coronation of a king, or the dedication of a temple. Social or corporate identity of a people is associated with their liturgical practice.

Church vessels and altar furniture represent an important area of Christian artistic effort. Fine examples of modern church vessels are found throughout the Christian world. Enamel, silver and gems are combined to produce simple shapes and symbolically meaningful decorations.

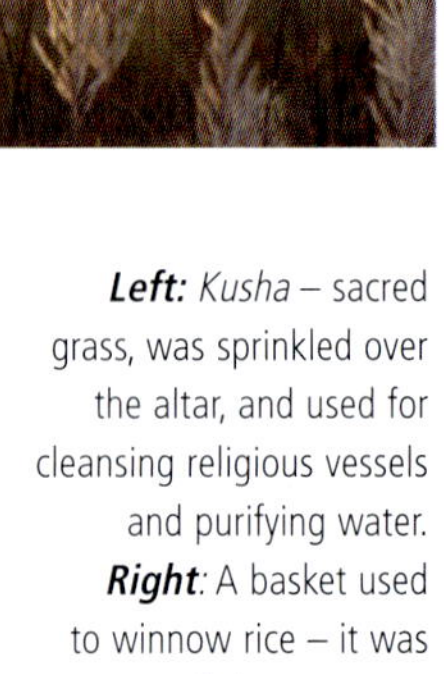

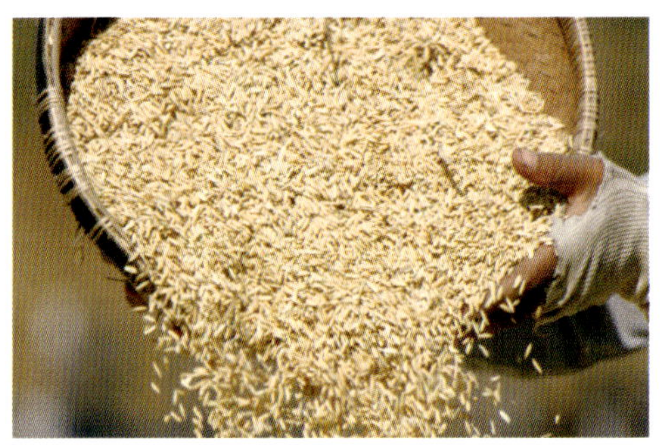

Left: *Kusha* – sacred grass, was sprinkled over the altar, and used for cleansing religious vessels and purifying water. ***Right***: A basket used to winnow rice – it was one of the numerous vessels used for performing the fire rituals in ancient times.

Liturgical systems typically exhibit an interplay of symbols and actions drawn from dimensions of experience as diverse as the psychological, the domestic, the socio-economic, the natural, and the celestial. Liturgy generates the world of shared human experience.

The earliest rituals practised in India date back to the time of the Vedas. A variety of implements and vessels used during the fire ritual are described and illustrated in texts. Complicated rituals promised riches in cattle and progeny, long life, and bliss in the next world. Materials used for manufacturing such implements were stone, metal, baked clay, wood, bamboo, grass, skins and horns.

Stone implements were used for pounding rice and crushing Soma. Winnowing baskets were made from bamboo or reeds. *Kusha*, the sacred grass, was sprinkled over the altar, and was used for cleansing wooden or metallic vessels, for purifying water, and for several other such purposes. Numerous kinds of vessels made of gold, silver, bronze and copper were used in the rituals. Big and small jars, deep and broad plates, and round jars, made of clay, were meant to hold liquids, carry live coals, and facilitate cooking. The design of the vessels used in the milk-offering ceremony was different from others. Rod-like implements were used for churning the fire. Swords were made in three different shapes. A cart was used symbolically for carrying rice during the new or full moon ritual.

The metalwork of the Jews is entirely utilitarian. There are some fine incense stands and tripod basis, the stands bearing openwork representations of priests making offerings or praying to images of seated deities, the tripod with a garland of leaves as its sole ornament. However, pottery figurines and plaques are more common than the metal objects. They depict nude women holding flowers, tambourines, doves, or playing the flute. The number and variety of types indicate that despite biblical prohibitions the popular worship of Canaanite gods continued in Israel. Other Israelite works include figurines of riders and chariots, miniature representation of tables, beds and chairs, and models of shrines.

INCENSE

Since ancient times incense has been an important part of religious rites and practices across the world. It has been used to appease the gods, sanctify a place or an object, and display reverence and respect. It plays a major role in purification rites and customs. Its fragrance is believed to please the gods. It is used in ceremonies of offering, prayer, intercession, etc. It is used to exorcise evil or harmful forces. In Japan it is a part of the tea ceremony. In Chinese Taoism, incense was used to disperse evil and to appease the gods. It was also employed in ritual for the cure of disease, and to measure time.

In India, incense is used in both Hindu and Buddhist rituals. In temples it is used as an act of homage before the image of a deity in order to make an offering and evoke blessings. Fragrant incense was also used to convey prayers to the gods and to drive off foul-smelling demons. According to Hebrew scriptures, incense was considered a holy substance in Israel. By the 9th century, incense was used in some of the churches for the dedication and coronation of the altar. It was later incorporated into the liturgical services of both the Eastern Orthodox and the Western churches.

In the Islamic tradition, incense is burnt to create a pleasant aroma in places of worship. Muslims burn incense sticks on auspicious occasions such as weddings, births and religious festivals. Incense is offered to the tombs of saints to obtain blessings.

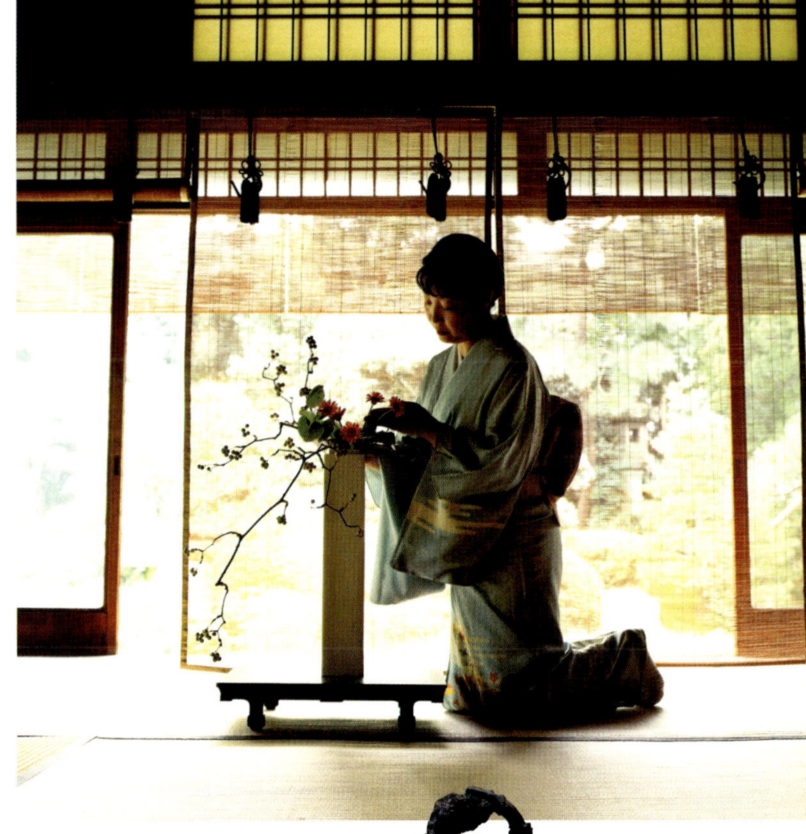

Top: Japanese woman arranging an Ikebana, the art of flower arrangement introduced around the 6th century AD.
Above: A Japanese Ikebana basket.

FLOWERS

Flowers are offered as a part of the five types of offerings known as *pancopacara* – *puspa* (flowers), *dhupa* (incense), *dipa* (lamp), *gandha* (fragrance) and *naivedya* (eatable offering). Different kinds of flowers and flower garlands are prescribed to be offered to various deities in Hinduism and Buddhism. The art of flower arrangement was introduced in Japan in the 6th century AD and is known as *Ikebana*. A number of Chinese priests worked as teachers and exponents of the art in connection with various religious ceremonies. There is a good deal of symbolism involved in the choice and arrangement of flowers. A fairly large amount is spent to train people in arranging flowers. The Japanese study the growth and habits of the plant that produces a flower. The Japanese Buddhist monks arrange flowers to reflect the profound meaning of *karuna*, which is compassion for all life, and the cosmic law of growth and change as flowers are a divine creation of nature.

Lotus flowers are often linked with the world of the spirits. These flowers, made of gold or silver paper, are carried at funerals, and

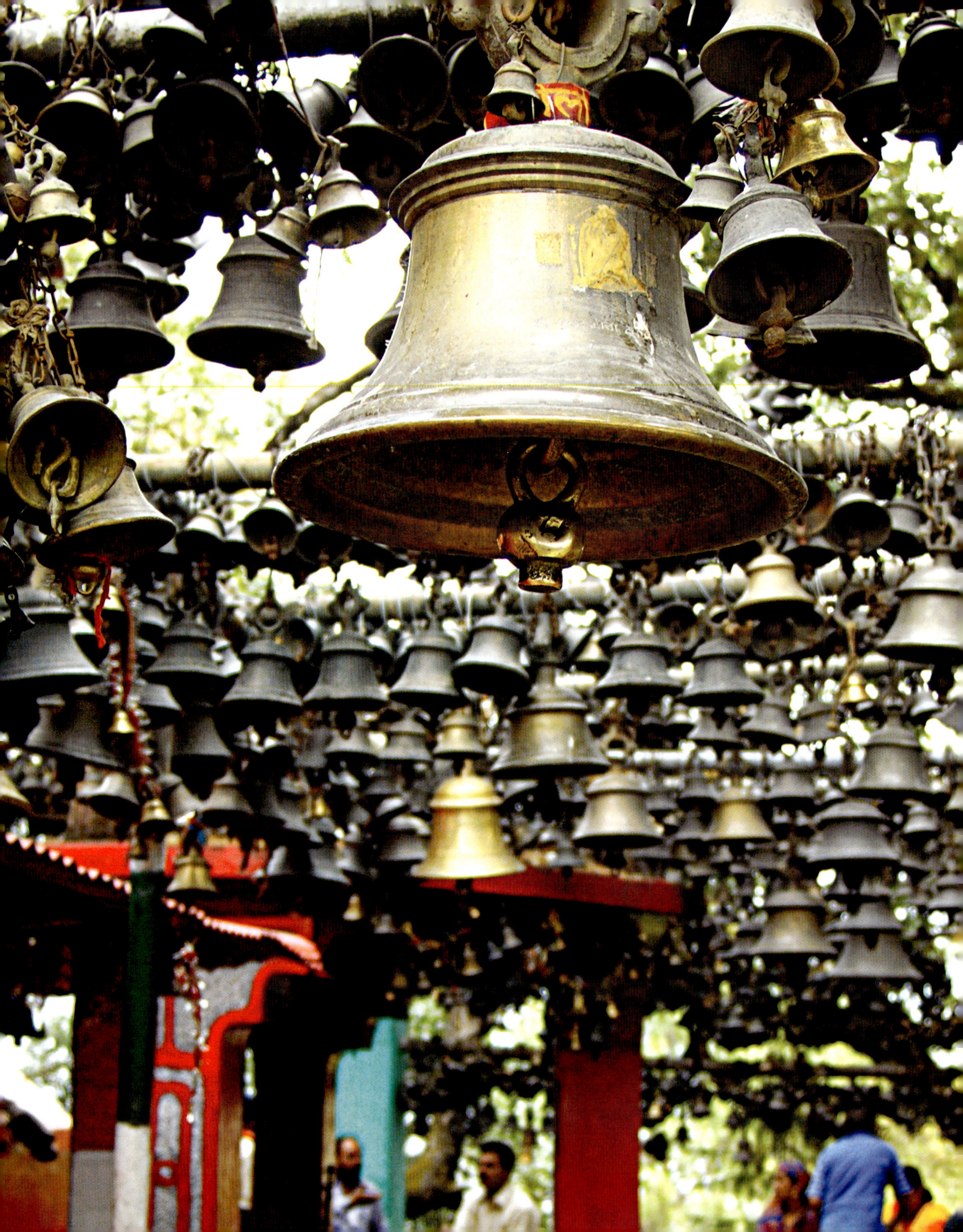

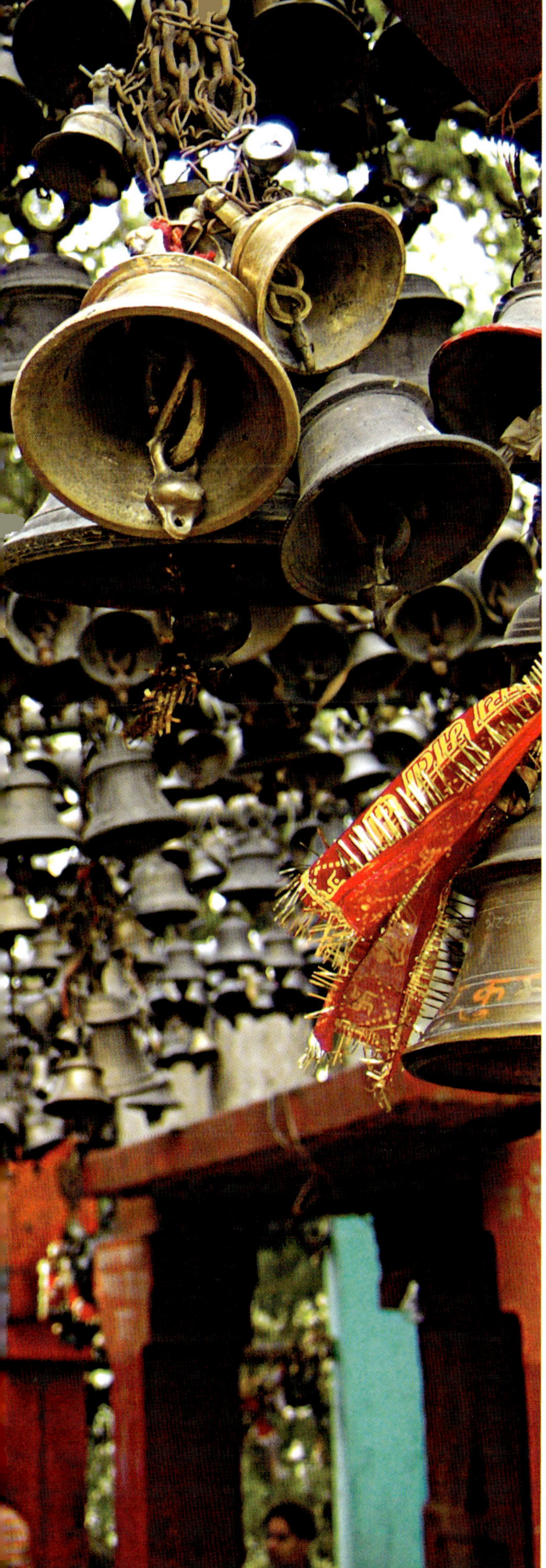

tombs are decorated with them at the memorial festivals for the dead. Lotus leaves are also used to wrap the food offerings for the spirits of the dead.

Facing page: Hanging bells at the temple of Golu Devta in South India.

VAJRA CROWN

The bell-shaped crown is worn by Nepalese Vajracharyas, Tantric Buddhist ritual masters, when they perform deity initiation ceremonies, fire ceremonies and other rituals. Such crowns are made of copper with gilded plaques, with a gilded band around the bottom. The crown shows five Tathagatas – Vairocana, Akshobhya, Ratnasambhava, Amitabha and Amoghasiddhi. There can be Taras in the middle register. On the top is a lotus plaque, then a vase, then lotus petals, and finally a moon disc surmounted by a five-pronged half *vajra*.

The important ecclesiastical objects used in churches are the rosary with large and small beads, the chalice used during Mass, for the communion of the laity, the portable holy water vat, the holy water sprinkler, the sanctus bells, the reliquary, and the clapper. There are three important rituals in Christianity: christening of a child, marriage ceremony, and burial. They require a variety of implements. Ritual implements in churches are placed within the interior altars. The decoration of altars varies from church to church. In a Protestant church, a candle, a box with the communion wafers, the crucifix, a communion cup and the Bible are placed on the altar covered with a cloth. In a Catholic church there are three altar canons, a crucifix, a candle, and an altar piece. For the ritual of Baptism, there is a pillow upon which an infant is carried, and a baptismal veil, a bowl and an ewer are kept there. For the marriage ritual, there is the marriage cushion, the myrtle

Priests during Holy communion, where they take the consecrated bread and wine as part of the Eucharist rite. It is part of Christian religious ceremonies performed at birth, marriage and death.

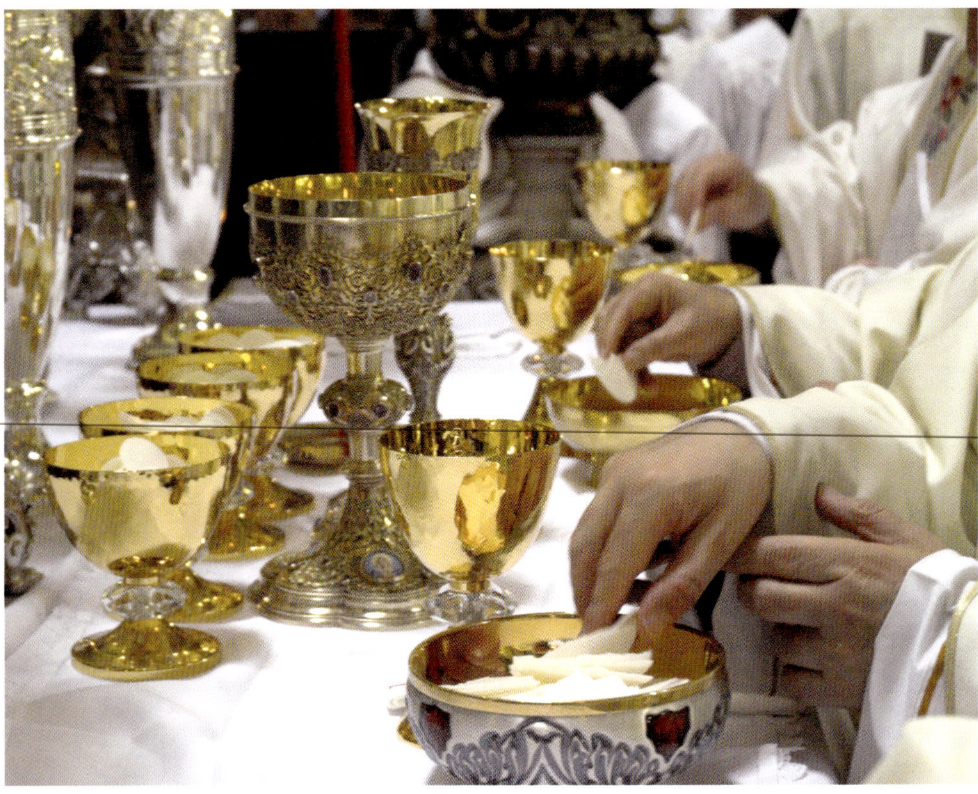

wreath, and the bridal veil that covers the face till the couple are pronounced husband and wife. A funeral procession and the ritual in a burial ground require different kinds of implements. Horses proceeding towards the burial ground are muffled, a man carries the wreath, another holds the cross, and the coffin is decorated with flowers and wreaths with streamers. The burial ground is decorated with candelabras, laurel trees and wreaths with streamers.

The Latin cross is called the 'Cross of Passion', St. Antony's cross is the T-cross, while the Tau cross is Y -shaped. The shape of the cross of St. Andrew is that of 'X'.

ROSARIES

A rosary is a string of knots or beads, designed as an aid to memory, and when used in religious exercises, providing a convenient method for reciting prayers or the names of the deity. Its use is widespread. Rosaries are blessed with prayers and holy water by some authorised priest in order to make them instruments of grace. Different kinds of rosaries are used by particular religious bodies or for special ceremonies.

The oldest reference is found in the Jain canon. It is also known as *japamala*, muttering chaplet, *smarani*, remembrancer, *ganayitrika*, the counter, and *kanchaniya,* gold or shining, *malika*, garlands, etc. It is used as a means of promoting contemplation by the ascetics.

The number of beads in a rosary differs from sect to sect. Normally it is 108, but for a Shaiva worshipper it may be thirty-two beads or its double. A favourite bead is *rudraksh*, an 'eye of the god of Rudra', a form of Shiva. The beads made of *tulsi* are smooth. They may be made of thread, sandalwood, red coral, crystal, cornelian, emerald, pearl, silver, or gold. Their colour can be red, yellow, green, white, or black.

Rosaries are used for repetition of certain mystical formulae and incantations to appease and propitiate the *Navagraha*s (nine planets) or guardians and deities during the rites for pacification, bathing an image, ceremony of sanctifying images, opening of a newly built temple, or installation of images. In the Theravada cult, monks recite the names of the Buddha, the *dhamma* and the *sangha*. Sometimes monks wear rosaries with 72 beads called *bodhi*. In Tibet it forms an essential part of a Lama's dress. The Tibetan rosaries have a pair of pendant strings which are threaded with small metal beads or rings. At the end of these strings is a *vajra*, and the other string has a bell.

In China, apart from the standard 108-bead rosary, there is a smaller rosary of 18 beads representing the 18 chief disciples of the Buddha. Part of the Chinese official costume consists of a rosary with 108 beads, which are often large in size, with dividing beads. The rosary has reached its most complicated form in Japan. Each sect normally has its own rosary, but the one common to all consists of 112 beads, divided into two equal parts by two large beads. In ancient times, rosaries in Japan were made from the *bodhi* tree from India, but there are other alternatives available now. The rosary plays an important role in ceremonies. Special value has been attached to rosaries consecrated over the sacred flame and incense smoke of a venerated temple.

The rosary used by the followers of Islam generally consists of 99 beads. Its exact origin is unknown, but the custom was probably introduced by the Sufi movements of the first two centuries of Islam, inspired by distant Indo-Iranian origins. Long sessions of meditation indeed involve prayers which require the use of rosary. The recitation of the 99 full names of Allah using the prayer beads is an old

Below: Rosary beads on top of a Bible. The beads are used during chants and are often blessed with prayers and holy water in order to make them objects of grace.

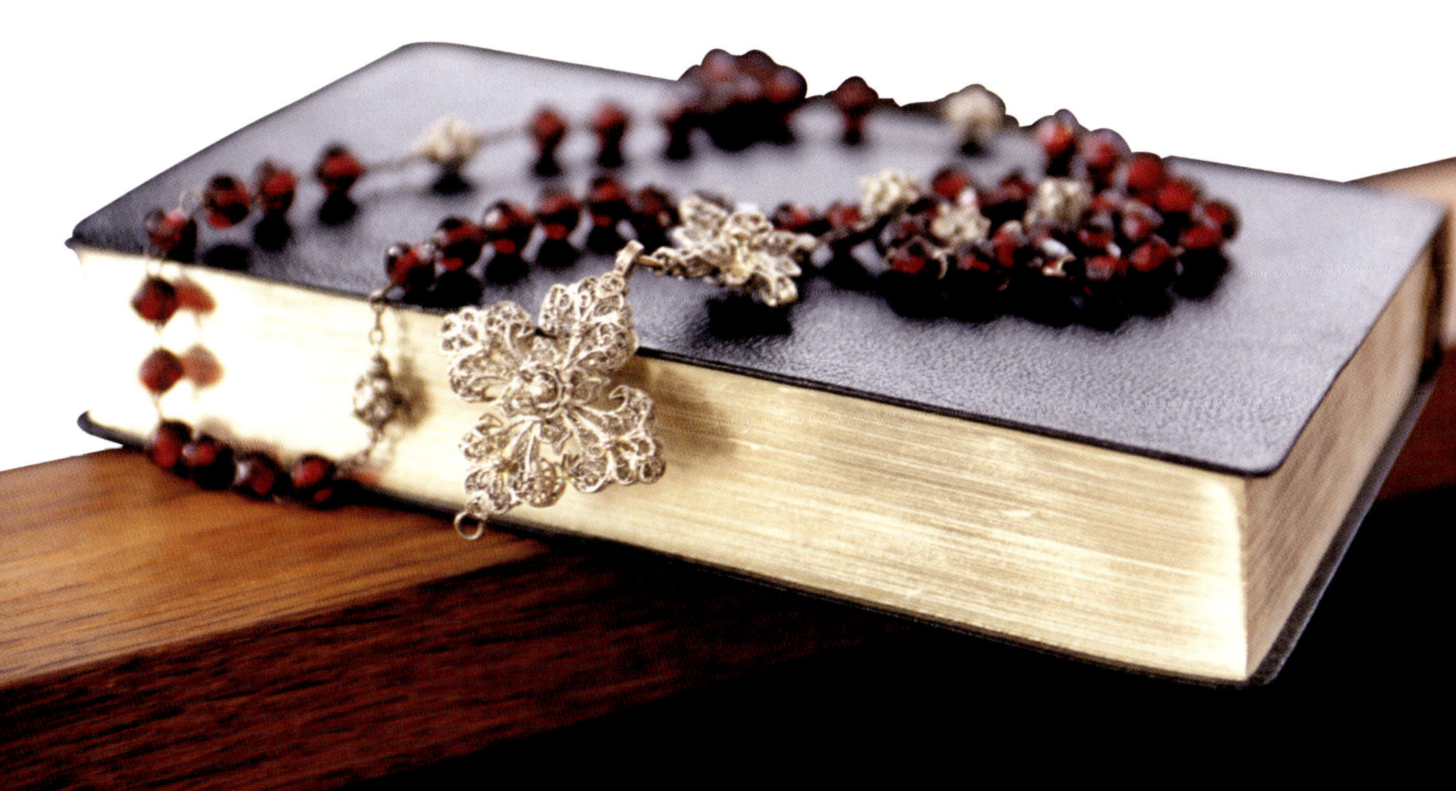

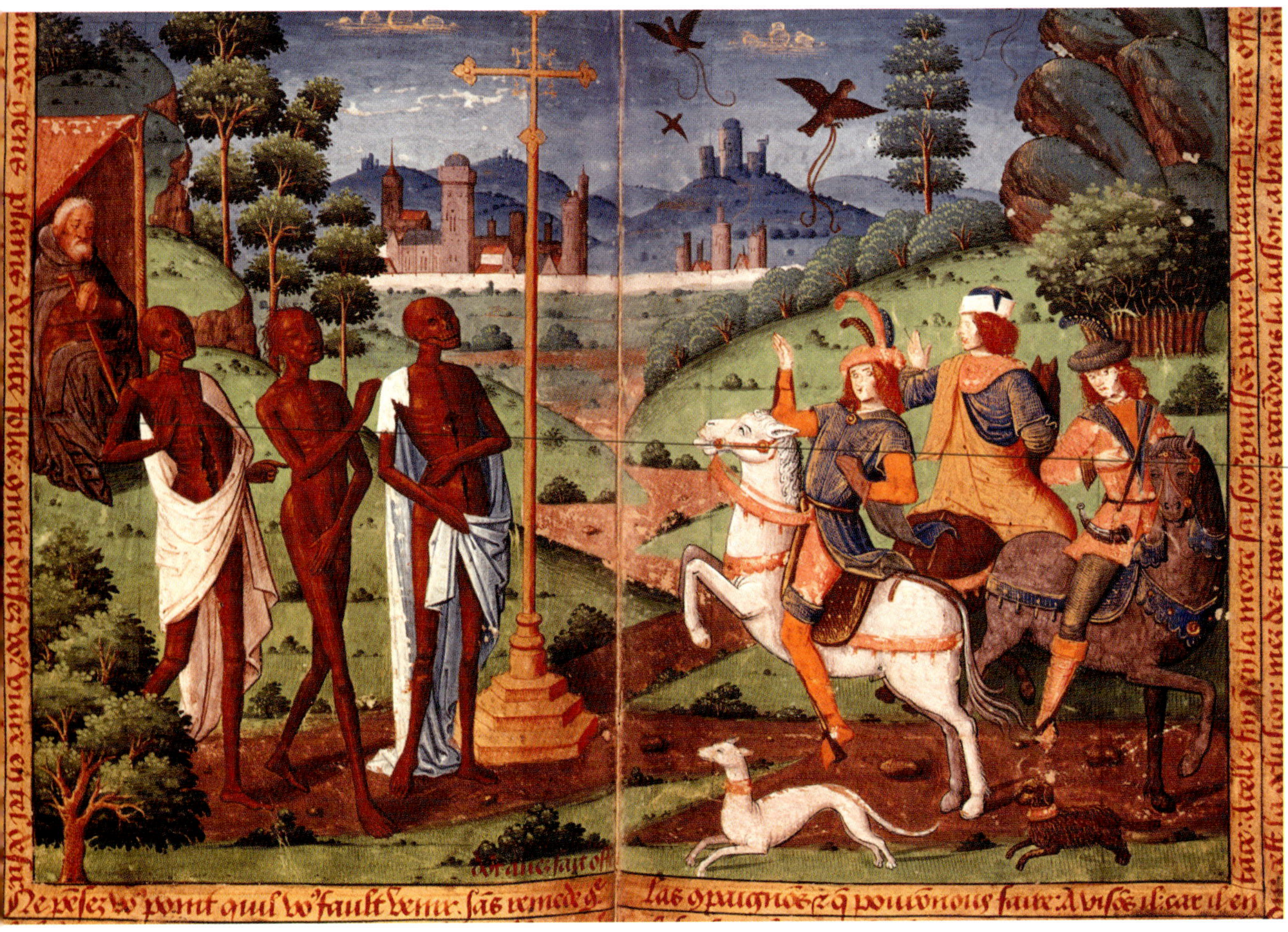

Manuscript illumination depicting the legend of the three lives and the three deaths from the Book of Hours of Charles V.

mnemonic practice used in every Muslim country. The symbolism connected with the prayer beads is that of the chain of worlds. Traditional formulas such as *shahada*, which recalls the unity of god, and *tahmid*, thanksgiving to Allah for his blessings, are also said on the beads. The rosary has become a visible reality in Muslim cities. Some believers never part from them.

Introduction of the rosary among Christians has been attributed to various sources. There has been a widely accepted theory that the rosary was introduced in Europe at the time of the Crusades. By the 13th century, the making of paternosters, as the beads were then called, had become a specialised industry in Paris and London. The complete Roman Catholic rosary consists of 150 beads, divided into decades by 15 beads of larger size. These beads form a chaplet. To each of the 15 decades is assigned for meditation one of the principle mysteries in the life of Christ or of Virgin Mary. These 15 mysteries are divided into three parts, vis-a-vis five joyful, five sorrowful, and five glorious mysteries.

ILLUMINATED MANUSCRIPTS

The invasion of Alexander was prompted by the vast quantum of golden tablets bearing

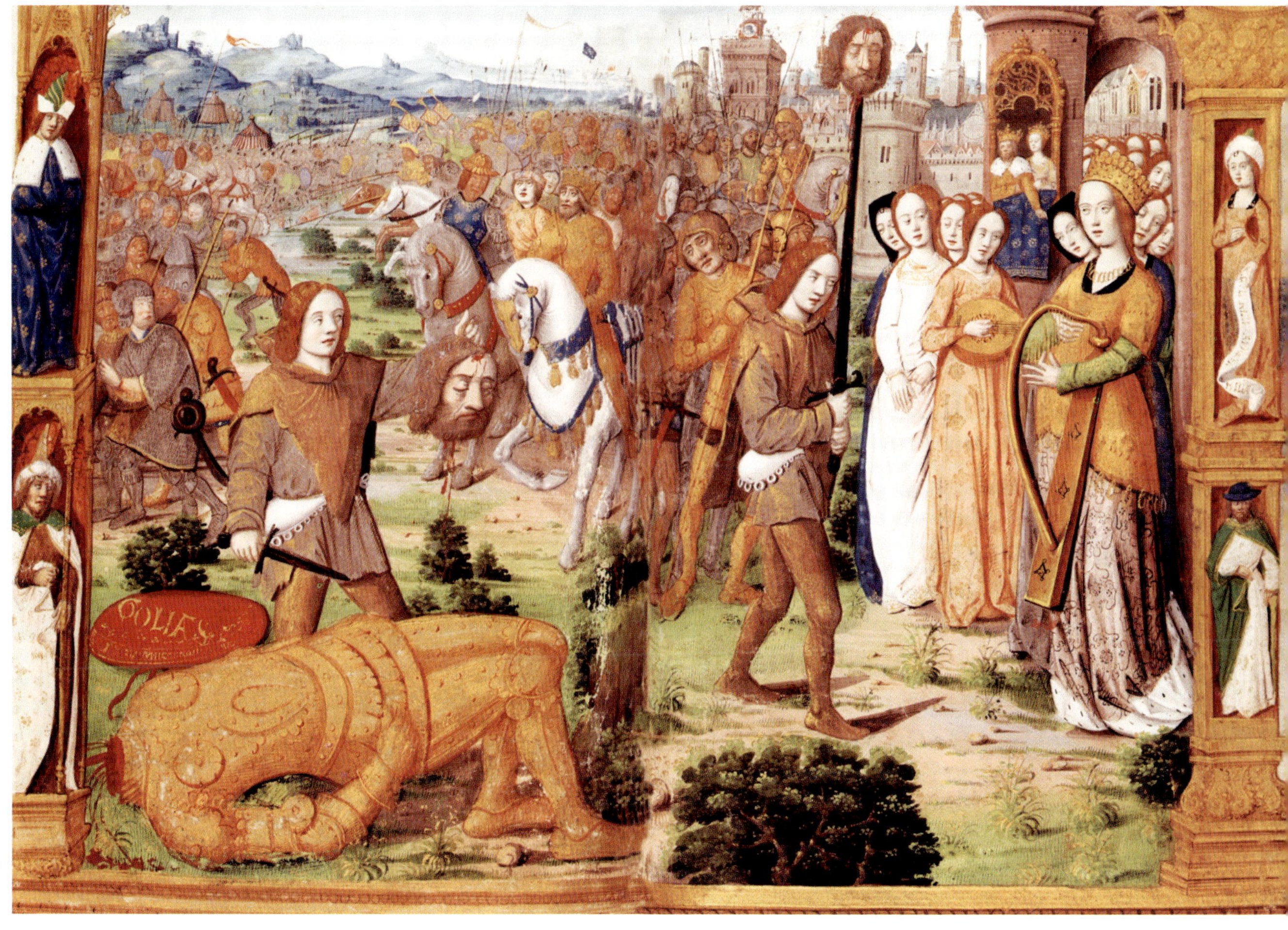

Zoroastrian scriptures, preserved with loving care under the Achaemenians. A sumptuous copy of the scriptures on gold was deposited in the 'Stronghold of Records' at Persepolis, and another set inscribed on golden tablets was preserved in the treasury of the fire temple at Samarkand. In Buddhism, *sutra* illustrations functioned in many ways – as illustrations and evocations of the *sutras'* content, as protective talismans of texts, as emblems of sponsors, and as pure adornment to an object of reverence.

Illuminated manuscripts produced in the monasteries of Nalanda, Vikramashila and Odantapuri belong to the late 10th century. The art reached a peak of technical perfection under the Pala monarchs – Mahipala II and Ramapala (c. 1075-1120). The text that was usually copied was the Perfection of Wisdom, or *Prajnaparamita*. It is illuminated with transcendental Buddhas, Bodhisattvas, and other divinities, as well as the eight great events of Buddha's life.

The art was effectively destroyed in India when the monasteries were looted by Muslim invaders. However, the tradition continued in Nepal, Tibet and other parts of the Buddhist world. Some 15th century examples are found from Bihar. Illustrated sutras were executed on paper that was cut, strung and bound in

Above: Illuminated manuscripts depicting the victory of David over Goliath from the Book of Hours of Charles V.
Following pages 130-131: Sassanian illuminated manuscript.

یدند تسخیر میسر شد اما فتح قلعه اندرون شهر بنابر حصانت و رصانتی که
در حیز توقف ماند و چون رای عالم آرای صاحب قران عدو بند
ی از قضیه حلب فراغت یافت نخست تسخیر قلعه حمص را وجهه همت
همت ساخت و علم دولت و بیرق بآن صوب برافراخت و چون هوای
از گرد سم کمیت لشکر جهانگشا معطر گشت اهالی آنجا از بالای قلعه
کثرت سپاه منصور مشاهده کرده از مخالفت و عناد پشیمان شدند
و ضراعت و التماس دیده با ترکات و پیشکشهای لایق بیرون
شاهزادگان و امرا که پیشتر آمده بودند شفیع ساخته بکان امان
حضرت صاحب قرانی جمیع اموال و غنایمی را که دران نوبت نصیب
آمده بود در مخدوم زادگان و خواص و مقربان تقسیم نمود و چون مدت
از تسخیر حمص گذشت و دولتخواهان بعرض رسانیدند که قرب دو
ند که هر یک مشقت سفر میکشیدند و چهار پایان بغایت لاغر بودند و دشمنان
عدلی تمام در خانهای خود نشسته اند اگر رای جهان آرا صواب
صحرای طرابلس رویم و این زمستان در آنجا بسر بریم و در اول
کشا و اقتدار روی باستیصال اعدا نهیم این سخن بر حضرت در نظر
ممدوح و مقبول نشاند بیت شه شیر دل خسرو پیلتن ٭ در آن داوری
صواب الجبان شد که آرام شتاب ٭ که آزرم دشمن نباشد
و رایات فتح آیات متوجه حمص شده و چون عرصه آن دیار مرکز

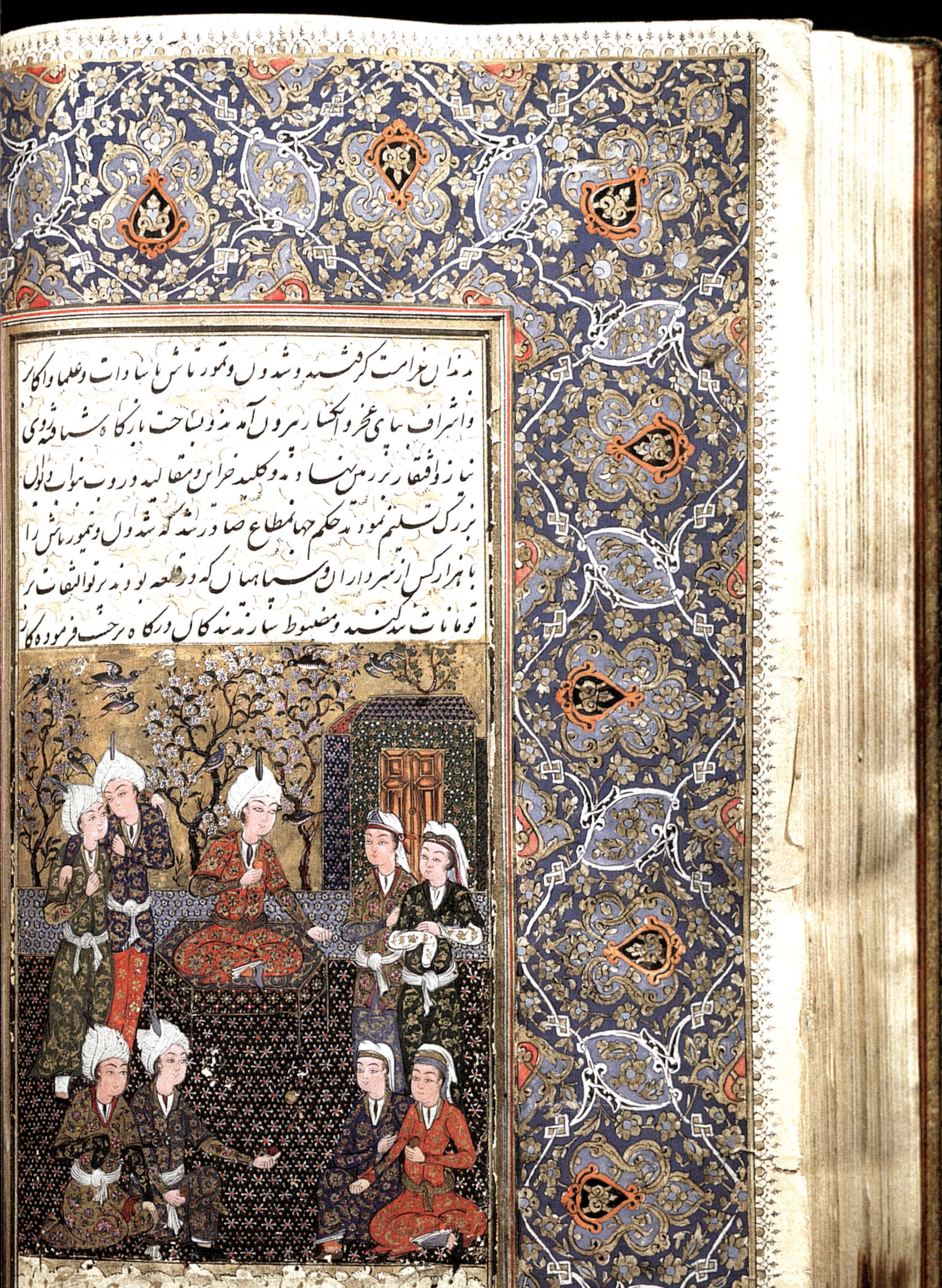

بدان غرامت گرفته شد و شدول و تیمور تاش با سادات و علما و اکابر
و اشراف بپای عجز و انکسار بیرون آمدند و بساحت بارگاه شتافته روی
نیاز و افتقار بر زمین نهادند و کلید خزاین و مقالید دروب نواب دولت
بزرگ تسلیم نمودند حکم جهانمطاع صادر شد که شدول و تیمور تاش را
با هزار کس از سرداران و سپاهیان که در قلعه بودند بر لوالبقات ر
تومانات بندکنند و مضبوط سازند تا بندگان درگاه بر حسب فرموده کار

Detail of a Book of Hours from the Convent of St. Clara.

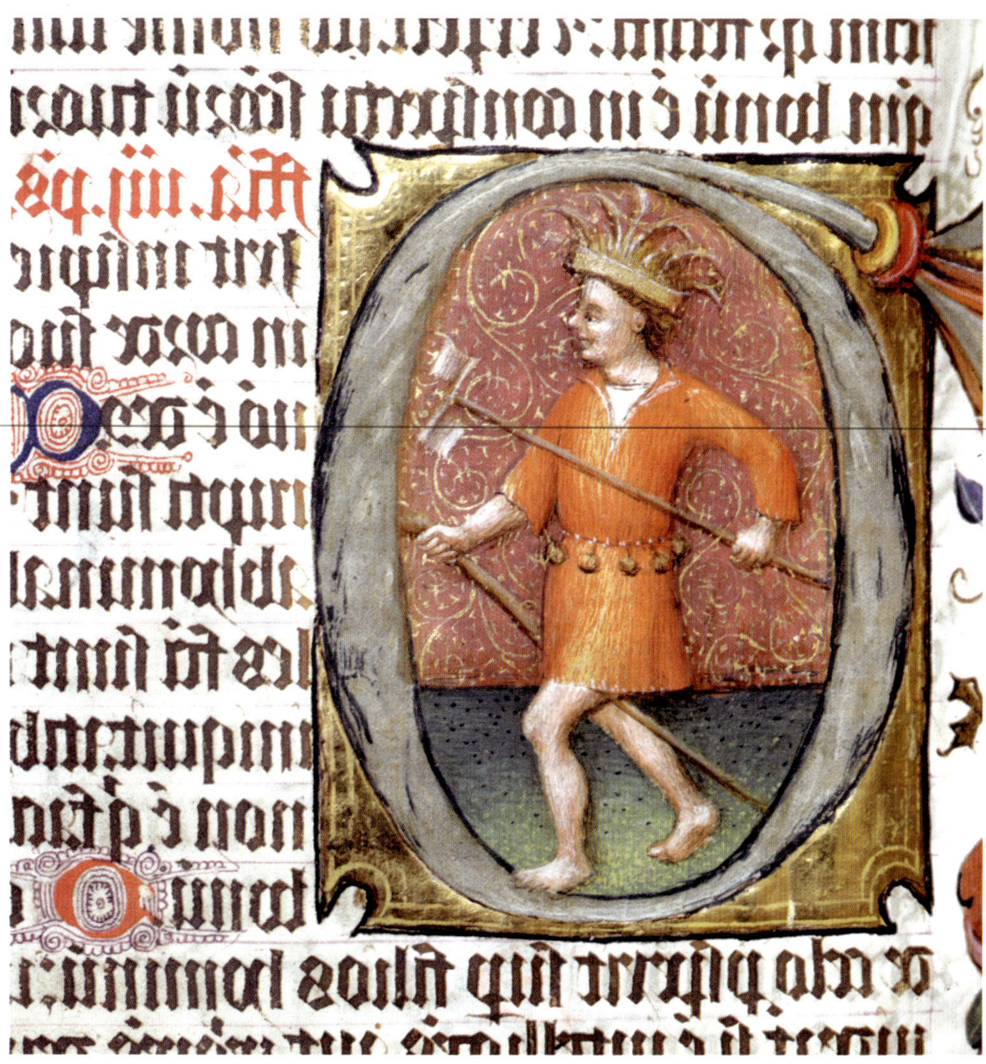

the shape and style of palm leaf manuscripts. In some manuscripts, figures are painted as symbols of protection and reverence for the text, while in some there were deities and narrative scenes based on the content of the *sutras*. In south and south-east Asia, the images were often painted in ink and gouache with gold and silver accents. Illuminated manuscripts saw a resurgence in Nepal, Tibet, Thailand and Burma both in number and quality, during 16th-18th centuries.

Illustrated manuscripts from Nepal have survived from *c.* 1000. This art form reached its peak in the last quarter of the 11th century. Exquisite vitality was maintained throughout the 12th century, but by the 13th century their quality and quantity began to dwindle. Illuminated manuscripts were revived yet again in the 16th century. By that time manuscripts were written on very dark blue paper in gold ink in Ranjana script. They were worshipped as embodiments of wisdom. Their commissioning was a pious deed bringing merit to all associated with it. The Nepalese style changed drastically in the middle of the 17th century with the coming in of the Rajput and Mughal styles to Kathmandu.

In the east, Hebrew books are found which are devoid of all ornamentation except the arabesque. In the west, on the other hand, there are numerous illuminated manuscripts in which biblical scenes are represented in rich landscape and architectural settings of Gothic art.

In Hebrew illuminated manuscripts the decoration is strictly aniconic. However, there is an interesting exception to be noted in a group of Persian Jewish miniatures that illustrate the biblical narratives vividly. Illuminated manuscripts of all kinds – prayer books, ethical treatises, etc – commonly found in richer households, constitute another aspect of Jewish art. The Hebrew manuscripts produced in Islamic countries are either not illuminated at all or, at the most, have only a decorated title page in which the decoration is based on arabesques.

Hand copied illuminated prayer books known as 'books of hours' are an art form dating back to medieval times. The Book of Hours was within the private devotional practices of the devout believer. Such books were considered expensive luxury items, handcrafted with precious pigments and gold leaf on sheets of vellum made from animal hides. A particularly fine example of such books is one commissioned for Mary, Duchess of Burgundy, in about 140 AD. The first illustrated page shows the duchess herself reading an illuminated manuscript, very much like the one that had been made for her.

PRAYER WHEELS

Cylindrical wheels which contain sacred texts have a special importance among the Buddhists. The smallest are made of silver attached to a wooden handle. They keep on revolving with a slight movement of the wrist, repeating the invocation engraved on the surface – *'om mani padme hum'*, salutation to the jewel in the lotus. Large wooden cylinders, coloured brightly and bearing the mantras in Sanskrit, are put up in the monasteries or at major crossings. In the monasteries such wheels were lighted with 108 lamps; they may also contain a shrine with some holy images and sutras that the devotee could use at the time of worship. Sometimes these wheels are placed above rushing streams and the current moves them unceasingly. They are also hung in temples and turned by hand or by means of a cord. Small metal wheels are fixed in the wooden pillars at the entrance of temples or pagodas in Japan. Such wheels are called wheels of fortune. The Japanese wheels have metal rings, which slide along the spokes and make a silvery sound. The Breton wheels produce the same effect by means of small bells with which they are decorated. The use of these instruments has a long standing in the Church. They symbolise human instability and function as instruments of purification.

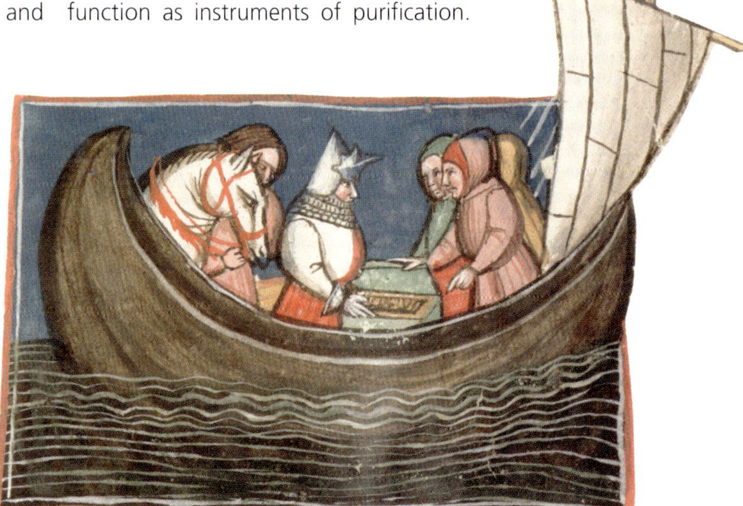

Illuminated manuscript portraying a knight travelling to the holy land.

Below the colonnade of Egyptian temples are placed movable bronze wheels, which are turned by those who believe that bronze is a purifier.

Bronze ceremonial objects began to appear in the bronze age. Ceremonial axes found from Indonesia may have been used at ceremonies and funerals. Decorations of the drums discovered from Southeast Asia include those of ships, scenes from everyday life, musicians, animals and houses.

PRAYER FLAGS

Prayer flags convey the pious wishes of the devotees to the divine. Tall flags, inscribed with sacred sentences, charms and prayers, are displayed aloft to gain merits and good luck, to increase the grandeur of the votary, to realise the material wishes, especially wealth and jewels, to gain victory over the enemies, or they are planted as a pious act by the lamas not merely to confer merit on the planter but for the benefit of the whole countryside.

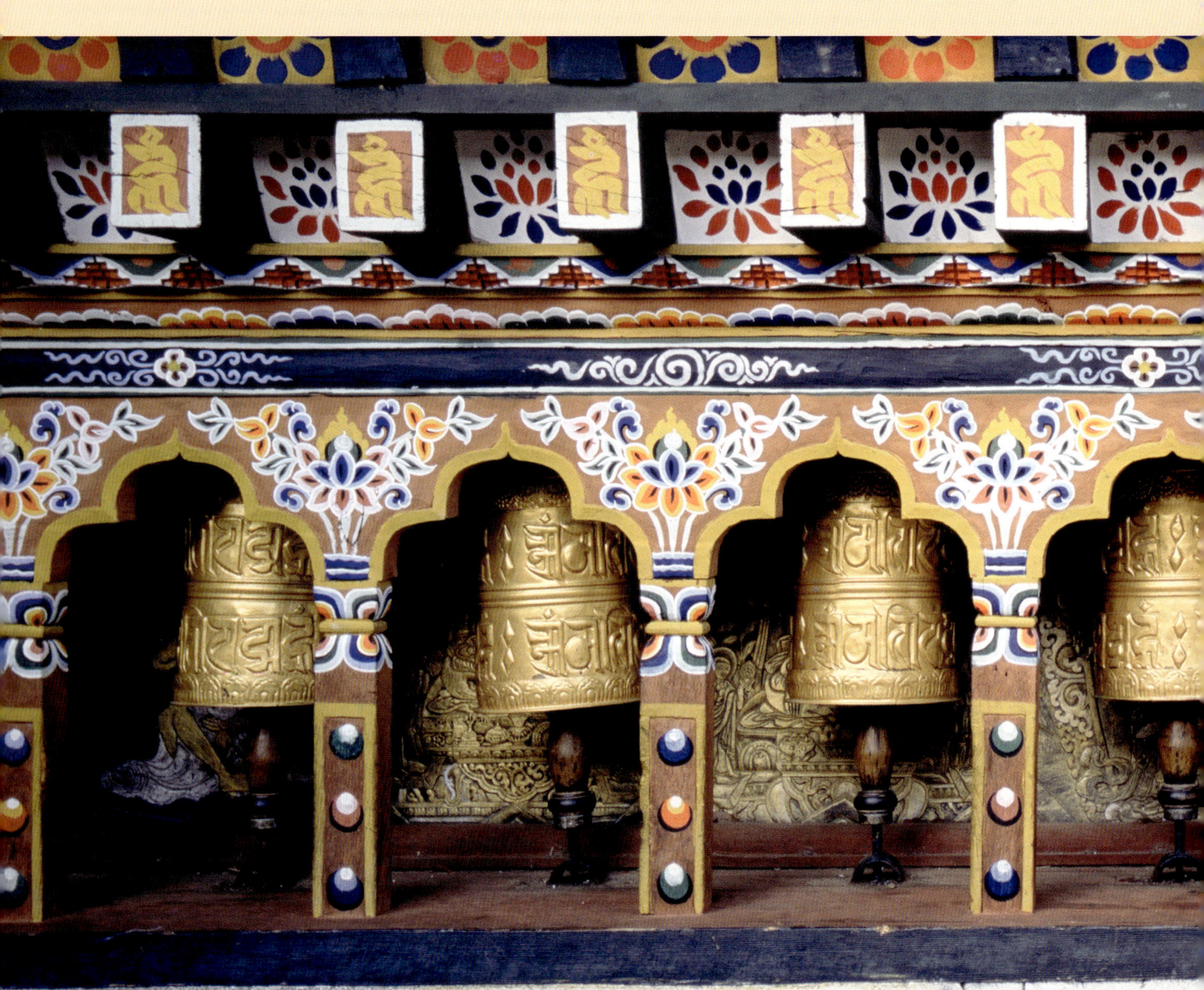

Prayer flags can often be seen in the Buddhist settlements, fluttering picturesquely. Tall masts with their streaming banners are fixed on the temple tops in Myanmar. The streamers are either flat or long cylinders of bamboo framework pasted over with paper, which is often inscribed with sacred sentences.

These flags are often used as talismans by the lamas, but they are also meant to spread the word of the Buddha. The concluding sentence of the legend inscribed on the flag is usually 'Let Buddha's doctrine prosper'. Tibetans call these flags Da-cha, evidently a variation of the Indian word *dhvaja*. The highly pious act has been practised by everyone at some time or the other. Sometimes such banners depict a horse carrying the eight emblems of auspiciousness: umbrella, fish, conch, lotus, *shrivatsa*, knot, banner and *cakra*.

These fortune flags can be compared with the prayer flags that the Burmese Buddhists

Colourful prayer wheels, containing sacred texts for the Buddhists, in a temple at Chimi Lakhang, Punakha, Bhutan.

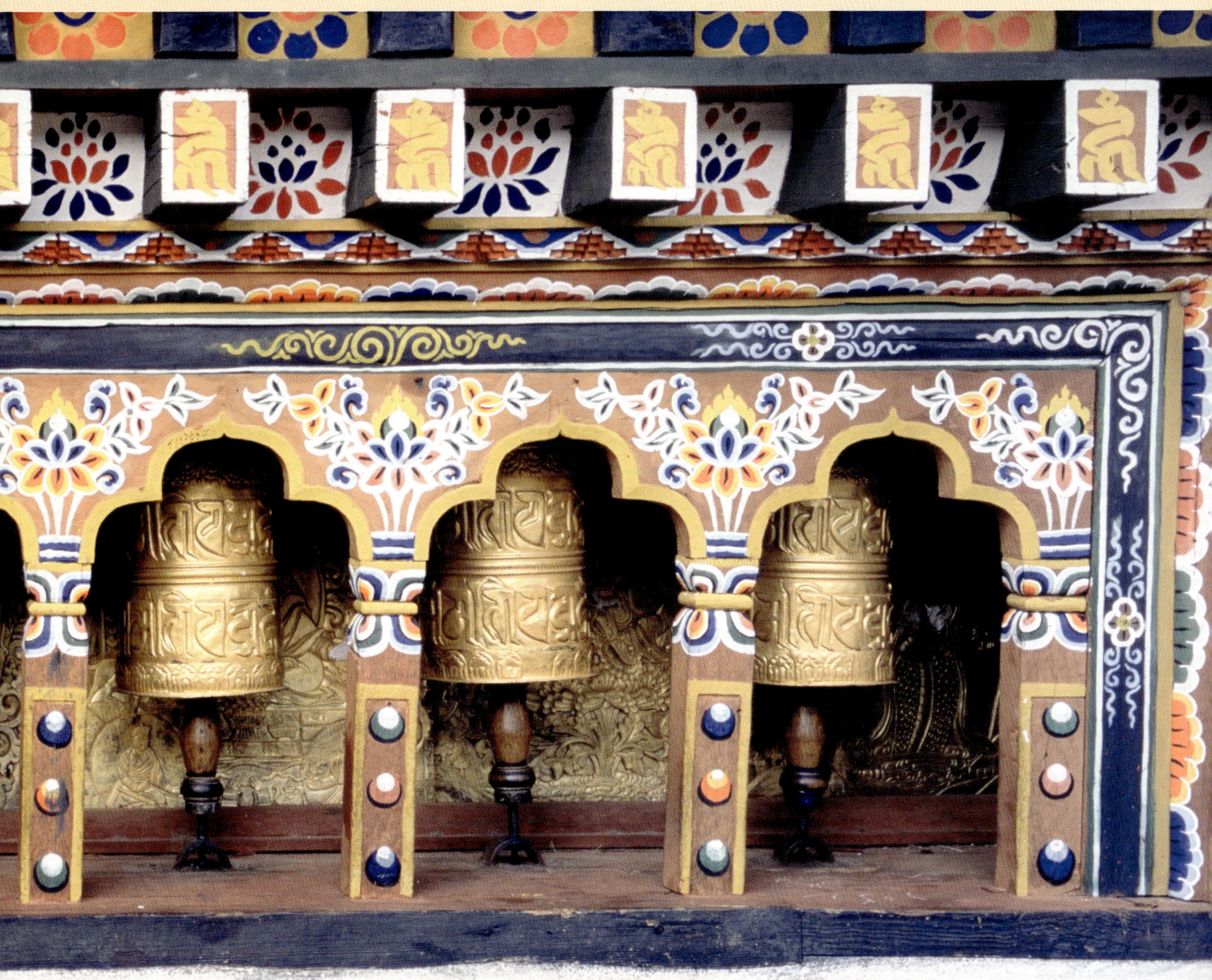

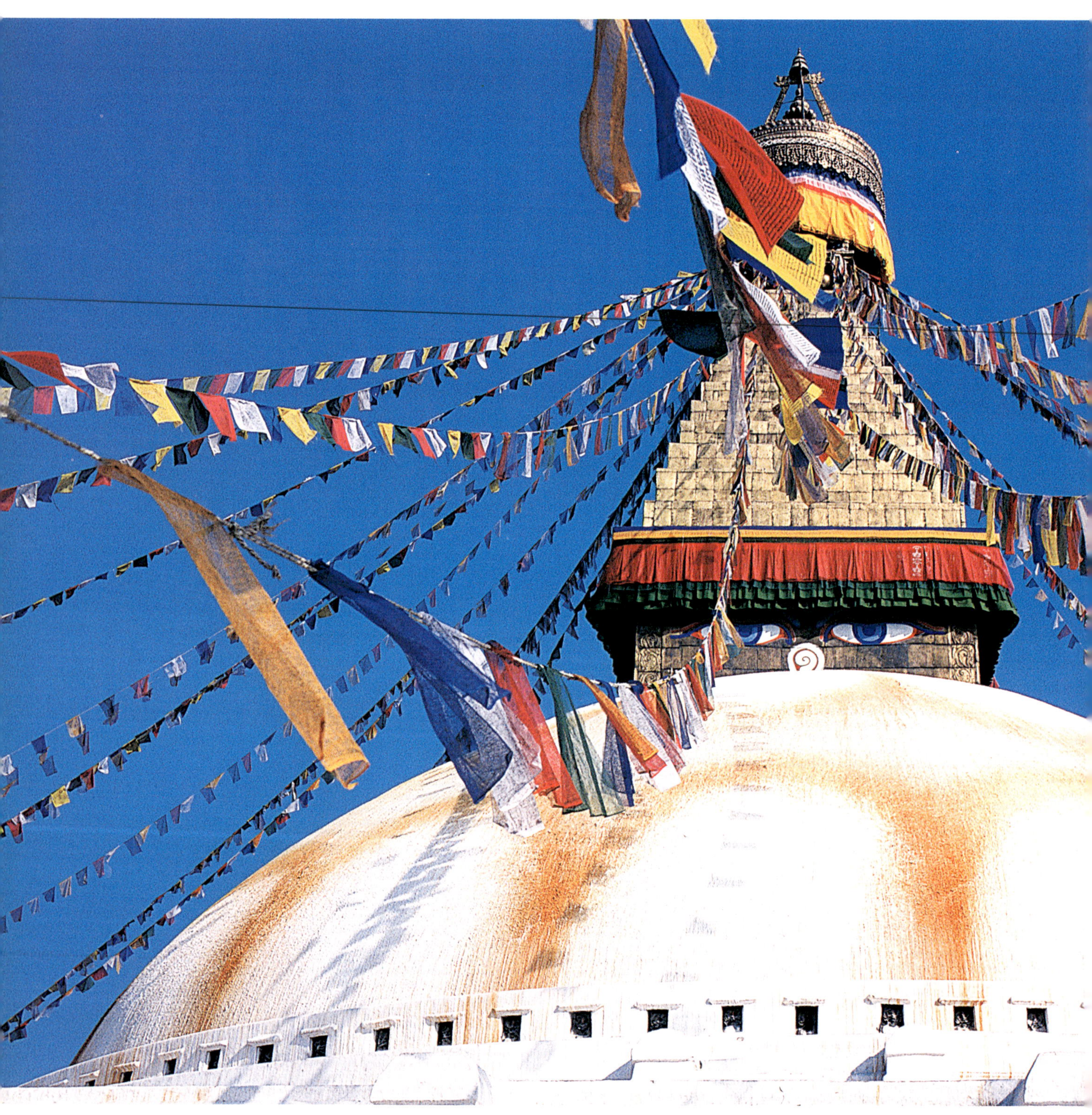

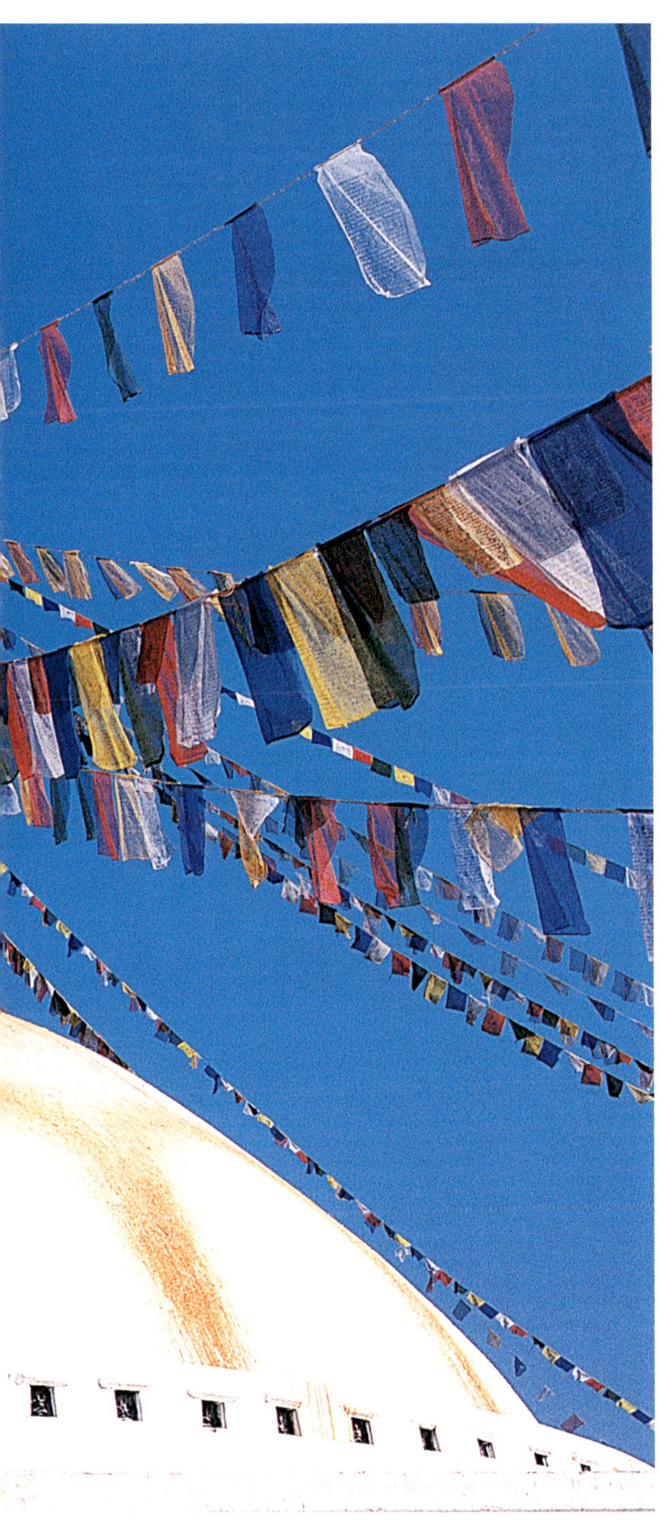

offer at their shrines. They are fancifully cut into figures of dragons and the like and in the centre contain sentences in Pali or the vernacular, seeking strength and blessings from the spirits, and freedom from all sorts of sickness and calamities.

OFFERING BANNERS

Votive banners were offered to the temples on special occasions for specific reasons. The largest number of such banners has been discovered from various sand-buried sites in Central Asia. Explorers and archaeologists from various countries, who travelled to these difficult sites, have collected these banners that are now preserved in museums like the Museum fur Indische Kunst, Berlin, and the Stein collection in the British museum, London.

These banners were painted on both the sides, and were made on silk, which was not transparent. They comprise of a head piece with hanging loops, side streamers, tail streamers, sometimes of darker colours, weighing boards, two bamboo stiffeners to be inserted on the top and bottom of the painted area, wound first with raw white silk and then diagonally with coloured silk. The banners made of hemp cloth, a coarser material, are more simply made and have survived rather better than those of silk. Banners made of paper show all features found in banners on silk and hemp cloth, from the hanging loop and triangular head piece to a stiffened piece of card at the bottom serving as a weighing board. Some banners are made of local paper, simply drawn and coloured. They are cheaper substitutes serving the same purpose as those made of more expensive materials.

Facing page: Colourful votive banners made in silk and hemp at Bodhnath Stupa in Kathmandu, Nepal.

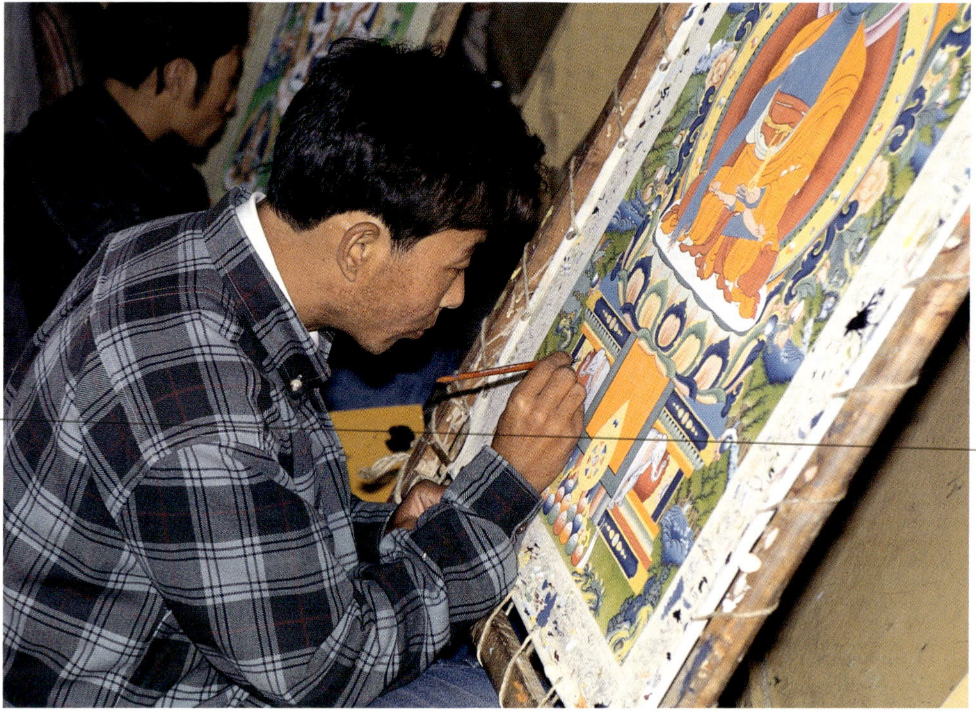

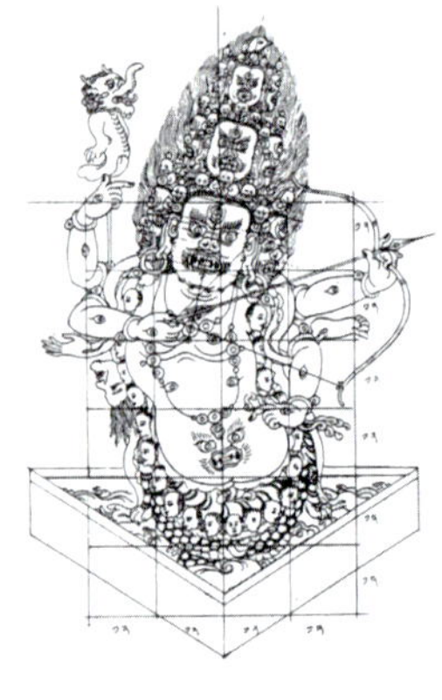

Top: A man painting a Mandala. It is a tri-dimensional geometrical representation of the universe, symbolising a combination of the enlightened mind and body of the Buddha. **Above**: The drawing of a standing deity with grid marks.

These banners were carried in processions to be offered with solemn rites. They range in size from a few inches to a couple of metres. They may display single figures of the divine beings or a series of Buddhas or a Bodhisattvas, seated or standing in almost identical representations, arranged one above the other. These banners may contain flying goddesses coming down from heaven or playing musical instruments, or *mandala*s of various divinities, birds, etc. The majority is executed in brush outlines only with little or no colouring; instead colourful effects are obtained by the use of colour in silk material itself.

BUDDHIST LITURGICAL IMPLEMENTS

The first Buddhist ritual implements were simple functional objects, permitted by the Buddha as possessions of the ordained mendicants. But with time, a greater number of implements were required as rituals became increasingly elaborate. The primary offerings made to the Buddha and the stupas were incense, flowers and candles. Incense and perfumed water were used for purification and flowers for paying homage. Candles were lit to eliminate the darkness of ignorance. Offering food symbolised the giving of alms. Special kinds of vessels were used to place the offerings.

Within esoteric Buddhism, rituals require a variety of implements to be put on the ritual platform. They can be broadly divided into four categories – those for protecting the practitioner, for purifying, for holding offerings, and for providing musical accompaniment. Weapons were used to imbue the officiant with extraordinary powers.

The *cakra,* one of the seven treasures of a *cakravrtin*, a universal monarch, helps in

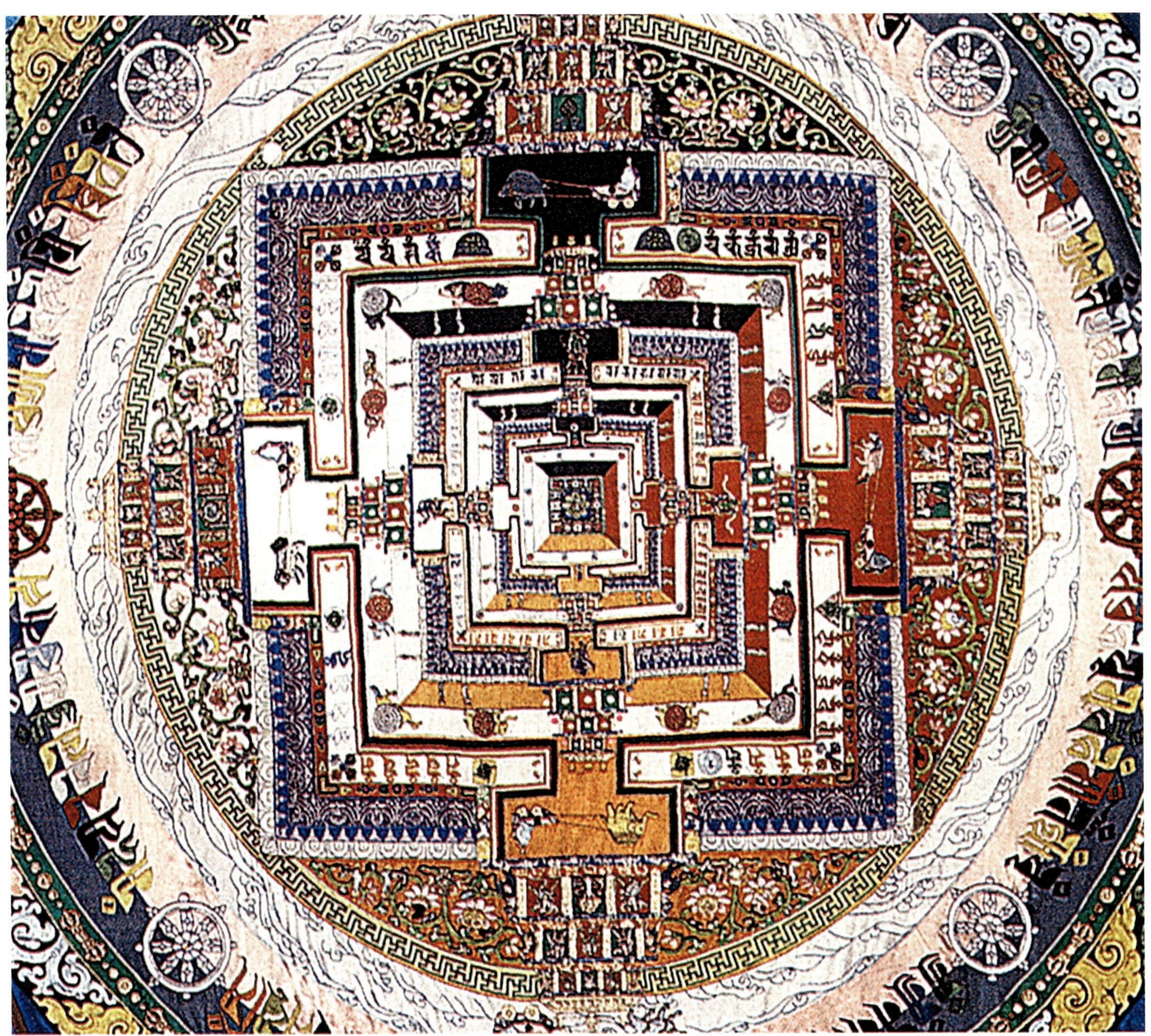

Kalachakra Mandala, a dynamic representation of the Wheel of Time.

conquering enemies. Water and powdered incense are put in covered containers generally made from gilt. Bells and cymbals are used to gain the attention of the deity, entertain it with sound, and then to provide it with melodious accompaniments upon its departure. Bells are also used to awaken the mind of the practitioner. A metal ritual tray consists of instruments to be utilised during the ceremony.

Tibetan butter lamps can burn for an entire day. They are beautifully decorated, often with eight auspicious signs, seven royal objects and eight lucky foods. They have a variety of shapes and designs. There can be a long-life vase forming the neck of the lamp, with coral and turquoise inset throughout.

Musical instruments like conch shell horns are often used in Tibetan rituals as sound offerings to the deities. The larger shells are

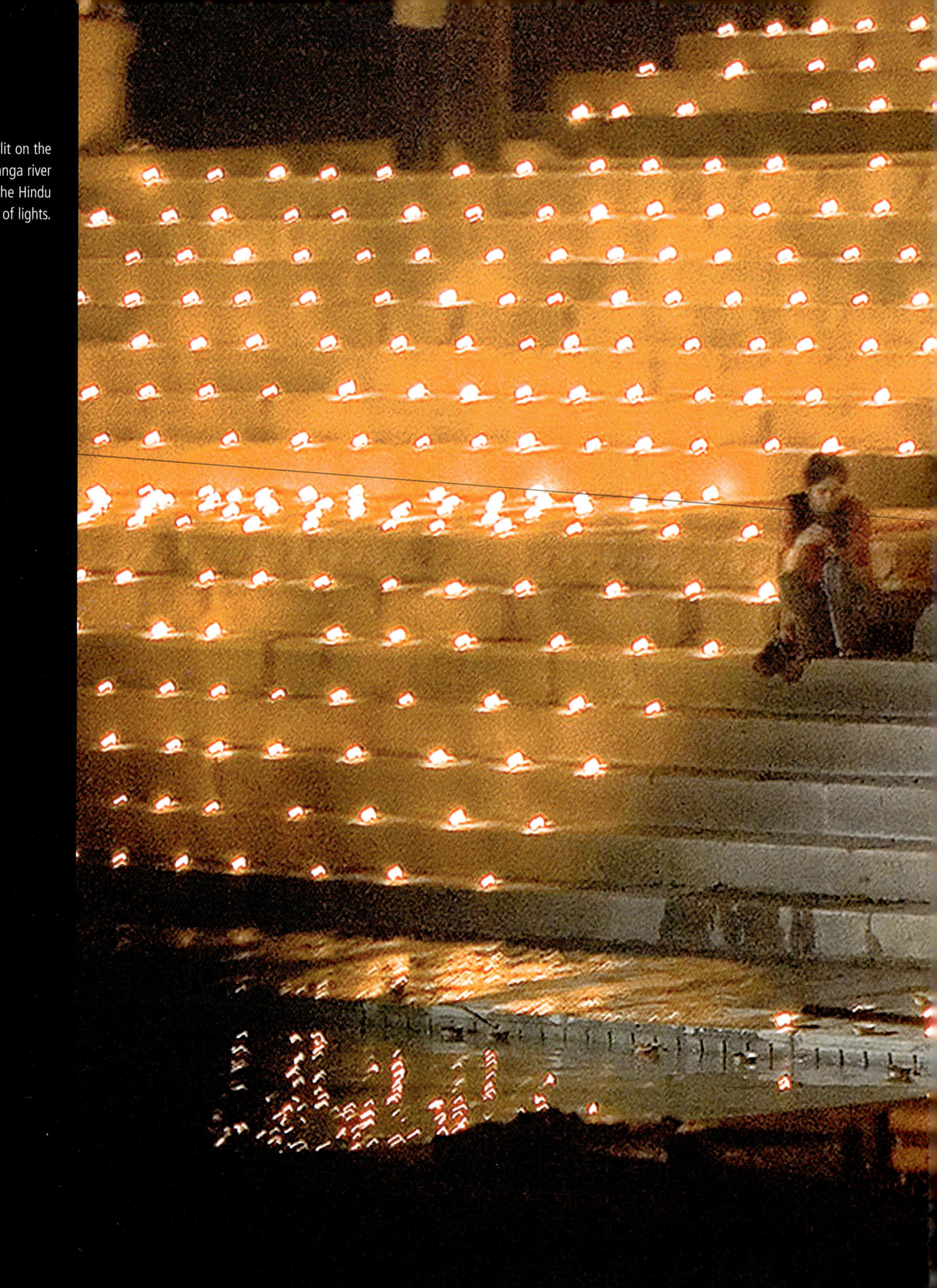

Oil lamps being lit on the banks of The Ganga river on Diwali-the Hindu festival of lights.

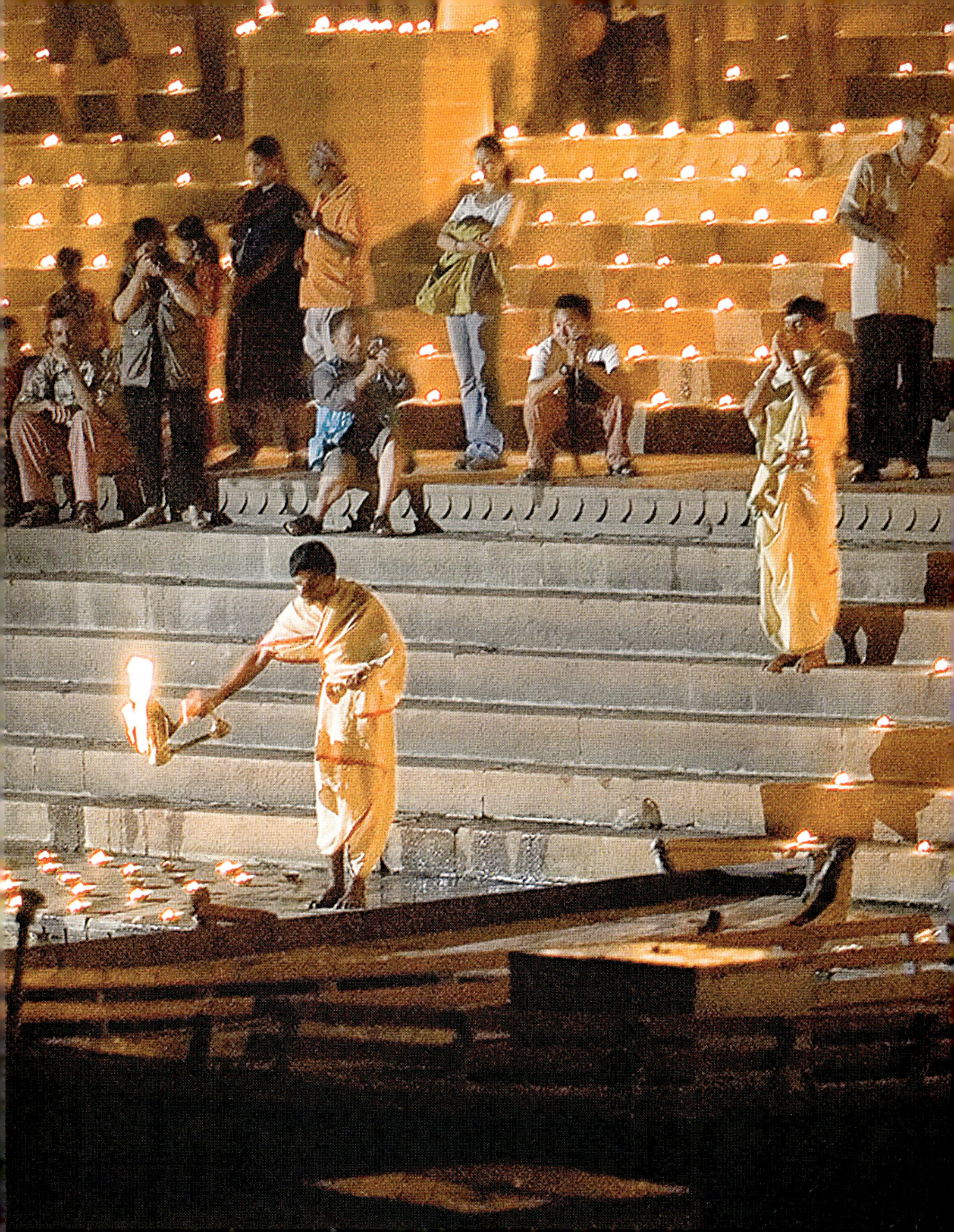

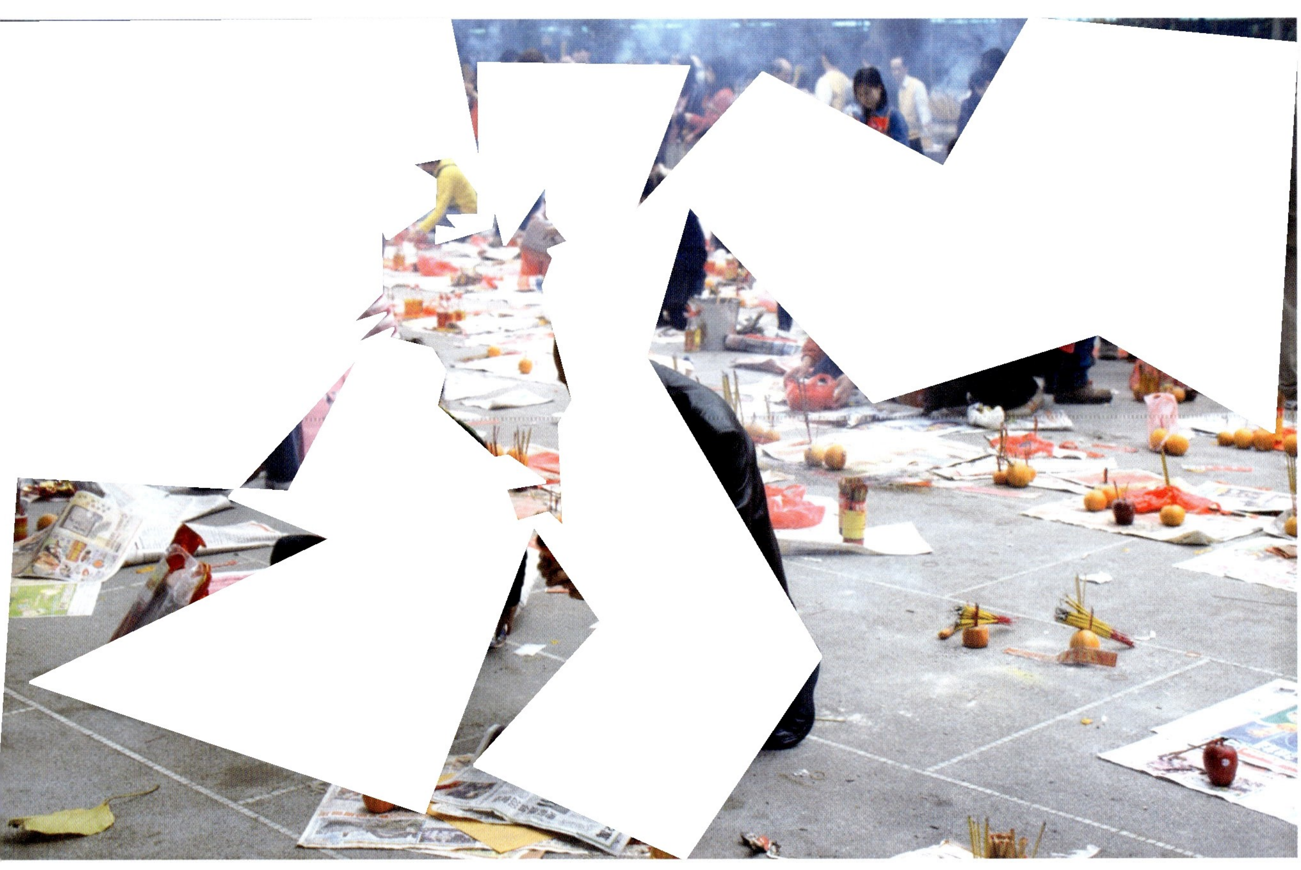

Buddhists performing religious rituals.

blown from monastery roof tops to gather the monks together. The metal shield and decorations make it more practical to utilise the shell, which might otherwise be broken, or may not be of the right shape or size.

The bell and the *vajra* are the most important ritual implements in Tantric Buddhism. The *vajra*, that is indestructible, supernatural and hard as diamond, symbolises compassion of all the Buddhas and the masculine principle. When used in ritual it is paired with a bell representing wisdom, the female principle. The bell is taken as the Buddha's speech teaching the dharma. A *vajra* can be used for evocation of the deities, while the bell is rung for protection during a Tantric ritual. During meditation of Vajrasattva, the *vajra* is placed on the chest of the practitioner, meaning that Vajrasattva is brought to the meditator and they become one and inseparable.

Use of skull cups and human bones in Tantric ritual symbolises death and impermanence of all things. These rituals are performed in secrecy. Tantrics offer objects which can be used by those who are initiated into the Tantras. A ritual skull may be made of gold, silver, or any other material, but must be designed as a skull. Spiritual masters are permitted to wear ornaments made of human bones when they perform special rituals or conduct initiation into the practice of Tantric deities, since they symbolise renunciation of the world and impermanence

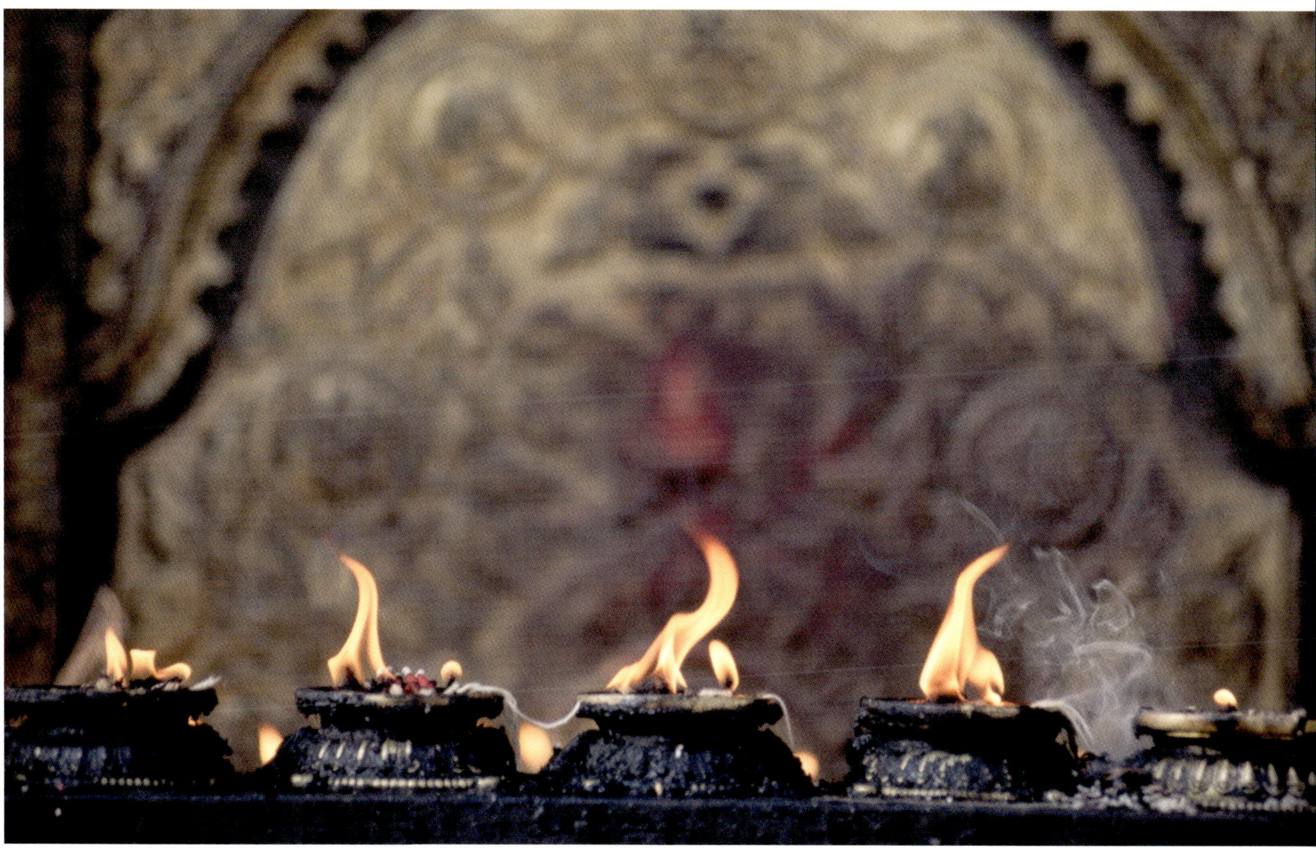

of life. A magical dagger, or *Khurpa* (a Tantric ritual object) is used by Tantric practitioners to conquer evil spirits or destroy obstacles coming in one's way. It is made of three separate pieces. The three-sided triangular dagger blade has an engraved serpent entwined around itself so that the head and tail point down. There is a *makara* head with a gilded decoration above each of the three corners.

A utensil is sanctified to be used in worship by Hindus by invoking deities so that the vessel becomes a suitable instrument for *puja*. It is filled with water. Fly whisk is waved by the priests during daily ritual offerings and festivals, to the accompaniment of music and chanting of the prayers. Lamps, known as *dipaka*s, are placed or waved in circles in front of the sacred images. A silver umbrella, an auspicious symbol and emblem of auspicious sovereignty, is offered to the divine during rituals. Crowns in south Indian temples are placed on the heads of the devotees to bless them with sovereignty.

Gongs and bells hold the first place among the instruments of percussion. The conch is also considered to be an auspicious symbol that bestows plenitude and fulfills wishes. The ringing of a bell is taken as signifying the arrival of gods and the departure of demons. An oil lamp dispels darkness and drives away evil spirits.

Above: Tibetan butter-lamps can burn for the entire day and are often decorated with eight auspicious signs.

Following page 144: The crescent moon, emblem of the mighty Sassanian empire, is a popular Islamic symbol.

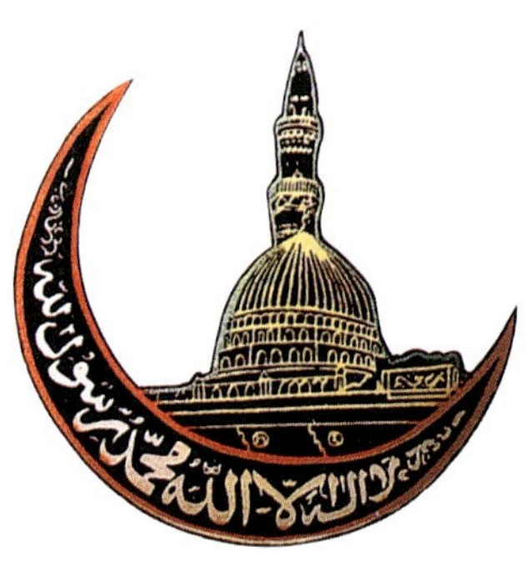

PHOTO CREDITS

CORBIS: Back cover, 2-3, 4-5, 8, 9, 10, 12-13, 14, 16,18, 22, 26-27, 31 (top), 32, 39, 44, 45, 46, 47 (bottom), 48, 49, 57, 58, 62 (top), 63, 64, 65, 66, 67, 70-71, 72, 73, 84, 85 (top), 85 (bottom), 86, 87, 88-89, 90, 91, 92, 93, 94, 95, 98-99, 102, 103 (top), 103 (bottom), 104, 105, 107, 108, 109, 110, 111 (top), 114, 118, 120, 121 (bottom), 122, 123, 124-125, 126, 128, 129, 130-131, 132, 133, 140-141, 142, 143

ROLI BOOKS: Front cover, 6, 7 (bottom), 20-21, 24, 25, 30, 31 (bottom), 33, 34-35, 40, 41, 51 (top), 52, 62 (bottom), 76, 78-79, 83 (extreme right), 96, 97, 112, 113, 115, 138, 139

GETTY: 27 (top), 111 (bottom), 127, 134-135, 136-137

AVINASH PASRICHA: 11, 50, 51 (top), 53, 54-55, 56, 59, 60-61

MADHU KHANNA: 1, 28, 36, 37, 38

SONDEEP SHANKAR: 68, 69, 80, 81; **AMIT PASRICHA:** 41, 101, 106

NATIONAL MUSEUM, NEW DELHI: 15, 83 (centre)

THOMAS KELLY: 17, 19 (top); **HANNAH SATZ:** 42-43

JEAN LOUIS NOU: 23, 50**; INDIAN MUSEUM, KOLKATA:** 82

SANGEET NATAK ACADEMY: 117

GOVERNMENT MUSEUM, MATHURA, UP: 83 (extreme left)

SANJEEV SAITH: 19 (bottom); **ANGELO HORNAK:** 29

V. MUTHURAMAN 74; **GANESH SAILI:** 75

ASHOK KHANNA: 77; **JOEL FISHMAN:** 121 (top)

RANMAL SINGH JHALA: 144; **MUSEE GUIMET:** 47

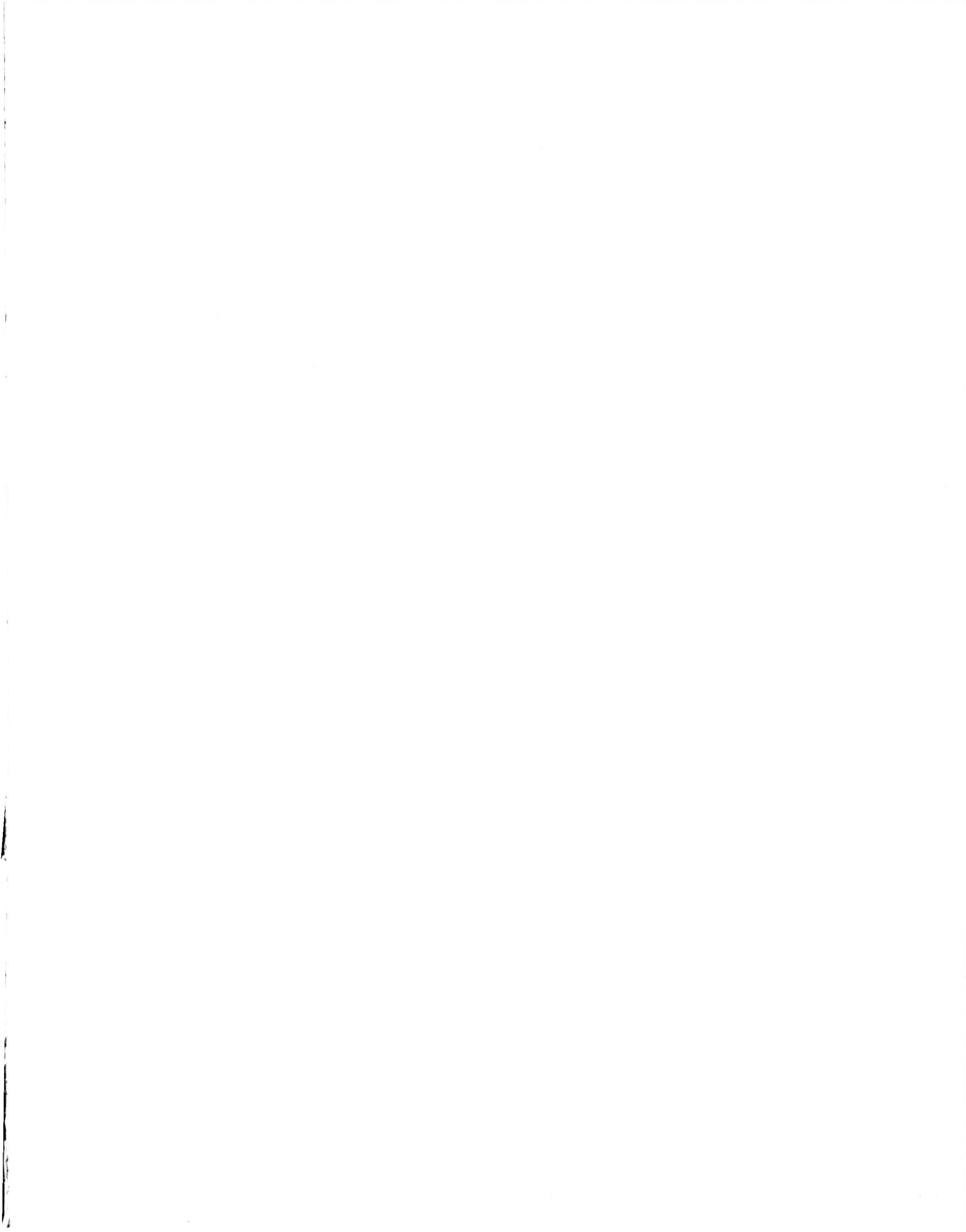